A15045 600420

ARISTOPHANES AND WOMEN

ARISTOPHANES AND WOMEN

Lauren K. Taaffe

PA
3879
.T3x
1993
West

London and New York

First published 1993
by Routledge
11 New Fetter Lane, London EC4P 4EE

Simultaneously published in the USA and Canada
by Routledge
29 West 35th Street, New York, NY 10001

© 1993 Lauren K. Taaffe

Typeset in Baskerville by Megaron, Cardiff, Wales
Printed and bound in Great Britain by T.J. Press (Padstow) Ltd,
Padstow, Cornwall
Printed on acid free paper

All rights reserved. No part of this book may be reprinted or
reproduced or utilized in any form or by any electronic,
mechanical, or other means, now known or hereafter invented,
including photocopying and recording, or in any information
storage or retrieval system, without permission in writing from
the publishers.

British Library Cataloguing in Publication Data
A catalogue record for this book is available from the British
Library

Library of Congress Cataloging in Publication Data
Taaffe, Lauren K.
Aristophanes and Women / Lauren K. Taaffe.
p. cm.
Includes bibliographical references and index.
1. Aristophanes–Characters–Women. 2. Greek drama
(Comedy)–History and criticism. 3. Women and literature–
Greece.
I. Title.
PA3879.T33   1994
882'01–dc20   93–18362

ISBN 0-415-09514-X

To my father and the memory
of my mother

CONTENTS

List of figures	viii
Preface	ix
List of abbreviations	xii
Introduction	1
1 THE REPRESENTATION OF FEMALE FIGURES IN ARISTOPHANES' PLAYS BEFORE 411 BCE	23
2 WOMEN AS WOMEN, MEN AS MEN: *LYSISTRATA*	48
3 MEN AS WOMEN: *THESMOPHORIAZUSAE*	74
4 WOMEN AS MEN: *ECCLESIAZUSAE*	103
5 THE LEGACY OF ARISTOPHANES' WOMEN	134
Notes	147
Bibliography	195
Index	209
Index of passages discussed	213

FIGURES

1 Dancers dressed as men and women   6
2 Bearded dancers dressed as men and women   7
3 Dancers with additional female heads (masks?)   8
4 Comic actors dressed as women   8

PREFACE

Near the end of several years of thinking about Aristophanes, comedy, and contemporary literary theories, as I contemplated the composition of this section of the following book, a variation on that old light-bulb joke kept creeping into my thoughts. Question: How many feminists does it take to screw in a light-bulb? Answer: That's not funny. I suppose this is because I know that feminists are often accused of being humorless (even Aristophanes' Lysistrata is stern (σκυθρωπός, 707), a character trait that critics relish, as if she proves the rule that the term 'serious feminist' is redundant), and scholars universally assert that Aristophanes' plays, despite their political references to fifth-century Athens and their age, are eternally hilarious.[1] In truth, a very small part of my point here is to say that Aristophanes makes jokes at the expense of women and that they are not necessarily funny. But contemporary readers are accustomed to lip-service being paid to feminism in this way; it is currently popular to acknowledge that jokes at anyone's expense serve to perpetuate racist, sexist, classist, and agist stereotypes. To point out that, over 2,400 years ago, the only whole extant works of ancient Greek comedy operated in such a fashion is not earth-shaking.

I hope that readers interested in an investigation into the workings of Aristophanes' 'woman plays' will read further, however, into what I have to say about why these plays were in fact probably quite funny to their original audiences and why modern readers, scholars, and actors need to consider much more about the conditions of the plays' ancient productions when evaluating their ostensible message. Reading against the grain, as the process of interpretation that I follow is often called, offers us new ways of identifying the relevance and meaning of Aristophanes' work today. The three plays that are my focus, *Lysistrata*, *Thesmophoriazusae* (*Women at the Thesmophoria*), and

Ecclesiazusae (*Women at the Assembly*), all appear to speak quite eloquently to contemporary concerns about women's rights and interests, the value of women's work, and the relationships between women and war, women and literary representation, and women and politics. It is not my aim to dismiss these works from the canon of great books because they perpetuate women's silence and invisibility. I have written this book rather to encourage an understanding of them on their own cultural terms, as products of late Classical Athens and its theater. I believe that if we strive to understand these works more accurately, then both the cultural distance and the cultural proximity of late fifth-century Athens to late twentieth-century America will become clearer. My view is bifurcated, then. On the one hand, I try to retrieve what an ancient Athenian audience, possibly an entirely male audience, may have taken away from the performance of any of these plays and what the plays meant within that culture. On the other hand, I look at the value of these plays for a late twentieth-century reader, specifically a female reader, and suggest ways of evaluating their current and future cultural relevance.

In a recent paper on travesty and transvestism in Aristophanic comedy, Suzanne Saïd describes her work as positioned at the intersection of three lines of research: scholarly inquiries into the image of women in ancient Greece, the spectacle and staging of Greek plays, and the process of mimesis and the nature of theatrical illusion (Saïd 1987: 217). With some finessing of differences, my inquiry is placed at that same Hekatean crossroads. In the introduction I will set out some explanations of the methodologies that have influenced my approach to Aristophanes' plays. This will also serve as an entry into the problems of conducting literary investigations into ancient Greek literature and provide a guide-map for readers. I encourage my classicist colleagues to skim over information that may be familiar to them and hope that my theoretical apparatus will enable all readers to look at the plays from a novel viewpoint.

This work began as a dissertation on *Ecclesiazusae* completed at Cornell University in 1987. My advisors there were Pietro Pucci, Phillip Mitsis, and Kevin Clinton; to them, and to the other members of the Classics department in residence from 1982 to 1987, I owe a debt of scholarly gratitude. Helene P. Foley taught me Greek at Barnard College and introduced me to Aristophanes. Her example and words of encouragement have guided me ever since. My colleagues at the State University of New York at Stony Brook helped me to formulate the theoretical framework of the book and to find a language to describe

PREFACE

what I have found; Dorothy Figueira, Adrienne Munich, and the members of the Humanities Institute Faculty Seminar in the spring of 1988 made especially acute suggestions. The Humanities Collegiate Division and the Classics Department of the University of Chicago provided great intellectual support for the two years that it took to complete the project, which by then had expanded far beyond the scope of the dissertation. Jayne Fargnoli, Marcia Mogelonsky, and Barry Strauss offered years of interest and friendship. Richard Stoneman has been an agreeable and faithful editor; Edith Hall was generous and thorough with advice and commentary. I am grateful to both of them and to Heather McCallum, also of Routledge.

Permission to reproduce the illustrations was kindly granted by Dr Geralda Jurriaans-Helle (Allard Pierson Museum, Amsterdam); Dr Gertrud Platz (Antikesammlung, Staatliche Museen zu Berlin); and Dr Hildegrund Gropengiesser (Archäologisches Institut der Universität Heidelberg). Parts of the Introduction and Chapter 4 were published as 'The Illusion of Gender Disguise in Aristophanes' *Ecclesiazusae*' (*Helios*, vol. 18. 2, 1991, pp. 91–112).

Jerome F. Hajjar has displayed endless patience, interest, and good humor about my work, without which I would probably not have completed this book. Finally, this work is dedicated to my father, James G. Taaffe, and to the memory of my mother, Donna C. Taaffe, in appreciation of the professional, scholarly, pedagogical, and humane examples they gave me, and still give me, to follow at home.

December 1992
Minneapolis, Minnesota

ABBREVIATIONS

AJP   *American Journal of Philology*
CA   *Classical Antiquity*
CP   *Classical Philology*
CQ   *Classical Quarterly*
G&R   *Greece and Rome*
GRBS   *Greek, Roman and Byzantine Studies*
IG ii² J. Kirchner (ed.), *Inscriptiones Graecae*, vol. 2, 2nd edn
JHS   *Journal of Hellenic Studies*
LCM   *Liverpool Classical Monthly*
LSJ   H. G. Liddell and R. Scott, *A Greek–English Lexicon*, revised by H. Stuart Jones and R. McKenzie
PCG   A. Kassel and C. Austin (eds), *Poetae Comici Graecae*
TAPA   *Transactions of the American Philological Association*
YCS   *Yale Classical Studies*

INTRODUCTION

A clever citizen founds a city in the sky, rules over the birds, and replaces Zeus; a poor farmer negotiates a private peace with his city's arch-enemy; war-weary brides refuse sex with their husbands and an army of old women seize the city's treasury to force a peace treaty; a man disguised as a woman sneaks into a secret women's festival to save his relative from death; a group of women dressed as men overthrow the government through a peaceful *coup d'état*: Aristophanes' plots present readers and spectators with wonderful worlds that long for peace, plenty, and happiness for the underdog. Yet, the interpreter of ancient Greek comedy faces a problematic and frustrating task. Not only do we possess a relatively small number of representative texts – tragedy remains in better condition than comedy, with whole extant works by three central authors compared to comedy's one author – but these texts also often appear fragmentary or spurious in part. The manuscripts contain no stage directions, actors' notes, or author's revisions. We have no information about the original productions, no reviews, no detailed history of any play's reception. Our information about almost every imaginable aspect of ancient Greek theater production is extremely limited. Hence, the enterprise of this book will require a stretch of imagination. We can, however, approach the circumstances surrounding the original production of Aristophanes' plays with educated guesses and imaginative suggestions based on the little retrievable evidence. This chapter will review the available information about the conditions of theatrical performance and production in ancient Athens as well as describe the current state of research on the images of women in ancient Greek literature. At its end, I will describe the theories of feminist performance critics and develop a methodology for looking at the construction of the female figures in Aristophanes' plays.

COMIC THEATER IN ANCIENT GREECE

Theater at Athens occurred under the auspices of the government at two official festivals, the City Dionysia (sometimes referred to as the Great Dionysia) and the Lenaea. Both festivals were organized forms of worshipping Dionysus, the god of wine. From the earliest times, Dionysus is associated with all the features of theater: singing, dancing, changes of identity, and role-playing revelry. At the height of Athens' power, tragedies, satyr plays, and comedies were all performed at these festivals, and the playwrights, actors, choruses, and producers all competed for prizes. The Lenaea appears to have placed emphasis on comic competition, the City Dionysia on tragic. The first recorded victor in the tragic competition is Thespis, whose victory was in 534 BCE, although it is not clear whether he won at the City Dionysia or at another dramatic festival. Comedy was initiated at the City Dionysia some fifty years later, in 486 BCE. The Lenaea began comic performances in 442 BCE and added tragedy in 432 BCE.[1]

The City Dionysia was held in March or April. A religious celebration of spring and renewal, the City Dionysia was attended by people from all over Greece and the rest of the ancient Greek-speaking Mediterranean as well as Athenians, since the weather was gentler and the seas more navigable. The Lenaea, held in January or February, was by contrast a more local festival attended only by Athenians. Where in Athens the Lenaea was held is not known for certain; the City Dionysia was held in the Theater of Dionysus on the south slope of the Acropolis, which could seat as many as 17,000 spectators.[2] These festivals lasted for several days. Before the Peloponnesian War (431–404 BCE) tapped Athens' time, attention, and financial resources, the City Dionysia held dramatic competitions for five consecutive days. During the war, the competitions were cut back to three days.

Each day of the festival saw dramatic performances of three types: tragedy, satyr play, and comedy. In the morning, four plays by a single tragic playwright – three tragedies and a satyr play – would be performed. The tragedies may have formed a trilogy, as Aeschylus' *Oresteia* did, or three plays may have embraced a single theme in different ways, or the plays may have been ostensibly unrelated. A satyr play, which would farcically dramatize traditional myths, followed. The chorus featured mischievous satyrs, mythological half-goat, half-human, male creatures associated with Dionysus. The satyr play seems to have made an effective bridge between tragedy and comedy.[3] Its gentle and silly humor may have eased the audience from tragedy into comedy. In the afternoon, a single comedy would be performed. On the last day of the festival, judges would vote and rank the tragic and comic plays for prizes.

The purpose of the Lenaea and the City Dionysia remains multifold. The offering to Dionysus not only of dramatic works but also of the preliminary procession, sacrifices, and other ritual performances surely honors the mysteries of the god. The occasion also provided an opportunity for public celebration of Athenian power and wealth; foreign visitors to the City Dionysia would be especial observers of the display of Athenian public spirit. The public and civic nature of the festival also ensures its effectiveness as a vehicle of ideas for collective identity and action.

In order to have a play performed at one of these festivals, a playwright would present his plans for the play to the appointed archon in hopes of being 'granted a chorus' (χορὸν διδόναι). After receiving approval, the playwright would be granted actors and a stipend for production expenses. Playwrights thus often produced their own plays. The transfer of this responsibility to another expert was not unheard of. For example, Aristophanes turned the matters of production for *Lysistrata* over to Kallistratos. Still, in addition to bearing responsibility for composition of the dramatic text, the playwright held the responsibility of teaching his actors their parts in the play; he is often referred to as the 'teacher' (διδάσκαλος). He would also be assigned a sponsor, called a *choregos* (χορηγός). The *choregos* was characteristically a wealthy Athenian citizen who, perhaps, sought to increase his reputation and influence by defraying the costs of a winning play and financially sponsoring its author. Typically, a victorious *choregos* would erect a monument of some sort commemorating his, and the poet's, success; the tripod presented as a prize would adorn the monument (Pickard-Cambridge 1962: 86–91). This *choregos* was responsible for financing the production; he was charged with obtaining and paying for the members of the chorus, whom he would probably select from the members of his own tribe. He also hired the chorus-trainer (χοροδιδάσκαλος) and the musicians, arranged for the chorus' costumes, and covered any other expenses incurred by the chorus. The prizes and payment to actors and playwrights came from the public treasury and were subject to a vote of the assembly. For those unfamiliar with ancient Greek theater, the important point here is that the circumstances surrounding the original performances of these plays indicate a great deal of state control and supervision as well as religious significance. In addition, the patronage of the *choregos* may or may not have influenced the final content of the drama. [While Aristophanes' political satire indicates that the poet retained quite a bit of freedom of expression, theater and theatrical performances formed and constituted a large part of Athens' ideological identity (Goldhill 1990; Henderson 1990; Longo 1990). In fact, the audience would have attended through religious and civic duty as much as through a desire for entertainment.]

As is well known, all the parts in Greek drama were played by male actors. [In performance, ancient Greek comic actors wore highly stylized costumes, the bottom layer of which consisted of bodysuits that had heavily padded arms and legs, often with extra wrinkles at the wrists and ankles. Bellies and rear ends were enlarged by more pads. Exaggerated and perhaps grotesque masks (depending on the nature of the character) covered their faces. While Old Comedy relies on physicality for much of its humor, it does not rely on malleable facial expressions. Over this comically constructed body, an actor wore the street dress appropriate for his character's type. Finally, male characters also wore large leather phalloi attached to their bodysuits. These phalloi were adjustable; they could be rolled up and hidden from view, extended straight out and visible, or manipulated for comic effect to any possible position in between.[4] Female characters were played with pads underneath their clothes as well. Since female characters do not become conspicuous in what remains of Old Comedy until *Lysistrata*, I will say more about the comic costume in discussion of that play.

Ritual role-playing and role-exchange have long been associated with festivals in many cultures, and so transvestite dramatic performances are historically a traditional phenomenon (Ackroyd 1979; Baker 1976; Davis 1978).[5] Boy actors played all the female parts in Shakespeare's plays, for example; female actors first appeared on the English stage in 1660. Interpreters of ancient Greek drama, however, seldom mention this central phenomenon of Greek theater. The convention of male actors is usually dismissed as a practice accepted without further thought by audiences, actors, and playwrights alike.[6] Because of the dearth of information surrounding the ancient performances of Aristophanes' (and others') plays, [we are unable to determine how ancient audiences would have perceived the appearance of female characters on the comic stage. Would they have been conscious of the male actor impersonating a woman,] as modern audiences are when they watch female impersonators sing in the guise of Judy Garland or when they watch old videotapes of Flip Wilson's Geraldine?[7] That prizes were awarded to the best actors certainly suggests that the audience, or at least the judges, remained aware and constantly evaluative of the individual actor underneath the costume. Given human differences, there was most likely a multiplicity of audience responses. The plays themselves beg the question: just as in modern transvestite comedies like *Some Like it Hot,* transvestism, acting, and disguise by costume all form a self-conscious part of the plots of *Lysistrata, Thesmophoriazusae,* and *Ecclesiazusae.* To provide a background, some information about the visual phenomenon of the actor on the ancient comic stage is in order.

Unfortunately, relatively little evidence also remains to us of the actual stage appearance of ancient comic characters. Vase illustrations of dramatic performances offer the only visual information about ancient performance practice. In addition, all the vases featured in the few published illustrations of male actors in pre-dramatic performances or in comedy playing women, with one exception (Fig. 1), were commissioned for someone involved in the performance's production.[8] Although these vases and their paintings were made to order in some fashion, that women are so rarely represented as true to life, as they often are in illustrations of tragedy, strengthens the possibility that men in comedy were not to be thought of as really becoming women. Vase-painters remained aware of dramatic convention in comedy and, perhaps, so did audiences.[9] The first two vase-paintings I discuss illustrate actors' performances in rituals which are dated to the time before the Athenian tragic and comic festivals began. Although the evidence here is from the pre-dramatic chorus, it nonetheless looks forward to the phenomenon of male actors portraying women in fifth-century Attic comedy.

Figure 1, an Attic red-figure column-krater dated to 600–550 BCE, shows a padded male pre-dramatic chorus with some members dressed as men and others as women (Trendall and Webster 1971: I. 1, 7). It is the only surviving example of what was probably a stock *symposion* vase (ibid. 6).[10] White skin distinguishes the females from the males, a traditional formula for indicating sexual difference. Color-coded gender is not unknown in earlier art of the region. For instance, Minoan frescoes found at Knossos and other sites in Crete portray women with white skin and men with dark skin.[11] The women in Figure 1 wear the same costumes as the men and they dance in the same fashion. Trendall likens the male figures to later representations of satyrs and the female figures to later representations of nymphs (ibid. 20).

Figure 1 Dancers dressed as men and women
(Antikensammlung, Staatliche Museen zu Berlin; 1966.17).

Figure 2, an Attic black-figure kylix by the Heidelberg Painter and dated to 560–540 BCE (Trendall and Webster 1971: I. 1, 8), shows another chorus of dancers, some dressed as women.[12] Their padded bodies indicate that they are actors. Their beards underscore the artifice of representation: even though three actors wear long women's *chitones*, they retain their facial hair, a sign of adult masculinity. In addition, all the figures have dark skin. The painter reveals an awareness of costume and artifice in his representation of actors playing their roles here. As Trendall provocatively writes, 'Perhaps our artist thought of a chorus of men dressed up as maenads' (ibid. 20).[13] If so, he also means for us to think of men dressed as maenads, rather than the maenads themselves. Illustrations of other pre-dramatic choruses follow a similar pattern of representing an illusion of gender disguise. The Berlin Painter, in his well-known picture of a chorus mounted on horses (Attic black-figure amphora, 550–540 BCE), lets the chorus's faces peek out from underneath their horse-head masks (Trendall and Webster 1971: I. 1, 9), for example.

Some fifth-century illustrations of tragedy indicate the same awareness of the actor's sex. An Attic red-figure skyphos by the Penelope painter, dated 440 BCE, presents a scene from the *Oresteia*

INTRODUCTION

Figure 2 Bearded dancers dressed as men and women
(Allard Pierson Museum, Amsterdam; 3356).

(Trendall and Webster 1971: III. 1, 2). Two women stand with offerings at a tomb marked *AGAMEM[NON]* (ΑΓΑΜΕΜ [ΝΟΝ]). The word *KALO[S]* (ΚΑΛΟ[Σ]) is written near the woman on the right. Trendall writes: '*kalos*, "beautiful", without a name attached refers to one of the figures in the scene; as it is masculine, the painter shows that he thinks of a chorus-man performing a female part' (Trendall and Webster 1971: 41). Another Attic amphora, this one illustrating a scene from *Phineus* (Nikon Painter, 470–450 BCE), has the same *KALOS* written near the Harpies, who are running off with Phineus' food (Trendall and Webster 1971: III. 1, 25).

Other vases reveal the actor's sex as he prepares to play a female role in tragedy. Fragments of an oenochoe (470–460 BCE) found in the Athenian Agora indicate actors in various states of dress (Pickard-Cambridge 1968: fig. 32). One nude male, probably an actor's attendant, holds a female mask in his right hand. The foot and ankle of another figure show traces of a long *chiton*. The actors appear to be dressed to play the roles of women. A more intact bell-krater (*c.* 460–450 BCE) shows two men preparing for a choral performance of some kind (ibid. fig. 33). One wears a maenad's costume and a visible female mask. The other man remains unmasked and holds a male mask in his hand; he may be getting ready to play Dionysus. Finally, a pelike (*c.*430 BCE) shows two men dressing for a choral performance as women (ibid. fig. 34). They wear knee-length *chitones* and soft boots. The man on the left, with his mask in place, holds a *himation*.[14] On the right, his companion pulls on a boot; a female mask lies on the ground at his feet.

Vase-paintings of male actors as female characters in comedy similarly show actors not in full costume, but rather in the process of

Figure 3 Dancers with additional female heads (masks?) (Museo Artistico Industriale, Rome).

Figure 4 Comic actors dressed as women (Archäologisches Institut der Universität Heidelberg; B 134).

INTRODUCTION

putting on the costumes of female characters or with their own sex revealed in some other way. Figure 3, an Attic black-figure mastos cup dated to 520 BCE (ibid. pl. V b, no. 18), shows a chorus of eight padded male dancers, three with female masks placed on top of their heads. That the men with the extra 'heads' are nude makes this representation of male actors playing women rather unusual. The painter again portrays the reality that male actors played female roles. He, at least, never lost sight of the sexual identity underneath the costume. Like an X-ray, the illustration displays both the surface illusion and also the truth inside. The costume has all but disappeared; the female mask, almost a second thought, is all that is necessary to indicate the conventions of performance.[15]

For my study here, the most pertinent example of this deliberate exposure of the illusion of an actor's gender disguise appears in Figure 4, an illustration that commentators often think of as inspired by *Ecclesiazusae*. This Attic red-figure bell-krater, roughly dated to 390–380 BCE, is contemporary with *Ecclesiazusae* (Trendall and Webster 1971: IV, 4). In the painting, two chorus-men dressed as women and wearing long patterned *chitones* are dancing. The actor on the left is fully costumed as a woman. He has put his mask in place and wrapped a long *himation* around his *chiton*, draping it over the back of his head in the feminine style. The other actor dances without a *himation*, his chest and bare legs exposed, and his mask raised up to reveal his face. Of this illustration, Trendall writes:

> The need to maintain dramatic illusion is over and so the chorus-man can show his face. The moment might be either when the chorus dance off the stage at the end of the play . . . or when they danced in the procession which escorted the statue of Dionysus out of the theatre.
>
> (Trendall and Webster 1971: 119)

That the painter has chosen to portray this moment, rather than one in which both actors are in full costume, is important. While he does commemorate the actors' performances, he also commemorates a moment when their illusion of gender disguise is displayed. Just so, manipulation of costume and language constantly reveals the illusion of gender disguise in Aristophanes' plays.

Complete illusion does not often exist in the visual representation of dramatic choruses dressed as women. The iconographic tradition appears to call for a deliberate reminder of the artificial nature of dramatic performance. No male actor in female dress is pictured without some reminder of his own sexual identity; the illusion of 'woman' is often disrupted. The picture on a vase reminds us that the actor is a man in women's clothes, whether the reminder is made by exposing the actor's phallos under his costume, by marking a female figure with a masculine καλός, by teasing the viewer with a lifted mask, or by showing a fully costumed actor with another actor not fully costumed.

Later artistic representations of actors in comedy show that this trend continues even after Aristophanes' death. A Paestan bell-krater by Python, dated to 350–325 BCE, shows three male actors at a party playing *kottabos* (Trendall and Webster 1971: IV, 8 b). It is not clear whether they are in performance or not. A satyr sleeps on the floor in front of their couch; he is clearly an actor wearing a wrinkled Papposilenus costume. Above their heads float three masks, a young woman's mask flanked by a comic slave's mask and an old man's mask.[16] It may be that the play is over and the picture illustrates a cast party, with reminders of the parts each actor played.

These illustrations have been presented as a visual introduction to the discussion of the construction of gender in Aristophanes' plays. The paintings of male actors playing female parts show that neither the theatrical representation of women by men nor the visual representation of actors in women's parts were unequivocally complete. Because of what the vase illustrations tell us, [it is inappropriate to assume that the convention of male actors in female roles was accepted wholeheartedly and without further thought by ancient audiences and playwrights.]

WOMEN IN ANCIENT GREEK COMEDY

In recent years, the study of women in classical antiquity has grown from a subfield of classics into a legitimate and respected subject of inquiry on its own. Still, the common term 'women in classical antiquity' has to be divided into at least two parts. What began as an attempt to recover information about the lives and ordinary experiences of real women in ancient Greece now encompasses both historical inquiry into the lived reality of ancient women and also theoretical or critical analysis of the images of women in ancient literature and art.[17] My focus is on the theatrical representation of women and my historical impulses in this research extend only to the possible production and reception of particular plays. Unlike the study of women in other national literatures, which can include the works of women writers and other sources which may react to women's literary voices, the study of women in ancient Greek literature is limited to only one dimension. There are no compositions by the women of fifth-century Athens; the only works we have by ancient Greek women are the earlier lyric fragments of Sappho, Erinna, and a few others.[18] Inquiry into the area of women in ancient Greek literature by nature uncovers the representations and images of women in works of art composed by men.

Many scholars who delve into the issue of women in classical drama work under the assumption that women in Greek drama are exceptions to the rules of expected female behavior. For example, *Lysistrata* and *Ecclesiazusae* often receive critical attention because of plots that center on female political revolt. The women of Greek tragedy, however, have even more effectively captured the interest of critics primarily because of their often aggressive and unusual behavior. For some critics, female characters step out of their standard social roles to become tragic heroines in the male tradition. Medea, Antigone, and Phaedra, for example, all seem to pose this model (e.g. Knox 1964: 62–116). The women in tragic drama have long been a popular topic among scholars. Their number is relatively large in the corpus of extant plays, even though the little evidence there is about early drama suggests that women were not originally included as individual characters, and scholarly interest has followed suit. There are not many women in comic drama, again even though the earliest fragment of comic poetry expresses the apparently eternal paradox that men find it difficult to live both with and without women, and the scholarship has been proportionate.[19]

It is absolutely necessary to distinguish between the representation of women in comedy and the representation of women in tragedy, especially when entertaining ideas about the possible stage actions that male actors may have performed and in hypothesizing the range of audience expectation and response. Tragedy proves effective not only because, as Aristotle remarked, it is 'the imitation of a serious action' (*Poetics* 1449 b 24–8), but also because the emotional distance between audience, stage action, and actor is narrow. The action on stage must be believed, the validity of actors' representations must be solid, the integrity of the fiction must be unquestioned for the seriousness of the action to be upheld. Comedy by its very nature exists on a more fluid interface between reality and fiction. Costumes, plots, characters, and language confront the audience with artifice; jokes, parody, and mockery work because the audience is aware of that artifice. Comedy also allows the poet to have characters address the audience directly, a phenomenon which does not occur regularly in tragedy. By its very nature, then, Aristophanic comedy would play upon the theatrical convention of male actors in female roles for humor, for it certainly plays with every other theatrical convention.

Comedy, and humor in general, performs many functions in society. The expression of usually taboo or forbidden words, ideas, and actions, the reversal of the normal social order: these aspects of carnival release certainly play their part in Aristophanic comedy. Yet both the psychological and the carnival theories of comedy neglect the immediate political context of Aristophanes' work.[20] Aristophanes' comedy also functions as a literary and political critique, as well as an occasion for social bonding and the reinforcement of societal norms.

After twenty years of dramatic compositions with varied and fantastic plots, in 411 BCE Aristophanes invented a new comedy with an apparently new theme. It has since become one of Aristophanes' most well-known and popular compositions. In *Lysistrata*, the young wives of Athens and Sparta, frustrated by the long Peloponnesian War and the absence of men, initiate a sex strike as part of a plan to formulate a peace treaty and bring an end to the war. The evidence for plays with women as the protagonists of a comic plot is fragmentary and inconclusive. In fact, some scholars now believe *Lysistrata* to have been the first Greek comedy with female protagonists (Henderson 1987b: xxviii).[21] Aristophanes produced another variation on the theme of female rebellion, *Thesmophoriazusae*, later in the same year.[22] *Thesmophoriazusae* presents the women of Athens on the third day of the Thesmophoria, a festival associated with Demeter and the Eleusinian Mysteries. They have decided to put Euripides on trial for producing plays about women with bad reputations and for tarnishing all women's reputations as a result. Euripides discovers their intentions and convinces a relative to dress up as a woman, infiltrate the secret meeting, and defend him against the charges. The Relative complies, but is discovered and captured. Euripides rescues him by staging parodies of his own plays to trick a rather dim-witted Scythian guard.

Ecclesiazusae, produced some nineteen years later in 392 or 391 BCE, recalls the themes of *Lysistrata*.[23] In this play, the women of Athens are inspired through the leadership of Praxagora to dress up as men, attend the next public assembly meeting, and vote through a measure that turns the government over to them. After Praxagora is appointed as the head of the new government, she institutes social reforms that make all property, children, and sexual activity communal. The play ends with several scenes of these reforms in practice and closes with a feast.

These three plays are often grouped together and nicknamed the 'women plays'. Within such a category, the plays can then be dismissed as not serious, as trifles. Historically these plays have sometimes only been taken seriously when taken as parts of other categories: *Lysistrata* as part of the 'peace play' triad with *Acharnians* and *Peace*; *Thesmophoriazusae* as a 'Euripides play' with *Acharnians* and *Frogs*; *Ecclesiazusae* as a 'utopia' play along with *Birds* and *Peace* (e.g. Gruber 1986: 14). [The appearance of women in these plays is considered by most scholars to have been a novelty and a realistic impossibility; each play is thereupon dismissed as a light fantasy that could never come true.] It was not until the mid-1970s that classics scholars began to approach the topic of women in ancient Greek literature with some skepticism and methodological sophistication, and those beginnings have led to my present investigation.

Inspired by the work of structural and cultural anthropologists, some scholars have treated these Aristophanic plays in light of the anthropological equation 'female is to male as nature is to culture'.[24] Helene Foley has pointed out, however, that this equation constitutes an inadequate formulation for thoroughly understanding Greek culture and that women, particularly in *Lysistrata* and *Ecclesiazusae*, do not and cannot single-handedly represent nature (Foley 1981). She illustrates, through a realignment of the equation in terms more appropriate to ancient Greek culture, that the relationship between *oikos* (home) and *polis* (city), female and male, nature and culture, is a reciprocal one. In a related study, Nicole Loraux has considered the relationship between women and the polis, showing that in *Lysistrata*, Aphrodite and Athena serve one another and offer their differing feminine aspects a place on the Acropolis (Loraux 1981). [Women's issues should thus be considered both familial and political. In this book, I will show that Aristophanes considers the feminine to be an essential element of the polis, yet one controlled and represented by men.]

Other scholars have taken a psychoanalytic view of Old Comedy (P. Slater 1968; see also Foley 1975). This approach is based on the assumption that women were presented on stage as authoritative, powerful, and dangerous in the home because the relationship between Greek mothers and their sons was problematic, influenced by the combination of an often absent father and a seemingly domineering and seductive mother. Medea and Clytemnestra, deliberately fearsome wives and mothers, are prime examples of such women. This approach has its advantages for comedy: many jokes are based on sexuality and lead easily to a psychoanalytic assessment of social and psychological relations between the sexes. Given the dominance of masculinity in ancient Athens, its exclusively male focus seems a benefit as well. Yet the psychoanalytic paradigm does not help us fully understand either how female characters themselves behave or how modern women might respond to the texts in question. The identification of the ideal male spectator with a play's masculine protagonist and his desire for a female object, an assumption which often guides psychoanalytic critics, will nevertheless be central to my thesis here.

In Aristophanic and Euripidean studies, Froma Zeitlin's work has paved the way for new observations about the formulation of female figures and ideas about femininity. In her study of *Thesmophoriazusae*, Zeitlin examines the relationship between gender and genre, between the representation of both female and male characters in comedy and tragedy (Zeitlin 1981).[25] She finds in this play an intersection of ideas about the feminine, comedy, and mimesis. The feminine and the female, she argues, are inextricably linked with imitation: a woman both imitates and is imitated. This observation becomes a central theoretical jumping-off point for looking at women in other Aristophanic plays. In a later paper on role reversal and the imitation of women in Greek tragedy, Zeitlin pushes her hypothesis even further. She argues that the feminine is

> the mistress of mimesis, the heart and soul of the theater. The feminine instructs the other through her own example – that is, in her own name and under her own experience – but also through her ability to teach the other to impersonate her.
> (Zeitlin 1985: 80)

The feminine becomes, in her theory, an essential part of the discovery and construction of the self that theater, especially Euripidean theater, investigates. Zeitlin's work, which has been influenced by the thought of French structuralists like Vernant, is valuable, for it examines the process and meaning of stage play with cross-dressing and role reversal seriously, and it recognizes the festival of Dionysus and its ritual theater as a viable shaper of both civic life and individual identity.

Here the ritual and dramatic convention of male actors in female roles comes to the fore again. Scholars often see

INTRODUCTION

theatrical convention . . . as a form of translation in which the reality of the narrative is reproduced on the stage in such a way as to close off or suppress any irrelevant thoughts about the actors on stage. 'Convention' is seen as a stable controller of meaning, mediating between a stable text and a stable reality.

(McLuskie 1987: 120)

Neither the text nor the reality will prove to be stable, however, so it may not be fair to grant stability to the stage representation. This assumption paves the way for my analysis of the Aristophanic texts.

In designing an approach to interpreting the female characters in Aristophanes' plays, particularly the three plays that feature women, I have tried to combine the best parts of these previous and disparate tactics with both close readings of the texts and an awareness of theatrical techniques. I do not view the female characters in Aristophanes as representations of women taken from real life, although I recognize that the plays may in fact reflect real concerns, concerns of both men and women, about sex roles and public policy. Ancient actors performed these plays in a ritual event that aided in defining Athenian identity specifically and Greek identity in general. Finally, that the only concrete information available about these plays today lies in sometimes ambiguous or fragmentary texts places limits on any critical venture. While my suggestions about performance practice require leaps of imagination and sometimes faith, they are all based upon an examination of textual evidence.

FEMINIST PERFORMANCE CRITICISM

In this section, I will offer working definitions for the theoretical terms that inform my analysis. It will become clear here to what extent my approach has been influenced by developments in literary theory and feminist thought outside the traditional perimeters of the field of classics.

The three plays in question revolve around many social issues, among them war, peace, good government, and the role of theater in the city. Nothing jumps out at the modern reader more boldly than their emphasis on gender, however, and so I will begin with that. In general, I follow Joan Scott's succinct definition: 'gender is a constitutive element of social relationships based on perceived differences between the sexes, and gender is a primary way of signifying relationships of power' (1986: 1067). To ancient Greek men, specifically to the Athenian men whose viewpoint is the only one left to us, sex and gender were one and the same thing for women. That is, biologically female sex characteristics were thought, in general, to establish a female's social role. A female body determines the gender role 'woman'. Having a male body, however, meant dwelling within a system of gender categorization in which 'men' dominate and 'women' are dominated. Within this system, it was possible for males to be referred to, thought of, and treated erotically as 'women'.[26] A male adult might be called a woman if he wore no beard, for example. The plays show that different constructions of gender were possible for men, while impossible for women. Today, we tend to differentiate between sex and gender for both males and females. For us, sex is biologically determined while gender usually refers to a learned, socially determined, and culturally specific identity. In order to ease confusion between the ancient and modern ideas of gender, I will use 'sex' in reference to biological differences and 'gender' in reference to social roles. My term 'gender disguise', then, properly refers to the disguise adopted by a character that enables that character to presume a certain social role. 'Sexual disguise' would be a disguise that attempted to represent the opposite sex accurately.

These concerns about sex and gender have recently found a stronghold in feminist scholarship on film and theater. In particular, feminist film theorists' concern with the relationship between the spectator and the image on the screen can be applied fruitfully to theater as well. Feminist analysis of the way modern cinema works explains that the film narrative posits an ideal male spectator and then, through the positioning of the camera, the ordering of images, and careful editing, manipulates the spectator's gaze to replicate and reinforce cultural images and assumptions about women, men, and male-dominated society.[27] As all-pervasive aspects of modern life, mainstream cinema, television, and advertising, reinforce what is called 'the male gaze', which posits men as spectators and women as objects of vision and desire. Jill Dolan offers a clear summary:

> Feminist film theorists have debated the gender-specific meaning of pleasure in the viewing experience. By analyzing the cinematic apparatus through a psychoanalytic interpretive strategy, critics such as E. Ann Kaplan, Mary Ann Doane, and Laura Mulvey suggest that film offers visual pleasure by objectifying the women in the narrative for the active male protagonist with whom the male spectator is meant to identify. Women are also fetishized as objects to be looked at, thereby decreasing the threat of their sexual lack. These feminist readings

INTRODUCTION

of film spectatorship emphasize that classical cinema constructs
the spectator as male.

(Dolan 1988: 48)[28]

While the spectator's gaze in a theatrical performance cannot be
manipulated as forcefully as it is in film, it is still grounded in cultural
assumptions about gender, sexuality, and power.[29] The spectator's
gaze is manipulated by specific aspects of any theatrical performance
(set, props, costume, blocking, choreography, and the actors
themselves) that are aimed, by the director and perhaps the author, at
a particular type of spectator. As Dolan writes, 'theatre creates an ideal
spectator carved in the likeness of the dominant culture whose ideology
he represents' (1988: 1). Allowing for the differences between the
experience of watching a film in a darkened movie theater, watching a
play in a modern proscenium or black box theater, and watching an
ancient dramatic performance in the sunshine of the Theater of
Dionysus in Athens, this theoretical construction of the spectator and
his relationship to the performance becomes eminently applicable to
ancient Greek drama. It is not clear whether women attended the
dramatic performances in Athens, and if they did, what sort of women
(upper- or middle-class housewives, courtesans, slaves, merchants,
foreigners) they were.[30] Even if they did attend, it is a common – so
common that it is often dismissed – scholarly observation, based on the
type and content of the jokes, that the audience to whom Aristophanes
geared his plays was male.[31] The ideal spectator for Aristophanes was
certainly a middle- or upper-class adult Athenian male, without a
doubt a member of the dominant culture. It is also clear that the
business on stage would have been intelligible to him in a way that it
may not be to us. Finally, Athenians were bombarded with visual
expressions of ideology, too: for example, the friezes on the Parthenon,
the statues and monuments in the Agora (see Keuls 1985; DuBois
1982). It hardly seems necessary to explicate this male gaze as one of
the general features of Greek drama. An insistence upon and interest in
the function of the male gaze as a determiner of meaning for the poet,
the actor, the spectator and the reader, however, does elicit something
new.

The issue of male actors in female roles forms a crucial part of this
line of inquiry. This aspect of performance practice has become a
provocative issue in other fields; in English Renaissance drama, for
instance.[32] The scholars whose work has inspired my investigation here
do have more information about theatrical practices and the reception
of plays than does the scholar of ancient Greek comedy. Yet some

17

imagination and educated guessing about ancient performance, based on textual evidence as well as theory, can transform our view of Aristophanes' work. At this point feminist theory and theater studies merge.

Performance theorists argue that any actor playing any role is recognized, remembered, and assessed by an audience; in addition, they claim that theatrical conventions are significantly recalled and manipulated in performance. Sue-Ellen Case has, in fact, recently called for a re-evaluation of Greek tragedy based on what we know about historical performance practice (1988: 19). She argues that modern feminists involved in contemporary performances (actresses, directors) may find some female roles that were once considered attractive for their assertions of the female voice, feminine power, and womanly strength, now unattractive in light of their origins as drag roles for men and as part of texts that originally functioned as vehicles of an ideology that required the silence and invisibility of women. Aristophanic studies may profit from her ideas. Certainly, it is possible that at a dramatic festival in late fifth- or early fourth-century Athens, a playwright may have played with gender roles and social power by means of the strategic use of costume, travesty, and transvestism. Knowing what the performances may have meant originally should highlight the great changes worked on an ancient text when roles are played by women and/or for women.

I have approached the plays of Aristophanes as a classicist and as a female reader in late twentieth-century America. As I have outlined above, it is quite clear that the intended audience of these plays is male and that my predisposition does not conform to what may have been Aristophanes' expectations for an audience. I ask the same question, then, of these plays that the feminist performance theorists ask of more recent comedies: how does a woman view performance constructed for or with the male gaze? And when she does look at the performance, what does she see? Can we retrieve more closely what Aristophanes may have meant for his audience to take home from the festival of Dionysus? By recognizing that my gaze differs from the gaze of the theoretical, original ideal spectator, that ideal spectator is 'decentered' or 'denaturalized'. The advantages of this position are many: from it, a critic is able to 'point out that every aspect of theatrical production, from the types of plays that are produced to the texts that are ultimately canonized, is determined to reflect and perpetuate the ideal spectator's ideology' (Dolan 1988: 1).

INTRODUCTION

A feminist viewpoint, informed by the methodology of performance criticism, leads to the following questions about Aristophanes. How are we to understand the role of women in the early plays? Are they simply the passive representatives of fertility and objects of male sexual desire, elements essential to a fantasy utopia, that many scholars would have them be? What is Aristophanes' purpose in playing with gender roles and the ideology of the city in *Lysistrata*, *Thesmophoriazusae*, and *Ecclesiazusae*? What were these plays like in performance, and how were male audiences meant to understand the representation of women in the plays? How does the representation of gender in these plays subvert or reinforce Athenian ideologies? What do Aristophanes' plays, especially the plays that feature female characters, tell us about the social construction of gender in ancient Greece? Does the representation of women on stage in Attic comedy have any relationship to the representation of women in other literary traditions? What are modern readers, spectators, actors, and teachers, male and female, to make of these plays today?

My treatment of Aristophanes' plays proceeds under the following assumptions. First, theater is a system of signs and representations. Meaning is construed by the audience's interpretation of the given signs. Cross-dressing is theatrical by nature: a person dressed in clothes representative of the other gender acts the part of that gender, taking on a new identity just as an actor in costume for a dramatic performance does. In a play like *Ecclesiazusae*, for example, originally performed under the aegis of strict costume requirements that included masks, clothes define a character as much as words and actions do (see Muecke 1977 and 1982a). Second, masculinity and femininity are cultural constructions set in a relationship of mutual resistance and cooperation. As a cultural construct, gender becomes a category of analysis that offers insights into structures of power. Third, a culture's values and assumptions are represented by its theater and its theatrical practices. Theatrical conventions may or may not be accepted and ignored by audiences. The conventions of Athenian play production call into question categories of gender and the representation of sexual difference: the standard practice of male actors 'playing women calls into question the relationship between the actor and his role, the nature and limits of theatrical representation, and the connection between the theater and the world beyond' (McLuskie 1987: 120). One point to keep in mind is that, since men play all the parts and the author is male, the representation of women on stage is the representation of a male interpretation of woman. It follows that the representation of man is also a careful social construct. Fourth, and finally, a society stages many activities following the basic pattern of elements in theater. Performance theory tells us that theater is marked by: '1) a special ordering of time; 2) a special value attached to objects; 3) non-productivity in terms of goods; 4) rules. Often special places – non-ordinary places – are set aside or constructed to perform these activities in' (Schechner 1988: 6).[33] Activities which are governed by the ritual basics of theater include religion, sports, and government.

In Chapter 1, 'The representation of female figures in Aristophanes' plays before 411 BCE', I examine the appearance of female characters, both personified feminine abstractions and 'real' human females, in the six extant Aristophanic plays produced before *Lysistrata*: *Acharnians*, *Knights*, *Clouds*, *Wasps*, *Peace*, and *Birds*. While there are no female characters of central importance to the action of these plays, every time a female figure appears, it is within a self-consciously theatrical context. Each scene with a female figure highlights her 'natural' trickiness, emphasizes that she is a comic character in a play, or plays with the dramatic convention that she is an imitation female played by a man. Female figures in these plays tend to manipulate language and costume, deliberately or incidentally, for comic effect. This treatment of the feminine allows for such standard comic devices as disguise and word-play, manipulation of the dramatic illusion, and metatheater. From its beginnings, perhaps, Old Comedy (as represented by Aristophanes' plays) never included real women, and by nature played with the stereotype of woman as a tricky fiction.

Chapter 2, 'Women as women, men as men: *Lysistrata*', looks at *Lysistrata* through the models of spectatorship that contemporary feminist theories of representation construct. In this case, the first appearance of a centrally important comic woman calls attention to the representation of women and the illusion of theater. In fact, the plot, the characterization, and the stage-play all posit theatricality and role-playing as the backbone of the play. Lysistrata's plan for peace requires that the young wives play stereotypical women's roles: as objects of desire within the field of the male gaze. This stereotype is not simply a temporary role, however; the women imitate who they really are. At the beginning of the play, Aristophanes carefully constructs his idea of 'woman', suggesting that 'woman' is a fiction, a creation of costumes and artifice staged for the male gaze. The characterization of Lysistrata has been a puzzle for scholars, however, for she does not adhere to the stereotype perpetuated by the young wives. Much of her character and her voice can be illuminated, if not fully explained, by recognizing that she is to be thought of as being of ambiguous gender, and quite clearly played by a man. Throughout the play, Aristophanes exploits the ambiguous mixture of gender and character that happens when women appear in comedy. The play highlights the absurdity of women in public life and, while it exaggerates masculinity, celebrates male sexuality and spectatorship.

Chapter 3, 'Men as women: *Thesmophoriazusae*', investigates this popular play as a continuous commentary on the fiction of woman on stage, in both comedy and tragedy. Everything in the play converges at the point of the representation of women. On stage, the audience sees a man representing a man who may or may not write realistic portrayals of women (Euripides), a man representing a man who dresses like a woman (Agathon), a man representing a man who unwillingly is disguised as a woman (the Relative), men representing 'real' women (the women of Athens), and a man representing a man who conducts his public life as a spokesman for women (Kleisthenes). *Thesmophoriazusae* attempts to turn comedy inside out through these complicated dramatizations. There is much manipulation of the power of costume to disguise and reveal, of the portrayal of women by men, and of the process of spectators' gazes and interpretations. Masculinity cannot be hidden underneath women's skirts, and the play confirms this ironic representative power as exclusive to comedy. After all, the men all wear the theatrical sign of Dionysus, the comic phallos. Staging false women as the objects of the male gaze becomes, in the end, the ultimate comic trick: it is what Euripides does to free his relative.

In Chapter 4, 'Women as men: *Ecclesiazusae*', an analysis of *Ecclesiazusae* reveals that the play presents both disguise and gender as dramatic illusions that exist on stage and in real life. This play creates an illusion of gender disguise that plays upon traditional divisions of authority based on gender and explicitly connects traditional gender roles with good government. Through its fantasy of women taking over the government, the play suggests that acting is a phenomenon at work outside the theater, particularly in the assembly. In fact, we are never encouraged to believe in any disguise that characters, male or female, adopt on stage, and so our faith in the basic disguise that makes female characters possible on stage is challenged. Both language and clothes become elements of disguise that make gender identity unstable and tricky. The play can be seen as a call for a return to masculine values and stable identities, not the call for revolution that it seems to be.

Chapter 5, 'The legacy of Aristophanes' women', offers some further thoughts on understanding Old Comedy through feminist literary theories and the relevance of such inquiry to modern readers, especially directors and actors. In addition to discussing the representation of women in Aristophanes' other two plays, *Frogs* (405 BCE) and *Wealth* (388 BCE), the chapter also discusses the link between female characters, gender identity on stage, and the convention of male actors in female roles in other comic traditions, using Shakespearean comedy as a comparative model. It also addresses the changes in meaning that actresses playing female roles originally written for men may facilitate.

1
THE REPRESENTATION OF FEMALE FIGURES IN ARISTOPHANES' PLAYS BEFORE 411 BCE

This chapter will review the presentation of female figures in the extant plays of Aristophanes that were produced before *Lysistrata* (411 BCE): *Acharnians* (425), *Knights* (424), *Clouds* (423), *Wasps* (422), *Peace* (421) and *Birds* (414). Although these plays do not focus exclusively on women, they all contain at least one female character. Most of these plays concern a man with fantastic plans for himself, his family, or the city; this man often has a wife or a daughter, and usually acquires some other type of female figure in order to realize his designs. Previous scholarship on the plays has correspondingly centered on this male hero and his schemes. Critics are likely to gloss over the flute girls and courtesans who appear at the ends of these comedies with a few words about their symbolic fertility and powers for the sexual rejuvenation of the male hero.[1] A close look at these figures, however, reveals new possibilities for the interpretation of each play and the configuration of the feminine in Aristophanes' comic plans. I shall be considering the following trends: (*a*) what functions female figures play in these early Aristophanic plays; (*b*) how the idea of the feminine fits into the scheme of the comedy; (*c*) any evidence in the text that points to the male actor playing the role of a female figure.

Several types of females are present in these plays: wives and daughters of the central male characters, representations of abstract concepts or mythological figures, and occasional older market women. Little girls appear in parodies of ritual and tragedy (*Acharnians*, *Peace*). Mythological females appear to help or to warn the hero (*Birds*, *Clouds*, *Peace*). Abstract feminine figures inspire sexual rejuvenation in the hero (*Acharnians*, *Knights*, *Wasps*, *Peace*, *Birds*). No matter the generic origin of her character, however, every female figure is presented within a similar framework. Female figures in these early plays are each represented within a highly theatrical setting. Each scene with a female figure is composed to reveal that she is a theatrical creation, or to point out that she is played by a male actor, or to expose that she is, as a female, generically false and tricky. Females tend to manipulate language and costume, deliberately or incidentally, for comic effect. They always display variations on traditional stereotypes of femininity. These variations are never stable; the representations of female figures double back on themselves to reveal their equivocation. Through such reversals, these figures become comic creatures in their own right designed for a specifically male audience. Even in the plays that do not feature women as important characters, the representation of femininity on stage calls attention to the inauthenticity and instability of the idea of 'woman'.

ACHARNIANS

Acharnians (425 BCE) dramatizes a war-weary country refugee's fantasy. Its protagonist, Dikaiopolis, is a farmer residing in Athens for the duration of the war (in compliance with Pericles' policy that brought all inhabitants of Attica inside the walls for protection while the Peloponnesian army raided the Attic countryside and burned the fields: Thuc. 2. 13–14, 16–17). Disgusted with the ineptitude and corruption of the assembly, Dikaiopolis establishes a private peace with the Spartans. The men of Acharnai, through which the Peloponnesian army has marched, become angry with him. In order to appease this fiery chorus, Dikaiopolis borrows the costume and character of Telephus from the poet Euripides; his parody of Euripidean strategies for pity works, and Dikaiopolis establishes himself and his family as a sovereign entity no longer at war, and so no longer subject to such hardships as the lack of food, wine, and sex that war brings on.[2]

Situations that resemble theatrical settings appear throughout the play. Even Dikaiopolis' opening monologue is addressed to the audience in the theater, for example (see Foley 1988; Muecke 1982a). When the assembly finally gets under way, Dikaiopolis interprets its artifice as though he were commenting on a theatrical performance: he laughs in general disbelief at the conflagration of characters and reveals their deceitful costumes and poses. Later, his elaborate solicitation of Euripides mocks Euripides' plots, characters, and style as effectively as any theater critic. Given these allusions to theater and theatricality, it should not be unusual to think of Dikaiopolis' other actions in terms of theater.

Dikaiopolis asks Amphitheus, a representative sent by the gods to make peace and who has been expelled from the assembly, to obtain the peace for him. After Dikaiopolis sets up a peace treaty and announces his private peace with Sparta, he leads out a celebration of the Rural Dionysia.[3] The procession is announced at a significant moment. With the peace, Dikaiopolis has also declared his political separation from the city of Athens. Now he is free to celebrate a renewed life without war (201–2), a life which he begins ceremonially. Dikaiopolis establishes an individual civic identity with this festival, just as a deme might.[4] He and his family alone benefit from the peace and celebrate on their own the institutions of the city.

The celebration is at once public and private. The family, primarily a private institution, imitates the public practices of the city. The procession will, they hope, affect the fertility of Dikaiopolis' *oikos* just as it might the prosperity of a separate state. Dikaiopolis' daughter leads the procession as the κανηφόρος, the basket-bearer; his slave follows behind with the phallos-pole. The daughter's basket contains offerings to Dionysus: a sacred cake and sauce. Dikaiopolis' wife is also present, but she never speaks. He tells her to go up to the roof after the procession and watch the proceedings from above (262); she seems to obey his orders.[5] Some editors have assumed from this passage that adult women watched the Rural Dionysia from the roofs of their houses; aside from this testimonium, there is no evidence to support such a hypothesis. It is, however, rather unusual that she appears at all. She is the only hero's wife to be present on stage in an extant Aristophanic play. Strepsiades' wife does not appear in *Clouds*, yet we know she exists from Strepsiades' complaints about her. Trygaeus does not mention his wife in *Peace*, but her existence is at least implied by the appearance of their daughter. It was common practice for men not to name upper- and middle-class women in public, and this practice appears to have carried over into the comic theater.[6]

Whether Dikaiopolis' wife is following a customary Athenian procedure or not matters little in the course of the play. For this scene, it is important that she watches from a distance. From her vantage point, she becomes the audience for the singing of the phallic hymn. The scene suggests a miniature reworking of the origins of comic drama, a play-within-the-play (Starkie 1909: 63).[7] The possibilities of exploiting her position on stage in performance are many. On the roof, as an audience for Dikaiopolis' parade, she is free to interact with the festival audience in the theater herself. There she becomes an intermediary between the play proper and the play-within-the-play for the audience in the theater. While her role as an observer (and not a participant) may be traditional, her position as a watched spectator becomes an important part of the comic action.[8] Our view of the procession is not filtered through hers, although she does complete the theatrical conceit on stage.

Dikaiopolis himself acts as the sacrificing priest, but his daughter has the central position in this proto-comedy: as the basket-bearer, the procession and hymn focus on her sexuality. We cannot ignore her and the contents of her basket; they are essential to the ritual performance. At one and the same time, she takes part in the procession for the good of her family and of her own future and she displays to the audience in the theater the origins of comedy, of which she, as the object of several sexual *double entendres*, is an essential ingredient.

With her first words, Dikaiopolis' daughter reveals her promise of fertility and her theatricality, not only through her role as the basket-bearer, but through the two levels of her speech. She addresses her mother: 'O mother, hand up the ladle there, so that I might pour the sauce over this little sacred cake' (ὦ μῆτερ, ἀνάδος δεῦρο τὴν ἐτνήρυσιν, / ἵν' ἔτνος καταχέω τοὐλατῆρος τουτουί, 245–6). Her words are not as simple as they seem, however; they carry obscene meanings as slang terms for male and female genitals.[9] Dikaiopolis' daughter appears not only as a young girl offering cakes to the god. She now becomes a comic character who parodies, with obscene *double entendres*, the sacrificial offering. The audience may see a girl naïvely expressing something only they and her father understand or a comic actor pretending to be a girl more knowing than her looks or age may suggest. Through either her knowledge or her innocence, she can turn a religious offering into a joke. This girl is an astute manipulator of the ritual text. The incongruity of her innocent presence – she is just a young girl and presumably should not speak about sex – along with the *double entendre*, makes the moment comic.

After her comment, Dikaiopolis invokes Dionysus (247–52), the god of theater, and then he turns to address his daughter (253–8). He refers to her strictly in terms of her future sexuality.[10] She should carry the basket well, he says, and look as though she has eaten savory (βλέπουσα θυμβροφάγον, 254). Dikaiopolis here calls attention to her mask, which may have a cute, parodical expression – she is encouraged to play to the male gaze.[11] The direction seems pointless; her mask cannot change expression at all, so she might not appear as prim as Dikaiopolis wishes anyway. At this point, she is the main physical comic on stage and our attention is focused on the parts of her costume that define her character. Her father, aware of both the internal audience (his wife and the chorus, which entered at 204) and the external audience in the theater, coaches his daughter as a director would an actor.[12] In fact, we are encouraged to see her as an actor playing a part.

Aristophanes sets this celebration as a ritual performed in front of an audience to enhance its position in the account of Dikaiopolis' peace negotiations. Dikaiopolis has just founded a new city, populated exclusively by his own family, performed a traditional civic ritual, and imitated, in miniature and in parody, the beginnings of the dramatic genre in which he exists. As Dikaiopolis does this, Aristophanes suggests that comedy is basic for the religious and public health of the city; after all, we do not see Dikaiopolis recreating tragedy. The daughter is not only identified with the *oikos*: as the daughter and κανηφόρος, she performs a function that is simultaneously public and private. Aristophanes makes her, as a comic character, speak and be spoken to about sex. To the audience, her *double entendres* are funny and controversial, another level added to the text. Her mother watches the performance from the top of the house as a spectator; in this way she both takes part in a public function and also frames the ritual theatrically. Finally, the first females (human females, to be exact) to appear in the earliest extant Aristophanic comedy are found within a clear theatrical and metatheatrical context. While female characters are not always necessary for metatheatrical play (Dikaiopolis ridicules and borrows from Euripides perfectly well on his own), whenever they are present, theatricality or metatheatricality appear in one form or another.

By theatricality, I mean that these female characters help establish a sense of themselves as creations of theater, not necessarily of real life. Take, for example, the obscenity of Dikaiopolis' daughter. On one level, her comment is in agreement with what a basket-bearer might say. On another, she is offered up as a sexual object, as a female figure in theater often is. It is unlikely that an Athenian father would prefer his daughter to be seen in this way. Dikaiopolis also gives her acting directions. By metatheatricality, I mean that female figures often help establish the theatrical framework of the scene and encourage us to see, for instance, ritual (or even life in general) as theater. In *Acharnians*, the ritual of the Rural Dionysia is presented as a theatrical procession with the help of Dikaiopolis' wife and daughter.

The wife and daughter are not presented here with any clear allusion to the male actors who play them. In the case of the wife, this would have to do with the cultural practice of good wives not appearing or being referred to in public; it is not necessary or preferable to call attention to her any more than Dikaiopolis already does. In the case of the daughter, her sexuality is so immature that the purpose of calling attention to the actor who plays her seems equally inappropriate. We may still speculate that Dikaiopolis' comments about her potential sexual attractiveness highlight the incongruity between the audience's knowledge that she is not really a girl but an actor dressed as a girl and her image on stage, although the text gives us no confirmation of this confusion.

Girls do not appear again until Dikaiopolis has opened his private market up for business and a hungry Megarian arrives with his young daughters (729–835).[13] He decides to sell the girls, with their permission; this seems to be the only solution to certain starvation. The episode, arguably the most gruesome example of black humor in Aristophanes' repertoire, brings home the effects of war effectively. When asking permission, the Megarian father addresses the girls' bellies, rather than their minds (733); their empty bellies make the decision.[14] The daughters do not remain in the guise of little girls for very long afterwards. Their father dresses them as sacrificial piglets (χοῖροι). In this scene, young girls are associated not only with theater and sexuality, but also with food, an important issue for Dikaiopolis after he establishes peace with the Spartans.

This man plans a Megarian trick (Μεγαρικά τις μαχανά, 738: an expression for a low, vulgar scheme) of which the girls are naturally the main instruments.[15] The mention of a Megarian μαχανά also recalls the origins of comedy.[16] In fact, the Megarian puts on a play for Dikaiopolis; he plays the merchant, the girls play the piglets, and Dikaiopolis plays the intended victim of the trick. Although their father disguises them in piglet costumes (hooves, τὰς ὁπλάς, 740; snouts, τὰ ῥυγχία, 744), the girls are not just the sum of all their parts as piggies.[17] Their new identity, piggies (χοῖροι), makes them living metaphors, synecdoches to be exact, for girls: χοῖρος is also a slang term for young girls' genitals.[18] After putting on the costumes and getting into the sack, even their speech ceases to be human and echoes their new identity. Now they say only κοῖ κοῖ (780; MacMathúna 1971: 30).

Dikaiopolis cannot quite believe his eyes when he sees what his salt and garlic can purchase, and the Megarian succeeds in passing his girls off as 'piggies' for sacrifice to Aphrodite.[19] The girls' costumes combine feminine sexuality with feminine theatricality. Dikaiopolis asks the 'piggies' what they like to eat, describing their food with obscene *double entendres*.²⁰ The girls respond with their piglet sounds (800–3). Stripped of language, the girls are no longer human, yet they remain totally female.

On the one hand, we can interpret this scene with reference to the traditional alliance of females and fertility. The two men who possess these 'piggies' perform functions with them which are generally for the continuance of life. The Megarian sells his daughters so that he may eat (although what he receives in exchange is only salt and garlic). With language and costumes he transforms them into two distinct organs, both with life-related functions: bellies and genitalia. Their disguises also resemble sacrifices to Demeter, a fertility goddess, but it turns out that even they have a double reference. Dikaiopolis buys 'piggies' for sacrifice to one fertility goddess, Demeter, and discovers that they can also be sacrificed to another fertility goddess, Aphrodite.²¹ How he sacrifices these 'piggies' to Aphrodite involves himself as well.

On the other hand, inherent feminine theatricality comes into play as well. Here, female figures don costumes and pass themselves off as what they literally both are and are not. Female figures appear as two things at once. The humor stems, perhaps, from this double fantasy: one man disposes of his female dependents for money (and food), another acquires females for sexual pleasure. Each man gains something in the exchange. Here male characters manipulate females for their own gain; without the feminine element, however, there would be no gain and no joke. Dikaiopolis becomes the last trickster, however. The garlic and salt that he trades with the Megarian are the last things that the Megarian needs: these items were Megara's chief exports.

Both the staging of the Rural Dionysia and the Megarian charade require women for their sexuality and for their theatricality. Each scene works a variation on the device of a play-within-the-play, offers a parody of ritual, alludes to the invention and practice of comedy, links food together with sex, and features women as central comic characters, as both the subjects and authors of humor. By definition, certain types of comedy must include feminine characters and certain types of jokes benefit from a feminine presence. Again, there appears to be no clear indication of the male actors under the costumes of these female figures.

Further appearances of female figures in *Acharnians* reflect a tendency to emphasize this female penchant for trickery by means of sexual *double entendres*. A Theban merchant with a bottomless bag of gourmet goodies offers Dikaiopolis some Copaic eels, apostrophized as maidens, and he tells of the pleasure gained from eating them (878–909). A banquet at the play's end abounds in *double entendres* for eating and sexual activity. The banquet celebrates the union of Dikaiopolis and Diallage, Reconciliation, a mute, nude female figure who enhances the abundance of peace and food with her suggested sexual fertility and who facilitates the theatrical magic of Dikaiopolis' sexual rejuvenation.[22]

The inclusion of female figures in *Acharnians* seems inextricably tied to the establishment of the play's comic perspective. Dikaiopolis uses tragedy to his own benefit here, and female figures have little part in that (unless the situation of the Megarian's daughters is considered tragic). Dikaiopolis initiates his newly formed city with a proto-comic festival, however, and his daughter plays an important role there; in addition, his market is initiated with an exchange of elaborately costumed females. Both these events enhance the theatrical message of *Acharnians*. While arguably and ostensibly a 'peace play', it also strongly establishes Aristophanes' identity as a poet who will reinvent comedy on the stage, as a reaction and tonic to tragedy. In 425 BCE the Peloponnesian War was only six years old. Aside from the simple fantasy of a personal peace and the lambasting of ineffectual politicians, *Acharnians* still presents peace as a positive and affirmative possibility and femininity as a humorously tricky aspect of both peace and comedy.

KNIGHTS

Aristophanes' *Knights* (424 BCE) features very few female figures. This play concerns a character named Demos, who represents the Athenian people, his slaves Demosthenes and Nicias (named for two prominent generals at the time), and the current favorite slave Paphlagon (a thinly veiled caricature of the popular and, according to Thucydides, subsequently dangerous demagogue Cleon). Demosthenes and Nicias discover that Paphlagon is about to be replaced as the favorite of Demos by a Sausage-seller. When the Sausage-seller appears, a chorus of cavalrymen (the Knights) offers him its support. Most of the play consists of a lengthy and heated argument between Paphlagon and the Sausage-seller in which all the dirty laundry of Athenian politics is aired. The Sausage-seller wins, of course, and is hailed as the savior of the city.[23]

Quite near the end of the play, the Chorus-leader tells a story about some Athenian triremes (1300–15). They are female, by custom and by linguistic gender (ἡ τριήρης), and their conversation (recreated within the story) is meant to be comically feminine.[24] The elder trireme (γεραιτέρα, 1301) speaks. She calls the other ships 'maidens' (ὦ παρθένοι, 1302). Through the personification of the ships, the passage becomes a comic treatment of a loss of virginity and innocence: the ships debate their 'maiden' voyages and the policies of the Athenian naval command. The passage admittedly tells us little about the comic representation of real women, yet the vivid analogy between real Athenian maidens and new triremes is telling. These vessels, built and run by men, have stereotypical feminine concerns (sex) and a facility with language (the *double entendre* between sexual experience and their first naval venture is suggested by the trireme herself). The appearance of these imaginary female figures in the Chorus-leader's fable does not represent female figures on the comic stage in any theatrical fashion. It does, however, offer a clear suggestion that female figures may appear in other than human female guise.

At the very end of *Knights*, the Sausage-seller calls out the Spondai as a gift for Demos (1389). The Spondai – the same pun on truces and wine-libations that appeared in *Acharnians* (178–200) – are just what Demos wants 'to satisfy his thirty-year peace' (1390–1). Female figures incarnate this pun; they are at once desired and abused, however. They function as signs of peace, signs of festivity, and signs of Demos' rejuvenation, much as the mute Diallage did at the end of *Acharnians*. Unlike *Acharnians*, however, it is not clear that *Knights* ends on a truly joyous note. Henderson writes:

> The rejuvenation of Demos is not developed much beyond a plot device, and the entrance of the two naked Truces at the end seems to be a perfunctory gesture made to satisfy an almost obligatory tradition in Old Comedy of staging the good old days this way.
>
> (Henderson 1975: 88)[25]

Still, a feminine component (the Spondai) is necessary for this finale, perfunctory or not. *Knights* contributes relatively little to the overall picture of female figures in earlier Aristophanic plays. Yet it does continue some of the trends for the representation of females found in *Acharnians*: females are necessary to comedy, staged, whether they speak or not, for a specifically male audience, and often appear in an ambiguously configured form.

CLOUDS

Problems between a father and his son form the impetus for *Clouds* (423 BCE).[26] Upon failing to convince his son Pheidippides (as his name indicates, he loves horses) to attend the school of argument (the Phrontisterion, 'the Thinkery') run by Socrates, Strepsiades ('Twisty') decides to enroll himself. He believes that if he learns how to twist words in an argument, then he will be able to talk himself out of his – and his son's – debts. Once Strepsiades confronts Socrates, and meets the goddesses who attend him (the Clouds), it becomes clear that he is too stupid to learn anything. Strepsiades and Socrates hold a debate between the personified Just and Unjust Arguments; Pheidippides reluctantly agrees to become the student of the victor. Unjust Argument prevails. Learning through observation, Strepsiades eventually succeeds in cheating his creditors of what he owes them. Pheidippides learns too, however, and beats up his father, justifying the beating with an argument. The play ends when an angry Strepsiades sets fire to Socrates' school.

Real women never actually appear in *Clouds*. The only glimpse we have of them is through Strepsiades' eyes (41b–55).[27] Strepsiades' opinion of his wife is neither positive nor unusual, although their marriage is rather odd. He is a poor farmer; his wife is a wealthy woman from the city. This woman and her sophisticated ways, her devotion to luxury and her worship of Aphrodite, are, to him, highly unnatural. Her sexuality is contrived; she smells of perfumes, expense, and two different cults of Aphrodite, Aphrodite Genetyllis and Aphrodite Kolias (51–2). She is also the source of his problems: her relentless instruction of Pheidippides has made the boy horse-mad (60–77). This could be a kind of 'odd-couple' joke: the poor old farmer has found a terrible and incompatible spouse, but at least she is wealthy. On the other hand, one also wonders whether this is a reflection of one of the possible consequences of Pericles' strategy of bringing those who inhabited the Attic countryside within the walls of the city for the duration of the war: some social classes may have intermarried.

Like the other females in Aristophanic comedy so far, the chorus of Clouds that Strepsiades meets in Socrates' Phrontisterion possesses a feminine talent for rhetoric and deceptive language. At first glance, we might see them as nature goddesses (Segal 1975). In their *parodos* (275–313), the Clouds ally themselves with nature. The strophe (275–90) tells of how they aid or assist fertility. They are ever-flowing (ἀέναοι), dewy (δροσεράν), and bright (εὐάγητον). They watch over the fertile land, rivers, and seas (281–4). Yet the Clouds are not wholly removed from human culture. The antistrophe (299–313) tells of Athens' fertility in religious and ritual terms. Their status is presented in human terms: they are maidens (παρθένοι). A παρθένος usually performs the function of the κανηφόρος and carries the basket in ritual processions (cf. Dikaiopolis' daughter in *Acharnians*). Here, the cloud-maidens are rainbearers (ὀμβροφόροι, 298) instead of κανηφόροι (298/99). They mention the mysteries and pride of Eleusis (302–4); it is appropriate for the Clouds, who bring rain that causes the crops to grow, to think of Demeter first, for she also helps the crops. They praise the abundance of festivals in Athens and the gifts to the gods from the Athenians in all seasons (307–10). All the Clouds' concerns here are feminine. They are, apparently, the first female Aristophanic chorus, and their linguistic gender is thus intentionally feminine (αἱ νεφέλαι).

Strepsiades calls our attention to the chorus's costumes with a question: why do the Clouds look like women (340–1)? When asked to describe what real clouds look like, Strepsiades says that real clouds look like spread-out wool, and not like women, and that these clouds have noses (342). Socrates' explanation is that the Clouds can take any shape they wish; because they happened to see Kleisthenes, an effeminate man, in the audience, they chose the shape of women (348–55; see Dover 1968: 148 *ad* 355; cf. *Ecclesiazusae* 167–8). On one level, the comment aggressively attacks Kleisthenes' masculinity. Theatrically, however, the comment may call our attention to the male actors underneath the costumes of the feminine Clouds. The word for nose here, ῥίς, can be used as an obscene term for phallos. Reference to the phallos does not necessarily cancel out the predetermined gender of the Clouds. Rather, it complicates the image on stage and offers a path of vision through the dramatic illusion. In other words, we may be asked to recognize that the chorus is made up of male actors dressed as women dressed as clouds (Brown 1983). This is the first instance in an extant Aristophanic play where we may say that the actor in a female costume is deliberately highlighted for comic effect.

Why would Aristophanes compromise the representation of the Cloud-chorus with a joke that reveals the actors underneath the costumes? The answer may rest in the trends of representing women in comedy. Clouds excel at imitation (they can take any shape they wish). According to a traditional strain of Greek thought, so do women.[28] In Hesiod's account of the creation of woman in *Works and Days* (42–106), for instance, femininity is allied with imitation and linguistic craftiness.[29] The personifications of clouds in this play are correspondingly conceived of as female.

Hesiod's account emphasizes the first woman's outward appearance and her clothes, her trickery with words and her crafty mind (see also the account of Pandora in *Theogony* 570–612). The story offers an explanation for the human (i.e. male) condition. Angry at Prometheus for stealing fire and giving it to men, Zeus has the gods create a deadly gift for man – a woman – and has Hermes deliver it to Prometheus' brother Epimetheus as his wife. Ignoring his brother's warning against accepting presents from Zeus, Epimetheus takes her in. This woman opens up the box she has and lets out troubles, diseases, death, and other bad things, causing sorrows and work for men (*Works and Days* 47–106). Once woman was created and given to Epimetheus, the world changed. Men had to work. She opened the jar and let terrible cares out to roam among men; in addition, her beauty and character inspire desire and envy. Thus, woman is allied with the invention of civilization; her ability to speak tricky words associates her with the invention of rhetoric (Pucci 1977: 100–1).

The Clouds are also allied with certain cultural institutions, such as education, especially education in deception. They function as Muses, as creatures who watch over the tricky logic of Socrates' school. Socrates tells Strepsiades of their talents:

ἀλλ' οὐράνιαι Νεφέλαι, μεγάλαι θεαὶ ἀνδράσιν ἀργοῖς,
αἵπερ γνώμην καὶ διάλεξιν καὶ νοῦν ἡμῖν παρέχουσιν
καὶ τερατείαν καὶ περίλεξιν καὶ κροῦσιν καὶ κατάληψιν .
... οὐ γὰρ μὰ Δί' οἶσθ' ὁτιὴ πλείστους αὗται βόσκουσι
  σοφιστάς,
Θουριομάντεις, ἰατροτέχνας, σφραγιδονυχαργοκομήτας
κυκλίων τε χορῶν ᾀσματοκάμπτας, ἄνδρας μετεωροφένακας,
οὐδὲν δρῶντας βόσκουσ' ἀργούς, ὅτι ταύτας μουσοποοῦσιν.

(316–18; 331–4)

They are clouds of the heavens, great goddesses for lazy men, who give over to us judgement, dialectic, intelligence, storytelling, circumlocution, striking with a point in argument, and checking the audience's reaction in debate. . . . Nor, by Zeus, do you know that these are the ones who nourish the most sophists, prophets of Thurii, healers, long-hairs with signet-rings, twisters of the songs of circular choruses, and astrology-quacks, and they nourish lazy men who do nothing, because they compose songs for them.[30]

This recalls the role of the Muses and, in some respects, the legacy of Hesiod's first woman. The Clouds cast man into misery as woman did (1458–64). She has a crafty mind and so do the Clouds.

Clouds have one more attribute that their femininity requires: they are protean, physically as well as linguistically deceptive. As Socrates says, the Clouds can imitate anything. That first woman, from whom all other women are descended, is not very substantial. Her appearance is just an image (εἶδος). She has a human voice, but she is not human. She has the face of a goddess but she is not a goddess. She is mud disguised as an alluring creature; her form is changeable.[31] Hesiod even describes her as a trick, a deception (δόλον αἰπὺν ἀμήχανον, 83), and not as a woman.

The trickery of Socrates' Clouds lies in their natural talent for imitation; they reveal the nature of things by concealing it, conceal the nature of things by revealing it (see L. Strauss 1966: 21). Hesiod might say that femininity exhibits the same talent. Aristophanes repeats the thought with this representation of the Clouds: Strepsiades' remark about the Clouds' apparent femininity and their 'noses' reveals the imitative nature of femininity and the impossibility of representing women as unequivocally stable in nature and form. Just as *Acharnians* represents female figures consistently within a theatrical framework, highlighting the representation of femininity as representation and not reality, so *Clouds* represents femininity as a protean, deceptive, and ultimately false construct. There are always men underneath.

If we regard the chorus of Clouds in *Clouds* as significantly female, then Aristophanes plays with the deceptiveness of nature, of woman, and of language. The chorus is deceptive; not only does it help Socrates teach the deceptiveness of words, but it deceives the audience and reader as well. At the end of the play, when the chorus seems to defend the institutions of *polis* and *oikos* and explain their reasons for punishing Strepsiades, we do not know if the Clouds are sincere or tricky. In fact, they appear trickier if they have deceived Strepsiades all along. Aristophanes conceives of this trickiness, in appearance and in language, as female. Conversely, he thinks of the female as a deceptive creature in form and in speech. In this play, Aristophanes mocks current trends in intellectual investigation and in education; by allying the sophists with feminine duplicity, he casts aspersions on their integrity and their sincerity. Yet Aristophanes has it both ways: the sort of duplicity that femininity provides Socrates with here is the same sort of duplicity that Aristophanes needs for his comedy.

In *Clouds*, femininity in comedy becomes deceptive itself, and this treatment of the feminine most clearly anticipates the use of femininity for comic purposes in *Lysistrata*, *Thesmophoriazusae*, and *Ecclesiazusae*. Woman is used as an emblem of both deceptive culture and fertile nature, allied with the way femininity appears in the tradition of invective poems against women. Real women, like Strepsiades' wife, may be contrived by city ways, but they are close to nature in their habits. Natural phenomena, like clouds, may be feminine by nature, but even that natural femininity can be represented as a false construct; on stage, we see that they are men underneath. Femininity is deceptive by nature in both appearance and practice, and its theatrical representation calls attention to its very falseness.

WASPS

Wasps (422 BCE) dramatizes another conflict between a son, Bdelycleon ('Hates Cleon'), and his father, Philocleon ('Loves Cleon'). Philocleon has become an addict of the courtroom: he loves to sit as a juror, vote to convict every defendant, and then collect his pay. He loves Cleon because the demagogue keeps the courts full and the payroll hefty. Bdelycleon tries to cure his father's addiction by imprisoning him in the house. The chorus of jurors, wasps who love to sting defendants, help Philocleon escape. Bdelycleon eventually manages to bring the chorus around to his way of thinking; he convinces them that the jurors are slaves to the rulers (namely, Cleon). In order to cure Philocleon's obsession, Bdelycleon tricks him by holding a trial at home. Through his son's chicanery, Philocleon acquits the family dog of the charge of stealing cheese. Philocleon gets the last laugh, however, for when Bdelycleon takes him out to dinner, he gets riotously drunk. The play ends with a celebration of Philocleon's outrageous behavior.[32]

Like *Knights*, the play has few female figures. A female bread-seller, Myrtia, appears near the end, after Philocleon has been cured of his jury-sickness and gotten drunk at his son's expense. She claims that the drunken Philocleon has hit her with his torch (1388). On the one hand, Myrtia is probably costumed as a fat, old hag, and she appears to be a stock comic interloper (cf. *Clouds* 1214–302; see Henderson 1987a: 121; Stone 1980: 303). Yet she presents herself with dignity; she has been wronged by Philocleon and she wants justice. She swears a serious oath to Demeter and Persephone (1396; cf. *Ecclesiazusae* 155–9), which appears to legitimize her femininity – only women swear by these two goddesses. She also names her citizen parents, Sostrate and Ancylion

(1397), to legitimize herself, but undercuts their respectability while trying to establish it. Sostrate has been identified as a stock comic name and Ancylion as a legendary rogue, known for beating his mother (Sommerstein 1983: 240 *ad* 1397). Only within the comic world would such lineage grant authority. By naming her parents this way, Myrtia also reveals herself as a creation of comedy, a theatrical figure. Myrtia's figure does not reveal itself as an imitation in the same way that other female figures have, and there is not enough information about her to determine whether or not the male actor compromises the illusion. She has a small part, and it may be enough just to display her comic ancestry.

Myrtia suggests a witness to the crime, but her own description of him undercuts his potential authority. She says that he looks 'like a yellow-faced Ino'. This probably means that he is sickly or pale.[33] His pale skin suggests effeminacy. At best, his masculinity would be compromised and the authority of his testimony weakened. At worst, the witness might be mistaken for a woman and so not be able to testify in court. Myrtia's choice of witnesses is silly. The interesting point, however, is the manner in which the authority of the witness is obliterated by establishing doubts about his masculinity, a masculinity that can itself be established through a certain physical appearance.

The flute-girl who appears at the end of *Wasps* (1341 ff.) functions as a clever source of rejuvenation for Philocleon (he asks her to use his phallos as a rope to help her get on stage). Her name is Dardanis (torch, 1371), the girl from Dardania ('Torchville'). She personifies the pun that Philocleon makes when he describes his phallos as a torch. In *Wasps*, where they are arguably of quite minor significance, female figures are drawn nevertheless with reference to traditional comic female characteristics: theatricality and its secrets of costume and deception, and the double nature of language and puns.

PEACE

Peace (421 BCE) recalls the desperate plans for peace of *Acharnians*. In this play, the farmer Trygaeus decides to fly up to the gods on the back of a dung-beetle in order to get some bread for his family's dinner. When he arrives, he discovers that Zeus has left and Polemos (War) has taken charge. Polemos has barricaded Eirene (Peace) in a cave and is now preparing to mix up Greece with his mortar and pestle (as if he were making a giant salad). As Polemos searches for his pestle, Trygaeus and some other farmers, with Hermes' help, retrieve Peace from the cave. Her return to Greece is celebrated with the wedding of

Trygaeus to Eirene's attendant Opora (Harvest) and the City Council to her attendant Theoria (Festival).[34]

Early on in Trygaeus' plan to fly to the gods on a dung-beetle, his daughters, upset about his departure, quiz him about the trip (114–53). The scene parodies Euripides' *Aeolus* and *Bellerophon* and becomes a play-within-the-play. After being summoned to her father's side by a slave, one of the girls asks him whether the story (φάτις) that has come to their home is true (ἔτυμος), that Trygaeus is leaving them with the birds, all alone, to go to the crows (114–17).[35] This is all hilarious, as the girl goes on to pervert lines from Euripides and make fun of her father.

The daughter sets Trygaeus up with questions; he provides the answers, and their dialogue is filled with literary allusions. Trygaeus announces that he got the idea for his adventure from Aesop (129). His daughter suggests that it might be better to fly on Pegasus, then he might look more like a tragic hero (τραγικώτερος, 136). Later, she warns Trygaeus not to fall, for then he might become a tragedy himself (τραγῳδία γένῃ, 148). She clearly knows about theater and drama, and so she understands his nature and identity as the hero of a comedy. This is one of the features of a comically configured female character.

Some aspects of the dialogue raise typically feminine comic concerns. Trygaeus initially appeases his daughters' worries by promising to bring them food if he returns successfully. Either they are hungry because of food shortages during wartime or they are hungry because women are always hungry. The girls also try to manipulate their father verbally. They call him πάτερ and παππία repeatedly, and ask for food in an ingratiating tone. Trygaeus resents this: 'I hate when you ask for bread by calling me "pappa" ' (ἄχθομαι ὑμῖν / ἡνίκ' ἂν αἰτίζητ' ἄρτον πάππαν με καλοῦσαι, 119–20).

Femininity contributes to the humor here in two ways. The daughter proves to be smarter than her father. She is able to parody Euripides and make her father look like a fool. Her objections to his scheme are all sound and rational, in fact; she asks nothing outrageous. At the same time, she forces Trygaeus into explaining the rationale behind his plan, a scheme which must seem particularly far-fetched to the audience. The daughter performs the part of 'straight-man' in the comedy routine, the performer who feeds perfectly reasonable and serious questions to a partner who gives ridiculous answers.

On another level, from the perspective of dramatic and parodic effect, the daughter proves to be a good reader and interpreter. She fully understands her father's situation. Having some knowledge of Euripides' *Bellerophon*, she sees a chance to make fun of it as she mocks

Trygaeus. She knows how to parody, to take words in one style and transform them, disguise them, as another. Part of the comic effect is the phenomenon of hearing a young girl parody tragedy. With Aristophanes, although we can always expect some parody, we never know who will deliver it. Aristophanes shows us, then, a feminine figure who controls the humor in a set-up gag by feeding lines to her partner, as well as a female who knows how to manipulate language and distort its original meaning in order to make fun of two people at once, in this case both her father and Euripides. This ability to parody, to disguise language, is essential to the characterization of the feminine in Aristophanes. There is no clear suggestion of the male actor here, so the theatrical integrity of the daughter's role is not in question. She serves rather to remind us of the theatrical and fictional nature of the proceedings. Finally, she is presented within a metatheatrical framework, just as the daughter of Dikaiopolis (perhaps her companion in age) was.

However, Eirene and her two companions, Opora and Theoria, make up the three central feminine figures in *Peace*. Their femininity is symbolic of fertility and necessary for peace.[36] Eirene was most likely represented on stage by a statue rather than an actor; she never speaks a word for herself.[37] Neither of her companions speaks either, but each of them is eventually married to a character in the play; they were probably played by live actors. When each aspect of Peace, each one feminine, is reunited with her masculine counterpart, then the war-ravaged community is restored and renewed.[38] That Eirene herself brings fertility needs little explication; the point is made obvious by the premises of the play. When she returns, Eirene brings with her all the pleasures of life, especially food, wine, poetry, and revelry (530–8). She and Opora provide happy procreation; while sex does return, neither one of them ever receives sexual abuse.

Theoria, unlike Eirene and Opora, is the object of blunt sexual remarks. In a series of *double entendres* for various athletic games and contests, she is threatened with beating (874), rape (876, 879–80, 882, 884–5), and roasting and scorching (sexual euphemisms; 891–3). After a description of the festal games (894–909), the Prytanis finally takes hold of her. This violence masked by euphemisms and code words, despite its potential amusement for some audiences, suggests that her return does not necessarily promise only procreative and mutually pleasurable relations between the sexes.

Eirene does not emerge from her cave without a few ambiguous suggestions underlying her return to the world, however. Hermes, the trickster god who gave Pandora linguistic cleverness and a thieving mind, always speaks for her. Hermes mediates the transaction between the gods and Trygaeus over these three creatures; he gives Opora to Trygaeus and Theoria to the City Council (*Boule*) just as Pandora was given to men (706–19). In preparation for removing Peace from the cave, Trygaeus invokes the same divinities who adorned Hesiod's Pandora: Hermes, Kharis, the Seasons (Ὧραι), Aphrodite, and Desire (Πόθος) (456; cf. *Works and Days* 65–6, 73, 75). Aristophanes suggests, perhaps, that the plenty Eirene brings may be tainted by her excessive femininity and her relation to Pandora. The craftiness of Pandora herself is left unmentioned, although hinted at through the appearance of and association with Hermes. Eirene's eroticism is emphasized, and that eroticism is her main similarity with Pandora.[39]

The events of 421 in Athens make an ambivalent reading of *Peace* attractive. The Peace of Nicias was not yet approved when *Peace* was produced at the City Dionysia that year. Although Athenians may have longed for peace, it proved to be not easily attainable and, once achieved, not long-lasting. According to Thucydides, the Peace of Nicias was a peace in name only (5.25.2; 5.26.2–3). Fears about the reality of peace are understandable. If we remember what Pandora caused for man, we might hesitate for Trygaeus to accept the gift. Aristophanes' message has a double edge: peace is better than war, but what will happen when there is nothing but peace, especially when Hermes speaks on Eirene's behalf? The world has already fallen. Society goes from war to peace in this play, not from the earthly paradise Hesiod claims existed before Zeus created Pandora, when men did not have to work, suffered no diseases, and did not die, to the present condition of human existence (*Works and Days* 90–104). Pandora is reborn from the earth in the form of Eirene. Things might be better for a while, but the one who picks up on these undertones might wonder what strife she could effect among men again.

The basic principle of peace and its attendant principles of fertility and festival are shown in female form here. Ostensibly, these are feminine principles of life and growth that have a proper place in society and without which man cannot survive. By recalling the basic relationship of Pandora to femininity and the subsequent degenerative condition of human society, however, Aristophanes casts suspicion on how much good females really bring. The feminine figures here embody one aspect of Aristophanes' vision of woman – as a creature of ambiguous value – and partially submerge another aspect, that of woman as a false construction. Femininity, whether abstract or embodied in a real woman, carries an ambivalent value in this play.

BIRDS

Peisetairos ('Persuader-friend') and Euelpides ('Hopeful') set off from Athens to find the city of the birds in *Birds* (414 BCE). They find Tereus, now a Hoopoe, who is acting as the birds' leader, and they discover that the birds have no city. Peisetairos convinces Tereus and the rest of the birds that they need a city to define their territory, which, he points out, lies between the territory of men and the territory of the gods. This strategic placement will allow them, he also points out, to regain their rightful power from the gods and change the structure of the universe. Persuaded, the birds accomplish the seemingly impossible and build themselves a city (Nephelokokkygia, 'Cloud-Cuckoo-Land') in the air. By blockading the airspace between Athens and Olympus, and through some clever persuasion and outright trickery, Peisetairos does manage to convince the gods to relent. Zeus hands his scepter and the maiden who holds his thunderbolts over to Peisetairos. The play ends with the marriage of Peisetairos to this maiden and the installation of Peisetairos as the new Zeus.[40]

The first female figure to appear in *Birds* is Procne, the wife of Tereus, who, according to a myth popular in Athens, became a nightingale in perpetual mourning for her son, Itys.[41] She has no spoken lines of her own, and she is asked to perform a perfunctory female function, providing entertainment for the audience by playing the flute (659). Once she appears, however, Euelpides can only see her as a potential sexual partner. He cannot kiss her because of her beak, so he announces his intention of cracking her shell and peeling her covering (668-74). In one sense, he means that he will have to remove her clothes. Perhaps he makes a subtle joke about a woman's ability to be different underneath than she is on the surface. Another reading yields a joke on the dramatic illusion. He means to remove her bird mask and see what – or who – is underneath. If he removes her costume, then the audience will see another actor inside. The inner workings of the production will be exposed and the validity of the dramatic fiction threatened (see Romer 1983). The representation of Procne, then, follows a familiar paradigm: she is presented in a way that threatens to expose her stage identity as false and calls our attention to the workings of theater and the illusion of costume. On the heels, perhaps, of Sophocles' apparently popular tragedy *Tereus*, she may also be a tragic parody herself.

Zeus' messenger Iris becomes the victim of Peisetairos' verbal abuse.[42] Upon her arrival in Nephelokokkygia, almost everything Peisetairos says to Iris involves a sexual slur. He asks if she is a ship or a dogskin cap (πλοῖον ἢ κυνῆ, 1203), a question that turns her into something else by ignoring her femininity and her well-established identity.[43] It also makes her a synecdoche for woman: κυνῆ puns on a slang term for female genitalia, κυννῆ (both from κυῶν, dog).[44] By ridiculing the actor's costume, Peisetairos once again highlights the falseness of the representation of a female figure.

Furthermore, he wants to know if some 'well-endowed bird' (τρίορχος) took hold of her, grabbing her when she came into the country (1205–6), or if the bird-guard shoved his stick (σύμβολον) into her (1214–15). He refuses to recognize Iris' authority by denying the existence of the gods who sent her (1233–5). Finally, if she does not accept his position and stop bothering him, Peisetairos threatens to rape her violently (1253–6). Faced with this possibility, Iris leaves. Here the female figure provides an occasion for Peisetairos' rejection of Zeus' traditional authority.[45] A messenger who exchanges information between men, she becomes an ineffectual stand-in for Zeus whom Peisetairos is easily able to dispatch.

Three-quarters of the way through *Birds*, after Peisetairos has set up his bird city in the clouds, organized the 'blockade' of sacrificial smoke to the gods, and has been visited by various merchants and other callers, Prometheus arrives on the scene (1494–1552). Prometheus hides from Zeus' sight under a sunshade and asks Peisetairos not to call his name out loud. He informs Peisetairos that the starving gods are about to give in to the birds' requests. He then advises Peisetairos to demand Zeus' handmaiden, Basileia, for his bride. After Prometheus departs, an embassy of Poseidon, Heracles, and the Triballian god arrive for negotiations. They eventually accede to Peisetairos' demands and the play closes with a song in honor of the marriage of Peisetairos and Basileia.

Prometheus cuts a strange figure in this play, hiding under a parasol in the fashion of attendant maidens (1508). He recalls his gift of fire and his traditional image as man's benefactor.[46] Prometheus is also a trickster traditionally interested in Zeus' downfall; his history is chronicled in Hesiod's *Theogony* (506–616) and *Works and Days* (47–106). Hesiodic allusions appear here when both Peisetairos and the bird Chorus parody the *Theogony* and the *Works and Days* as they tell the story of the birds' primordial powers (see Epstein 1981: 8–9, 12; *pace* Reckford 1987: 338–40). When Prometheus appears on stage, the audience should remember him as one who tried to deceive Zeus (e.g. *Theogony* 613; *Works and Days* 105). In this guise, he seems an appropriate adviser for Peisetairos, who wants to take Zeus' place. However, Prometheus' appearance and link with the acquisition of Basileia cast a shadow over the wedding festivities at the end of the play.

Prometheus' entrance is comic and slapstick. He parodies tragic diction (οἴμοι τάλας, 1494) while worrying about being recognized by Zeus, who watches from above (1494–1509). He apparently now knows that Zeus can see everything (this image is repeated several times: 1494, 1496, 1497, 1506, 1509). Prometheus' overactive desire to remain unrecognized in Nephelokokkygia suggests that his relationship with Zeus is not any better than it ever was in Hesiod. Either he is still at odds with Zeus, over one of his tricks, or he is about to perpetrate something Zeus may not like.[47] While his insistence upon anonymity makes for some comic play, it retains suspicious undertones.

Prometheus offers two methods for acquiring Zeus' power. First he suggests that men should continue withholding sacrifices to the gods. Peisetairos is also not to pour any libations until Zeus hands his scepter over to the birds and gives Peisetairos Basileia as a wife (1534–6). By denying the gods their usual nourishment, men will gain the upper hand in negotiations (1516–19). Furthermore, he briefs Peisetairos about the embassy of gods that will arrive for negotiations. Peisetairos then asks who this Basileia is (τίς ἐστιν ἡ Βασίλεια; 1537), and rightly so.[48] Prometheus answers, 'the prettiest girl, who distributes the thunder of Zeus, and absolutely everything, good will, good laws, moderation, naval bases, insults, flattery, and triobols' (καλλίστη κόρη, / ἥπερ ταμιεύει τὸν κεραυνὸν τοῦ Διὸς / καὶ τἄλλ' ἀπαξάπαντα, τὴν εὐβουλίαν / τὴν εὐνομίαν τὴν σωφροσύνην τὰ νεώρια, / τὴν λοιδορίαν τὸν κωλακρέτην τὰ τριώβολα, 1537–41). Clearly, Basileia is Zeus' source of power. Apparently anyone in possession of her can rule (see Auger 1979: 84–5; Pozzi 1986: 127). The token of exchange that signifies the transfer of power, she is of singular importance to the success of Peisetairos' *coup d'état*, even though she does nothing in terms of stage action. Finally, she is the centerpiece of a plan devised by Prometheus, the master of trickery against Zeus. Although she never speaks, her presence is crucial to the fulfillment of the hero's plan.

Prometheus' brokerage of Basileia recalls his involvement with another of Zeus' female creatures: Pandora, and the female gift from Zeus in Hesiod's *Works and Days*. In *Birds*, the Prometheus situation is somewhat reversed and recalls aspects from both versions of the story. Prometheus suggests a trick on Zeus that is the opposite of the one he played on Zeus originally, in this case a deceptive sacrifice. In *Theogony*, Prometheus burned a large offering to Zeus, with much smoke, sputtering, and fat, in order to test Zeus' omniscience and greed (*Theogony* 535–57). In response, Zeus ordered the gods to create Pandora and she is given to men as a beautiful evil (*Theogony* 585); her presence among men established the current human condition. In *Birds*, Prometheus advises an alternative appeal to the gods' greed. He suggests the denial of sacrifice as a trick for Peisetairos to gain power over Zeus.

Prometheus' second suggestion is also an inversion of the Hesiodic situation that involves the acquisition of woman. Prometheus advises Peisetairos to take the woman Basileia from Zeus, while he warned his brother never to accept a gift from Zeus.[49] The episode between Peisetairos and Prometheus is a comic reversal of traditional Prometheus themes. Instead of offering sacrifices, Prometheus proposes withholding them; instead of warning against gifts from Zeus, gifts that coincidentally include a woman, he proposes taking or stealing a woman from Zeus. This woman, Basileia, provides things necessary for culture, just as the first woman did for Hesiod's men.

Prometheus' appearance on stage immediately recalls his mythic heritage. By his secretive behavior, we remember his feud with Zeus. He tells us himself of his friendship with men (1545). Peisetairos, however, does not recall all of Prometheus' influence on human society. He remembers the gift of fire, but he fails to recall Zeus' retribution for that gift (1546). When he remembers that Prometheus enabled man to cook (and so make sacrifices to the gods), Peisetairos is very close to remembering the rest of the story. The comedy (and tragedy) of the scene is that he fails to read the situation and forecast the future. Peisetairos remembers the Aeschylean Prometheus, the benefactor of man punished by and reconciled with Zeus, but not the Hesiodic Prometheus, whose gifts to man were followed by a 'beautiful evil' from Zeus. Mention of Pandora is made conspicuous by its absence, and it is at this point that we may link Basileia and Pandora (and her nameless counterpart from the *Works and Days*).

Basileia presents the same problem for Peisetairos' reign that Pandora did for all mankind. She has the same double aspect, being lovely, powerful, and female. As Prometheus says, she distributes good things (εὐβουλία, εὐνομία, σωφροσύνη), bad things (λοιδορία, κωλακρέτη), and things of ambiguous benefit or harm (νεώρια, τριώβολα). These are all things of the city, particularly of Athens, and all things that Peisetairos needs to have a complete society, one that closely resembles the Athens that he and Euelpides have left. Prometheus recognizes the necessity of Basileia's presence and her fulfillment of Peisetairos' needs. He appeals to Peisetairos, saying 'If you have her, you have everything' (ἤν γ' ἦν σὺ παρ' ἐκείνου παραλάβῃς, πάντ' ἔχεις, 1543). In this case, everything includes the bad as well as the good.

When Basileia finally appears, the Herald describes her as 'a woman of unspeakable beauty, shaking the thunderbolt, the winged bolt of Zeus' (γυναικὸς κάλλος οὐ φατὸν λέγειν, / πάλλων κεραυνόν, πτεροφόρον Διὸς βέλος, 1713–14; cf. also 1537: καλλίστη κόρη). What does she forebode, this powerful woman, of whose beauty one may not speak and who brandishes thunderbolts? She is not without Pandora's allure and danger. Her alliance with Peisetairos suggests that he may become just another Zeus, with the same feminine power at his side (she is Zeus' πάρεδρος, 1753). Basileia appears to share this aspect with Hera and Athena, although their functions are not described with such specific detail. On the other hand, he may be another Epimetheus, who acquires beautiful, powerful women from Zeus, unaware of Zeus' overall plans. We have no indication that the figures of Basileia or the other mute figures at the ends of *Acharnians* and *Wasps*, for that matter, were made sexually ambiguous by virtue of the male actor playing them. They probably appeared to be fake women; any man in a bodysuit crafted to represent a naked female body is going to look quite clearly like an imitation of a nude woman.[50] Still, no certain conclusion can be drawn because of the lack of any solid evidence.

Some echoes of the Hesiodic Prometheus inform the situation surrounding Peisetairos' acquisition of Basileia, and so his seat on Zeus' throne. Basileia functions as a personified abstraction of ruling power, as a goddess without whom civilization cannot proceed, and as the bride of the traditional comic *exodos*. She can be all these things at once; after all, if Peisetairos has her, he has everything. Aristophanes concludes the play with a wedding just after Peisetairos has received Basileia. The scene seems joyful and optimistic, but the future of Nephelokokkygia is left up in the air. On the one hand, Peisetairos' marriage to Basileia represents his triumph over Zeus and his rejuvenation. On the other hand, Basileia is feminine, stolen from Zeus on advice from Prometheus, and as such forebodes possible retaliation and the downfall of this newly established society. Perhaps in 414, after the failure of the Peace of Nicias and in the midst of the disastrous Sicilian expedition, Aristophanes means to question the potential of changes in leadership, no matter how idyllic those changes may seem.

CONCLUSIONS

Young girls, older market women, silent wives, creatures of the natural world, and mythological personifications: no matter what their form, these female figures in Aristophanes' earlier plays all share common characteristics. Each of these figures, in one form or another, displays a facility with language and *double entendre*, an ability to change her appearance, and a natural trickiness. These aspects of femininity are presented within some sort of self-consciously theatrical setting. Although none of these characters enjoys any central importance to the primary action of the play, the feminine proves to be an essential component of Aristophanic comedy, and not just for a symbolic expression of fertility, under all circumstances.

The strain of Greek thought that equates femininity with an essential craftiness informs the spirit of Aristophanic comedy at a basic level. Even the most peripheral female characters possess essential qualities for comic moments. Sometimes female figures need only appear as sexual partners; their appearance is powerful enough to rejuvenate an elderly hero. But female figures also allow for elaborate and traditional jokes equating sex and food; their malleable natures let females substitute for either element of the joke. Play, with the dramatic illusion and with incidents of metatheater, both at the expense of the hero, are made possible through the natural skills of female figures. The traditional Greek view of woman, as a changeable figure, is fundamental to Aristophanes' comic sensibility.

Aristophanes' comic sensibility is not wholly free-spirited, however. Many critics find notes of seriousness and concern in the plays, and traditional views of femininity come into play there as well. The (at least) dual nature of the feminine makes disaster as well as fun possible. The ancestry of all females to the first woman in traditional Greek mythology taints the nature of femininity and makes all women suspect. Hence, the inclusion of the feminine at the end of these plays, especially as the Peloponnesian War continues and Aristophanes' plays begin to celebrate peace with marriage, also makes the peace suspect. With Basileia, for example, Aristophanes tosses a serious note into the *Birds'* final revelry. Even though a comedy may end with a vision of utopia, that utopia usually includes a woman; with femininity present, Aristophanes suggests that any utopia may not be as ideal as it seems.

In traditional Athenian ideology, femininity is deceptive by nature in both appearance and practice, and its theatrical representation in Aristophanic comedy calls attention to its own falseness. While these early plays do not all clearly call attention to the convention of male actors in female parts, those in which femininity is the most suspect (*Clouds*, for example) make a point of doing so. The female characters are not fully developed in these plays, however, and concerted emphasis on the dramatic representation of women will really take hold in *Lysistrata*. What evidence there is suggests that not until that play does Old Comedy appear to have featured real women, although it is fair to say that Greek comedy always relied upon traditional views of femininity for humor and inspiration. In *Lysistrata*, Aristophanes will take these aspects of the comic female even further and use them to great theatrical effect. By so doing, he may have changed Greek comedy forever and firmly established the basic Western dramatic representation of the comic woman.

2
WOMEN AS WOMEN, MEN AS MEN: *LYSISTRATA*

The younger wives' sex strike and their husbands' subsequent capitulation, the older women's occupation of the Athenian treasury and their physical victory over a band of decrepit and angry old men, and certainly the charisma of its eponymous heroine have all combined to make *Lysistrata* a favorite among scholars and students alike. Its frank recognition of heterosexuality titillates and amuses. Once bowdlerized, the play is now often seen as a statement of feminine solidarity and of universal truths about war, peace, and the battle of the sexes.¹ On top of that, it satisfies, as no other Aristophanic play does, an audience's desire for cohesiveness and clarity: its sustained plot has a beginning, a middle, and an end.²

Lysistrata turns upon clearly determined stereotypes of sex and gender. Its humor relies on role reversal to befuddle audience expectations. That humor is rather tendentious, for as the women deny their sexual urges in order to distract their husbands from the war, they become, more and more, emblems of a male vision of femininity. As the men turn away from fighting and succumb to sexual desire, their masculinity becomes more and more apparent. Understandably then, an analysis of *Lysistrata* with regard to the comic portrayal of women requires, for balance and contrast, some consideration of the portrayal of men and masculinity.³

Women have significant speaking roles in *Lysistrata*, which is the earliest extant ancient Greek comic play to feature women in central roles and possibly the first play of its kind altogether, although this cannot be determined for certain. That the first extant Attic comedy with women as main characters did not appear until 411 BCE, relatively late in the history of ancient Greek drama, has caught the attention of only a few critics. Most mention the phenomenon, praise Aristophanes' comic genius, and move on to other issues, arguably skeptical and interested in other matters.⁴ In contrast to tragedy, for which there are many earlier fifth-century female characters both major and minor, the only females found in comedy prior to *Lysistrata* were personifications (e.g. comedy in Kratinos' *Pytine*; Opora and Theoria in *Peace*), mythological figures (e.g. Iris in *Birds*), wives and daughters of male characters, with relatively few lines to speak (e.g. Dikaiopolis' wife and daughter in *Acharnians*; Trygaeus' daughters in *Peace*), or mute flute girls (e.g. Philocleon's companion at the end of *Wasps*).⁵

In spite of this apparent novelty, some important aspects of the apparent uniqueness of *Lysistrata* have been overlooked by scholars. Tragic and satyric actors had been portraying all sorts of female characters, from citizen women to aging nurses, regal queens, and goddesses, for years.⁶ For these actors there must have been a tradition of acting technique from which to draw for performance skills.⁷ An actor in the part of Lysistrata would be breaking new ground and establishing a way of portraying a woman in comedy. There may have been no model for the actor who played Lysistrata, nor for his fellow actors in the supporting female roles. How would he know the way that *comic* women should speak, dress, or walk? For that matter, how would the audience, accustomed to seeing masculine heroes and impersonations of mute flute girls on the comic stage, react? It is likely that, watching full-fledged females in comedy for the first time, the audience's attention would be drawn to the convention of male actors in female roles in comedy (see Cartledge 1990: 33).

An actor playing a woman's part, with or without a mask, faces a difficult challenge. Just as an audience knows how citizen men walk and talk and look, in real life and in comedy, so it knows how a citizen woman walks and talks and looks. Instead of portraying a divinity, whose appearance can be imaginative, the actor must portray a person wholly 'other' to his experience and yet wholly real. The illusion of woman was, then, a great task of representation, of *mimesis* (imitation).⁸ For the actor playing Lysistrata, a double difficulty arises: not only is he asked to play the 'other', but he is also expected to play her for laughs, possibly for the very first time. How realistically Lysistrata and the other women were played is highly speculative.⁹ Although Whitman, for example, argues for fairly realistic women on stage, the realism of any comic character is doubtful.¹⁰ It is more likely that the women on stage are so stereotypical that realism and the dramatic illusion are not necessarily appropriate terms to use.

Aristophanes is a poet always on the lookout for theatrical devices to exploit for humorous effect.[11] The portrayal of women by men on stage has a double edge. On the one hand, the female *persona*, or mask, may be fastened tightly. An audience may accept characters without question for the women that they appear to be. On the other hand, the mask may become somewhat loose and the text (as well as the performance) may let it slip to show the male underneath and to suggest an odd mixture of gender and character.[12] One of the few critics to mention this phenomenon is Gruber, who asks:

> Does the fact that 'Lysistrata' was a male in disguise have any bearing on the meaning of the comedy? We have every reason to think so. . . . Humor at the expense of women is integral to the play and was unquestionably relevant for Aristophanes' patriarchal audience.
>
> (Gruber 1986: 3)[13]

In his otherwise interesting chapter on the dramatic illusion in Greek comedy, however, Gruber never fully examines just how a male actor playing the woman's part informs a performance and makes *Lysistrata* an opportunity 'to figure forth mysteries of human identity' (ibid. 4). Instead, he discusses the metatheatrical nature of scenes in *Acharnians* and *Thesmophoriazusae*. Although Gruber does not mention it, his question carries not just theatrical interest, nor does it relate simply to the production of humor at the expense of women; it bears relevance for a complete understanding of the representation of women in drama and the social construction of gender in ancient Greece. In addition to discussing the origin of the comic female figure in traditional Athenian patterns of thought about women, this chapter will pick up Gruber's question and investigate how the fact that 'Lysistrata' and all her companions were played by male actors is central to any reading of the play.

The phenomenon of theater relies on role-playing: an actor steps in to represent or substitute for a character (who otherwise exists only in the imagination). These 'actors' are defined by their title: they act, do, perform. The metatheatrical nature of role-playing, both as a dramatic convention and as a plot device, will be central to an understanding of this play. In addition, costumes, make-up, language, and actions are aspects of gender identity as well as of acting. The play comments on both. In the complex world of *Lysistrata*, role-playing is healthy, healing, unitive, and funny; unlike the role-playing in *Thesmophoriazusae* and *Ecclesiazusae*, it involves only a little actual cross-dressing (and the cross-dressing in *Lysistrata* is silly at that). In fact, while the entire plot rests on the supposed absence of men, masculinity proves to be omnipresent, overshadowing any apparent femininity. When viewed through the lenses of performance practice and metatheater, however, the play calls attention to the dramatic convention of male actors in female parts, the absence of women from the Attic stage, and the social construction of gender identity.

In the opening scene, the actors playing women construct for the audience's eyes and ears a gathering of clearly unrealistic and comic women. When their sex-strike plan proves effective and a city magistrate challenges the women's actions, Lysistrata diffuses his power by making him play the part of a woman. Later, the teasing seduction of Kinesias by Myrrhine sketches a clear picture of fantasy femininity and masculinity. The representation of Reconciliation by a nude female figure brings the play to an appropriate conclusion: the polarized forces of male and female must come together; the pull is as inevitable as it is predictable. In addition, these figures play against the imposing and enigmatic figure of Lysistrata herself. The integrity of male identity is kept whole, while the absurdity of women in public life is played up. The play confirms and celebrates an ordered sense of gender identity in which male is stable and female is unstable, in need of control through marriage. Finally, the convention of male actors in female roles ensures that masculinity is always present on stage, even when all the characters are female.

STAGING THE COMIC WOMAN

The initial scene of *Lysistrata*, in which the heroine outlines her plan, does much to establish one layer of the play's metatheatricality. Lysistrata's proposal requires that the women borrow the most basic technique of theater: role-playing. Lysistrata requests that the women act to stop the war because the men's actions have failed to do so. Since public policy is traditionally the exclusive domain of men, the women here take the places of men in public life. In theatrical terms, they are acting or playing male roles.

Lysistrata's proposed scheme has a twist to it, however. The roles these women play entail their acting more like women than they already do. In stepping into the roles of men, they will assume the passive roles of women: as ideal images of sexuality in the eyes of their husbands.[14] In theatrical terms, the women will represent women as part of their taking on of the political roles of men. Then the plot twists again. The women's active (or acted) passivity entices its intended audience, their husbands, who approach with extended phalloi and in increasing discomfort. The husbands' appearance displays a dramatically exaggerated masculinity just as these men are stepping into the fictional and symbolic roles of women, as creatures physically representative of home-bound fertility, needful of and overtly preoccupied with sex, willing to relinquish control of public policy, and eager to return to the confines of home and marriage.

In the final analysis, we might describe Lysistrata's plan as a play in which women enact the roles of men by playing the parts of 'women' and men enact the roles of women by playing the parts of 'men'. This play is resolved when the middle, role-playing, level of character is eliminated and the super-feminine women reunite with their super-masculine men and recreate ideal marriages.

In addition to the central role-playing element, Lysistrata's plan contains other features basic to theater. It takes place in two special places, on two metaphysical stages: one part takes place on the Acropolis, the other in the home.[15] We see neither, in fact. When we do finally witness the wives' sex strike enacted by Myrrhine upon Kinesias, it occurs outside the Acropolis under the wall, where Lysistrata herself stands as a spectator just before Myrrhine's entrance. The actors in the play have special costumes: they discuss the sexy clothes needed for the plan (42–8; 149–54). There are special rules outlined by Lysistrata and agreed upon by the group: they take an oath which outlines the rules of the strike action (212–37).

All the while, the central figure in the action actually stands apart from that action. Lysistrata participates in neither the strike nor the seizure of the treasury. Her role is rather that of author, director, and producer; the women make up her dramatic troupe. Lysistrata's opening remarks about women's predilection for drunken revelry consciously separate her from 'them'. As the prologue progresses, she develops into a separate entity, representative of neither the wives nor the older women. Her speech is straightforward and serious; the wives' comments are silly and light-headed. Lysistrata herself, as the director of the plays-within-the-play (the sex-strike plot and the plan to seize the treasury), stands apart and watches the wives' comic selves undercut their staged femininity. Her separation also highlights the contrived imitation of women. How and why her character is so distinct will be discussed later on. For now, I shall focus on the portrayal of the wives.

WOMEN AS WOMEN, MEN AS MEN: *LYSISTRATA*

The plot and characterization in *Lysistrata* rely heavily upon two mythic patterns of domestic disruption, the Amazon myth and the story of the Lemnian women. The Amazons are well known; a tribe of women who excel in warcraft, especially riding and archery, they are said to live near the south-eastern coast of the Black Sea and to shun male companionship aggressively, kill men after becoming pregnant, and keep only female children.[16] Myths about the Amazons appear to have pervaded the Attic imagination deeply and to have been used to express both fears about female threats to male power and the ultimate domination of Athenian ideology over all representatives of the 'other' (see DuBois 1982; Hartog 1988; Kirk 1987; Tyrrell 1984; also Apte 1985; Gardner 1989; E. Hall 1989a). Like the Amazons, the women in *Lysistrata* come together in a group and refuse sexual relations with men, thus inverting the typical pattern of an upper-class woman's life as envisioned by men: kept in or near the house and accompanied by servants, nurses, children, or male relatives. Women in groups always cause trouble, the myths say.[17] Like the myth of the Amazons' invasion of Athens, women in *Lysistrata* occupy the Acropolis; in fact, paintings on the Stoa Poikile and the metopes on the Parthenon celebrated the victory of Theseus over those invading women as the mythic counterpart of the Persian invasion (Paus. 1. 15–17). The chorus of old men in *Lysistrata* even refers to the chorus of old women as Amazons, for they dare to seize and occupy the Acropolis (678).

The Lemnian women, according to sources much later than Aristophanes, for details about the story are scattered throughout Greek literature, were made by Aphrodite to develop an odor that offended their husbands (see Aesch. *Ch.* 631; Apol. Rh. *Arg.* 1. 608 ff.; Apollod. *Bib.* 1. 9. 17; cf. Hdt. 1. 146. 3; see also Burkert 1983: 190–6; on the Lemnian rituals, see Martin 1987). The husbands took some Thracian women as captives and concubines, and in response their wives murdered all the men on the island of Lemnos. Hypsipyle, the daughter of the king, refrained, however, from killing her father and instead disguised him and set him out to sea. She became ruler of the remaining women and when Jason and the Argonauts arrived in Lemnos, she married her subjects to the sailors, married Jason herself, and thus restored normality to the island. Like the Lemnian women, the women in *Lysistrata* are influenced in some way by Aphrodite to force a separation from their husbands. A battle takes place between men and women on Lemnos; in *Lysistrata*, a battle of fire and water occurs between the choruses of old men and old women. Both stories end with a truce and an affirmation of marriage. Aristophanes clearly

53

borrows from these story patterns and their ability to create cultural expectations for the behavior of women to structure and shape his play. As a comic poet, however, he works to overturn the tragic and destructive flavor of the myths.

From its very outset the traditional stereotype of woman determines the character of the Greek wives in *Lysistrata*. Waiting for the women to arrive, Lysistrata complains to Kalonike that '*according to our husbands* we're the best at clever schemes' (ὁτιὴ παρὰ μὲν τοῖς ἀνδράσιν νενομίσμεθα / εἶναι πανοῦργοι, 11–12; italics mine).[18] Kalonike proudly confirms the characterization, saying 'and that's the truth' (καὶ γάρ ἐσμεν νὴ Δία, 12). Nevertheless, the women's tardiness upsets Lysistrata. Kalonike's agreement appeals to an understanding of and sympathy with the stereotype: women are crafty and lazy, so lazy that they will even be late to a plotting session! So we are not to identify these women with real Greek women at all. They are theatrical, comic women, whose gender identity is determined by what men think, by exaggerated fantasies and fears. They are female figures completely created by men, on the stage and in the imagination. Moreover, femininity complies with the definition, for Kalonike agrees that the accusations are true.

Kalonike further embellishes the stereotype from which the wives are drawn. First, she imagines women busy at home and unable to get away from their morning's work (kissing husbands, waking up servants, taking care of children; 16–19). Surprised at Lysistrata's claim that the women will save Greece, she questions women's capabilities. 'But what can women do that's sensible, or grand? We're good at putting make-up on, designer clothes and wigs and necklaces, imported gowns and fancy lingerie' (τί δ' ἂν γυναῖκες φρόνιμον ἐργασαίτο / ἢ λαμπρόν, αἳ καθήμεθ' ἐξηνθισμέναι / κροκωτοφοροῦσαι καὶ κεκαλλωπισμέναι / καὶ Κιμβερίκ' ὀρθοστάδια καὶ περιβαρίδας, 42–5). For Kalonike, women are mostly good at dressing up in costumes. Kalonike is proud of her talents: she uses grand and elegant language here. This list of actions and clothes defines 'woman'. From the beginning, plot, character, and text all indicate that 'woman' is primarily a mimetic construct, a being whose outer appearance differs from the inner self (if there is one). Her outer image is constructed to be seen and so she is a kind of theater in and of herself.[19] Lysistrata's plan, however, will exploit this very talent: 'And that's exactly what will save us all: the little gowns, the perfumes, and the slippers, the make-up and the see-through lingerie!' (ταῦτ' αὐτὰ γάρ τοι κἄσθ' ἃ σώσειν προσδοκῶ, / τὰ κροκωτίδια καὶ τὰ

54

μύρα χαὶ περιβαρίδες / χἤγχουσα καὶ τὰ διαφανῆ χιτώνια, 46–8). Lysistrata's diminutives (τὰ κροκωτίδια) mock this talent while simultaneously proposing it as the solution to war. In fact, this conversation draws two pictures of woman, positing the stereotype as reality and the costumed seductress as a kind of mimesis. The real wife is the crafty and lascivious lush, eager to eat, drink, and meet her lover for a tryst, the well-established comic stereotype played by the actors at the outset of the play. The ideal wife is a chaste seductress, luxuriating in expensive sexy clothes and teasing her husband, yet nonetheless an imitation perpetrated by the wives in their strike. Women, endowed by nature with a multiplicity of appearances, can be both. Lysistrata envisions the seductress as the saviour of Greece. Indeed, Kalonike becomes interested in the role and offers to go out and buy a new costume (51–3).

Rosellini attributes these two visions of woman to traditional Hesiodic attitudes: the 'Pandora' type and the 'ideal housewife' type (1979: 21). Both visions are fantastic stereotypes, of course; a picture of a real woman would be more complex, combining both visions. Traditional Hesiodic influences can be seen in the composition of female figures in Aristophanes' earlier plays as well. Loraux also sees a dual feminine here, in the personified forms of Athena, chaste goddess of the city and war, and Aphrodite, goddess of love and sex (1981: 157–96).[20] Both critics are correct, to a certain extent. The women are a pest to men, by meddling in civic affairs and concerning themselves with the war – both of these behaviors are thought of, by men, as wrong for women. The women also display a certain kind of idealized behavior, however, through their temporary chastity.

Neither critic addresses the fictional and theatrical nature of the characters on stage, however. Aristophanes takes great pains at the beginning of the play to establish the women's personae. We are given example after example of their lasciviousness. All this works not only to tell us (in case we missed it) that we are watching *comic* women (whom we have not seen or heard to this extent before on stage), but also to call our attention to the actors themselves. Discussion about the outer image of women helps to create for the audience the illusion of women played by male actors, although not without some of the magic secrets on display. The parts are quite easily played, it seems: feminine costumes and behavior can be outlined clearly. Because we see the women discuss theatrical illusion, for a moment we may recall that male actors play the parts here. Later the plot will require the wives to play roles for a private audience, their husbands. When we see them struggling with their parts, we may again, by analogy, be reminded of the play as a play, and of the magical illusion of theater that turns both men and women into 'women'.[21]

The arrival of the rest of the wives presents more opportunities for play with costume and acting convention. For example, Lampito, the representative from Sparta, appears to have quite a masculine physique: 'What a gorgeous specimen, you lovely thing! What healthy skin, what firmness of physique! You could take on a bull!' (οἷον τὸ κάλλος, ὦ γλυκυτάτη, φαίνεται. / ὡς δ' εὐχροεῖς, ὡς δὲ σφριγᾷ τὸ σῶμά σου. / κἂν ταῦρον ἄγχοις, 79–81). The alleged masculinity of Spartan women was a common stereotype for Athenians (Henderson 1987b: 77; see also Cartledge 1981; Powell 1988: 243–6).[22] Still, Lysistrata's words emphasize a sort of mocking femininity, perhaps reminiscent of drag humor (Baron 1990). She exaggerates the compliments: Lampito is 'dearest' (φιλτάτη) and 'sweetest' (γλυκυτάτη), two extremely feminine attributes. Then, she admires Lampito's musculature and, presumably, her broad shoulders. The stereotypical Spartan woman may have been fitter and so more apparently masculine than her Athenian counterpart, yet the opportunity for metatheatrical joking seems too easy to resist here. While speculative in nature, some ideas about Lampito's costume and the subsequent stage-play are called for here. If Lampito wore a Doric peplos, its low décolletage would have enhanced not only the ambiguity of her gender identity but also the artificiality of her very being (Henderson 1987b: 77; also Baron 1990). Kalonike examines Lampito's breasts, perhaps manually (83–4). Visually and theatrically, this might not confirm Lampito's femininity so much as make fun of and question it.

With their admiration of Lampito's toned body, her breasts, and her overall good shape, both Lysistrata and Kalonike look at her with a male gaze. Lampito thus becomes for them a sexual curiosity, since she is so apparently different from the Athenian women. Yet with this body and its charms she will provide a powerful weapon for Lysistrata's plan. We are encouraged, through the gaze of Lysistrata and Kalonike, to look at Lampito as a sexual object. The text, however, does such a good job of establishing the way that we are to look at her that we may forget what the effect of her actual appearance on stage may have been. Instead of suggesting a sort of aggressive homosexual desire on Lysistrata's or Kalonike's part, the on-stage play may rather have called attention to the very parts of Lampito's costume that were the most artificial. Thus far in the prologue, Lysistrata and Kalonike have created an image of the Athenian woman as a wholly artificial creature who can and will enjoy dressing up for male admiration. Now, her Spartan counterpart appears, and she seems quite clearly to have a masculine interior and false (or at least, unbelievable) female attributes. Play with Lampito's breasts and her muscles on stage would provide the incongruity necessary for the audience to recall that she is played by a man. Finally, what better way to joke about Spartan women than to visually suggest that they resemble men in women's clothing, with false bosoms and broad shoulders?

The women from Boeotia and Corinth also receive pointed comments about their bodies that may serve to highlight their artificiality. The Boeotian woman would most likely have been clothed (we have no reason to think that she would defy logic and appear nude), yet both Myrrhine and Kalonike comment on her genitals (87–9). Perhaps she wore a sheer tunic that revealed a female body underneath. If so, she would represent a literal interpretation of my point so far, that the costume reveals an artificial woman whose very falseness reveals itself. The Boeotian woman has contrived her feminine attractiveness for consumption by a male audience. Why are the other women commenting on her depilation? They are looking at her as the ideal male spectator might. Again, they call attention to the aspects of her costume, and her gender identity, that are, on stage, the most contrived. The Corinthian woman's body, not surprisingly, receives similar treatment. In a way that anticipates the play's final scenes with Diallage, Kalonike admires her body: 'She's got some pretty gulfs herself. Here's one in front, and here's another one' (χαῖα νὴ τὸν Δία / δήλη 'στιν οὖσα ταυταγὶ κἀντευθενί, 91–2).[23] Once again, the audience's attention is drawn to aspects of the costume that ostensibly indicate femininity, yet also indicate ambiguity. We know for certain that she is not really female. The vision that we are asked to have is male; we are asked to see her as a sex object. The joke is that 'she' does not even really exist: she is a creation of make-up, costume, and our imaginative gaze.

Lampito's later lines continue to reveal masculinity lurking within her female exterior. When the women have finally assembled, she says: 'Well: who convenes this revolutionary cell of women?' (τίς δ' αὖ συναλίαξε τόνδε τὸν στόλον / τὸν τᾶν γυναικῶν, 93–4). The vocabulary of politics (συναλίαξε) and the military (τὸν στόλον) is male (Henderson 1987b: 79). She applies these male terms to women. The incongruence of gender and character is thus always present in Lampito.

ARISTOPHANES AND WOMEN

When Lysistrata proposes her plan to the wives, they are at first less than enthusiastic (124–8). Some start to leave, preferring the continuation of war to the denial of their stereotypical desires (129–35); they would rather walk through fire, says Kalonike, than live without the penis (133–4). In her despair, Lysistrata utters a revealing remark: 'No wonder tragedies are written about us, for we are nothing but Poseidon and a little boat' (οὐκ ἐτὸς ἀφ' ἡμῶν εἰσιν αἱ τραγῳδίαι· οὐδὲν γάρ ἐσμεν πλὴν Ποσειδῶν καὶ σκάφη, 138–9).[24] She refers to the story of Tyro, a woman who, seduced by Poseidon, set her newborn children adrift in a little boat. Lysistrata subtly recognizes the theatrical nature of womanhood: a vision of woman as a victim of rape and as bearer of ill-fated, often illegitimate, children informs tragedy regularly. Here, she means to write a new script, a new part, for women on stage, one no less stereotypical but comic rather than tragic. In this case, for example, the women will control the seduction. Still she follows the standard way of defining women in theater, through a list of attributes, in this case a male god and the skiff her babies are set adrift in. While Lysistrata plays to the weaknesses of these women (they have, in fact, done or said nothing to lead us to any other conclusion but that they care mostly about sex), she nevertheless means to create a comedy here, a story with a happy ending, and she is about to lose her players. This comment gets the attention of the departing women, and Lysistrata turns to Lampito for support.

Lampito agrees with the group that it is very difficult to live without penises, but finally sides with Lysistrata and consents to her plan (χαλεπὰ μὲν ναὶ τὼ σιὼ / γυναῖκας ὑπνῶν ἐστ' ἄνευ ψωλᾶς μόνας. / ὅμως γα μάν· δεῖ τᾶς γὰρ εἰράνας μάλ' αὖ, 142–4). This may be Aristophanes' biggest joke: the plan is motivated by the absence of men (and their phalloi) but the plan also requires the absence of phalloi. A comic audience is accustomed to seeing characters with oversized phalloi on stage; here, they have seen nothing but female characters, who naturally have none. Phalloi, arguably the most obvious feature of the Greek comic stage, do not come into view until Kinesias arrives much later in the play. After his arrival, more men continue to enter the stage with larger and larger phalloi. For all its absence, however, the phallos is actually quite present in the first half of *Lysistrata*, if only in the minds of the women on stage. The women's alleged inability to get along without the phallos increases its imaginative power all the more. The phallos is made conspicuous by its absence.

To make his point about the conspicuousness of the phallos even clearer, Aristophanes makes sure that Lampito receives the highest praise after she agrees to the plan. Lysistrata calls her 'the only woman among them' (μόνη τούτων γυνή, 145).²⁵ That old joke about the masculinity of Spartan women appears here again, for Lysistrata jokes by replacing 'man' (ἀνήρ) in the common compliment 'the only man among us' (μόνον ἄνδρα) with 'woman' (γυνή) (Xen. *HG* 7. 1. 24; Henderson 1987b: 84; see also Rau 1967: 144–7). By acting most like a man – by being able to resist sex, but ironically, doing so by pointedly rejecting the most obvious sign of masculinity – Lampito earns a male epithet in female disguise. The compliment recalls the theatrical convention of male actors in female roles, and we all know by now that Lampito *is* a man in a female disguise. She really only gives up the phallos for the sake, and for the duration, of the performance. Throughout the play Aristophanes employs two distinct lines of metatheater, and they are both present here. He consistently portrays woman as a creature of imitation, both by nature and in nature, created by men, and he suggests through language and jokes that male and female roles are, to some extent, easily played through certain behaviors. The plan's irony lies on a razor's edge: to become more like wives, and to get the men to act more like husbands, the women must take on some male characteristics while outwardly emphasizing their inherent femininity.

Another character who reinforces this image of a man in women's clothing is the female Scythian archer, the Scythaina (184). Her character functions much in the same way that male Scythian guards do in other comedies (cf. the Scythian archer tricked by Euripides at the end of *Thesmophoriazusae*). She is called out as part of the parody of the regular male assembly to perform as a guard, setting out the shield and the sacrificial victim (185–6), and to witness the women's oath-taking.²⁶ Lysistrata rebukes her for being distracted (184), just as the Proboulos rebukes the male Scythians who accompany him (426–7). She has no speaking role, and we can only speculate what costume she wears – perhaps she appears in a slightly feminine version of the usual attire for the male Scythian archer, although it has been provocatively suggested that her gender is indicated by a female mask and that she wears the same costume as a male Scythian would, since her appearance is meant to parody customary male practices (Stone 1980: 306). If this is accurate, then her silence matters little; she performs in pantomime the symbolic ambiguity of gender and sexual identity that occurs when female characters appear on the comic stage.

Lysistrata's plan places the women in the center of the action, ironically making themselves sexually desirable but denying their husbands sex in order to stop the fighting. The costume assures her that the plan will work:

> If we go home, and get ourselves made up,
> and slip on one of our imported gowns
> with nothing underneath, and show some crotch,
> our husbands will get hard and want to screw,
> but if we keep away and don't go near them,
> they'll soon enough make peace, you have my word.

> εἰ γὰρ καθήμεθ' ἔνδον ἐντετριμμέναι,
> κἀν τοῖς χιτωνίοισι τοῖς Ἀμοργίνοις
> γυμναὶ παρίοιμεν δέλτα παρατετιλμέναι,
> στύοιντο δ' ἄνδρες κἀπιθυμοῖεν σπλεκοῦν,
> ἡμεῖς δὲ μὴ προσίοιμεν, ἀλλ' ἀπεχοίμεθα,
> σπονδὰς ποιήσαιντ' ἂν ταχέως, εὖ οἶδ' ὅτι.
>
> (149–54)

Simply put, the women will make spectacles of themselves, by means of costumes and posturing. Lysistrata is quite aware of the effect of such a pointedly organized display. In fact, such a plan has worked before, according to Lampito, who recalls the story of Helen and Menelaus mentioned in Euripides' *Andromache*: when Menelaus met Helen after the fall of Troy, she revealed her naked breast to him and he was unable to kill her (155–6; cf. Eur. *Andr.* 627–31). Here Lampito brings to bear her own cultural identity. Not only is her allusion to this episode in the story of Helen and Menelaus amusing for its example of Spartan male weakness in the presence of a naked, sexually suggestive woman and for the historical precedent that it sets, but it also seems reasonably appropriate for a Spartan woman to use Helen as her point of reference. The mention of Helen's beauty by means of a Euripidean allusion links up with the general theatrical nature of woman here. While the story of Menelaus' response to Helen was well known, Euripides added the dramatic detail of her naked breast.[27] That Aristophanes picks a theatrical moment is as significant as his choice of a Euripidean moment. The very idea of Helen's use of her feminine charms and the exploitation of her body (represented by a man in a female costume) recalls the ambivalent nature of femininity. Love, or more bluntly sex, does conquer war, or more exactly death, here, but not without the frame of dramatic performance.

As the play progresses, it becomes clear that for the sake of Lysistrata's plan, real women must act like men; that is, they must be able to resist sex.[28] At the same time, they must act as much as possible like ideal wives, like irresistible sex objects. So far, their plot resembles a play: it has a special place, at home; specific costumes, filmy dresses, make-up, and special shoes; and special rules, teasing only. Lysistrata, however, exists on another plane; her character displays an odd mixture of male and female traits. From her first moment on stage, Lysistrata deliberately distinguishes herself from the other female characters. Her initial rebuke to the women, that if she had called them to a festival of Dionysus, Pan, or Aphrodite they would have come in enthusiastic and noisy droves (1–3), accomplishes much of this for her. For one thing, it tells the audience that Lysistrata herself is capable of dreaming up and organizing a unique activity for women. Henderson writes that 'Lysistrata assumes a role traditionally assumed to be a male prerogative: calling a meeting, possessing will-power and entertaining ideas rather than physical drives' (1980: 169).

In her defense of the other women, Kalonike helps reveal Lysistrata's distance from ordinary Greek womanhood. Kalonike's list of women's chores (16–19) elicits only Lysistrata's high-minded disdain: 'But they've got more important things to do than those!' (ἀλλ' ἦν γὰρ ἕτερα τῶνδε προυργιαίτερα / αὐταῖς, 20).[29] Lysistrata seems not only unaware of the day-to-day details of a woman's life but also unconcerned about them. She stays awake nights tossing about plans for the salvation of Greece, for instance, rather than tossing about a husband (26–7). She never mentions a husband or children, for that matter, and so may in fact lead a life quite different from the others. The only aspect of their lives which she admits to understanding is the absence of husbands and/or lovers (99–101; 107–10).

Lysistrata's attitude towards women differs greatly from Kalonike's. She recognizes and more or less confirms the comic stereotype of women through her plan. Instead of denying the inherent weaknesses of women and asking the wives to pretend to be the way that their husbands believe that they are (a request more distinctly modern in conception, perhaps), she simply accepts the characterization and determines to use it to her own advantage (42–9).[30]

Lysistrata's ignorance about women's ritual oaths also betrays some gender equivocation when she seeks guidance from the other women.[31] Lysistrata asks what the oath will be (191a), but comes back with a suggestion designed to appeal to this comic stereotype of woman: 'Something's hit me. Want to hear? Let's chuck the shield and get a giant wine-glass, and slaughter a giant bottle of red bordeaux, and swear we'll never fill the glass with water!' (ἐγώ σοι νὴ Δί', ἦν βούλῃ, φράσω. / θεῖσαι μέλαιναν κύλικα μεγάλην ὑπτίαν, / μηλοφαγοῦσαι Θάσιον οἴνου σταμνίον / ὁμόσωμεν εἰς τὴν κύλικα μὴ 'πιχεῖν ὕδωρ, 194–7).[32] It has been written that

> Lysistrata is portrayed as essentially different from and superior to both her allies from among the Attic wives and her Spartan counterpart Lampito. She possesses superior charm, will, vision, political insight, strategic and diplomatic abilities. She is also free of the stereotyped weaknesses of her sex: inability to resist the need for sexual and other sensual pleasure; ignorance of and lack of concern about anything outside the home; preoccupation with trivial matters.
>
> (Henderson 1980: 187)

The standard explanation for Lysistrata's nature, as well as for her name, is that her character alludes to the priestess of Athena Polias, Lysimache (Lewis 1955; Martin 1987: 86–7).[33] This explanation is accepted by most critics, including myself. However, my argument here leads to an additional observation. Lysistrata is separate from the other women not only because her character alludes to the priestess Lysimache. Lysistrata also bears many of the standard identifiers of masculinity. She has ideas and is concerned with the future of the city, not with sex, drinking, and domestic intrigue. She plays to the male audience's comic stereotype of women. She appears to have no husband or children. Finally, her language is neither distinctively feminine nor distinctively masculine. In mimetic terms, Lysistrata is an imitation of a woman (Lysimache) who represents Athena, who is herself a male creation. Her character, no less than those of the other women, becomes an example of a man speaking about women by speaking for women, and speaking about a specific woman (Lysimache) by speaking in her place.

DRESSING THE PART

After a water-and-fire contest between the battling choruses of old men and old women, a city magistrate arrives to see what havoc the women have wrought. He has a standard suspicious attitude towards women, speculating that they are celebrating a women's festival (388–90). As he speaks to the chorus of old men, he sarcastically blames his entire sex for the women's behavior: what can we expect, he asks, when we teach them to misbehave and nurture these plots (ὅταν γὰρ αὐτοὶ ξυμπονηρευώμεθα / ταῖσιν γυναιξὶ καὶ διδάσκωμεν τρυφᾶν, / τοιαῦτ' ἀπ' αὐτῶν βλαστάνει βουλεύματα, 404–6)? Significantly, he uses the word διδάσκω, the word that describes what the chorus-director (διδάσκαλος) does in instructing his actors. The Proboulos acknowledges male responsibility (first person plural: ξυμπονηρευώμεθα) for the female character. From a metatheatrical point of view he is correct, of course: the characters are completely male-authored. His further comments on the cuckoldry of shoemakers and jewelers only confirm what the play has shown us so far, that women are perfect comic tricksters.

The Proboulos displays a bitter attitude towards the women. While men were in the assembly debating the Sicilian expedition, he says, women were celebrating the Adonia and shouting from the rooftops (387–98).[34] There are several points to notice about his comments. First, he calls attention to the wide difference between male and female public speech. Men debate in the assembly about serious matters of war. Women sing and shout in religious festivities, actions necessary to the health of the city but not, from his point of view, of serious daily importance. Second, he echoes Lysistrata's own remarks at the play's outset (1–3): women would rather celebrate in drunken festivals than discuss 'serious' civic business. Lysistrata's masculine outlook is highlighted once again, appropriately by the man who will become an on-stage mirror for the representation of women.

The irony – indeed, the impossibility – of Lysistrata's very existence is perhaps appropriate to recall here. Women, the Proboulos reminds us, have no voice in public affairs. However, men have taught them to be tricky and to concoct plans. This man does not realize that his worst nightmare is about to come true: a woman has brought to fruition a plan that involves public policy and he will be silenced. The Proboulos' characterization lies on the opposite end of the gender spectrum from the characterization of the wives: as stereotypically female as they are, so he is stereotypically male.

Lysistrata begins the *agôn* with a clear statement of the roles of men and women in public affairs: women keep silent, according to the wishes of their husbands and out of their natural *sophrosyne* (507–8; see Rosellini 1979: 17–19). However, they are not happy without a say in public policy (509). When they ask nicely, smiling (γελάσασαι, 512), about these matters, they are told to shut up (514–515a). Her account of the typical husband's reaction to his wife's inquiries alludes to Homer. This typical husband responds, 'War is the business of men!' (πόλεμος δ' ἄνδρεσσι μελήσει, 520). The Proboulos heartily agrees.

63

Now Lysistrata declares that the women plan to save Greece and orders the magistrate simply to shut up and listen to her plan, just as the women have been forced to listen to the plans of men (527–8). The external components of gender identity become switched as the Proboulos' confrontation with Lysistrata heats up. She argues with him about a woman's role and he tells her to be quiet. Indignant, he addresses her by her costume: 'Me shut up for you? You who wear a veil?' (σοί γ', ὦ κατάρατε, σιωπῶ 'γώ, καὶ ταῦτα κάλυμμα φορούσῃ / περὶ τὴν κεφαλήν, 530–1; translation mine, after Henderson 1988). To silence the Proboulos effectively, Lysistrata has the other women dress him as a wife in a veil, give him beans to chew, and instruct him in working wool with a spindle (532–7). He will now play the wife's role and sit spinning silently as he listens to Lysistrata's analysis of public policy. Again, as far as these women are concerned, all it takes to represent one of them is a veil, beans, and a spindle: the costume and the work substitute for and create the image of the person. The Proboulos does not even have to learn any lines to speak, for silence becomes a woman in public debate. Other men dressed, to their distinct disadvantage, as women perhaps come to mind: Pentheus, for example (see Levine 1987; Zeitlin 1985: 63–8). This visual role reversal recalls the general role reversal of the plot. In this case, the magistrate bullies the women with his masculinity and must be disempowered. This is accomplished through costumes. Not only is the Proboulos robbed of his authority over the women, but his imperfect costume makes him a source of great amusement.

After the Proboulos has been silenced and 'feminized', Lysistrata triumphantly realigns his thinking. Revising that Homeric quote, she claims that 'War is strictly for the women!' (πόλεμος δέ γυναιξὶ μελήσει, 538). She has reversed the roles and plays the man's part while he plays the woman's. Lysistrata is able here to appropriate epic speech, and she rewrites epic just as she rewrote tragedy earlier (155–6).

Thinking of the scene in performance will reveal some provocative suggestions. The mixed gender of Lysistrata comes to the fore. Her figure on stage looks like a woman, but is characterized as male, both in action and in speech. The Proboulos looks like a man, but is re-dressed in women's clothes and keeps rather self-consciously quiet. The Proboulos, then, provides a distorted reflection of the actor as Lysistrata: a man dressed in woman's clothing, playing a woman's part. Lysistrata's mask slips a bit here. For all the ostensible visual evidence of her sex, the other evidence (attitude, knowledge, language, behavior) indicates that Lysistrata is a man. This is important for her subsequent speech: she will speak out on public issues, something only a man may do.

After their brief song of eagerness for action in support of the cause, a song in which they characterize their abilities by means of both male terms (ἀρετή, θράσος) and female (χάρις, σοφός), the chorus strengthens the masculine basis of Lysistrata's character. They call her ἀνδρειοτάτη, 'the manliest', and inspire her to steer their plan with the wind (549–50). Ironically, however, she responds with a feminine prayer to Eros and Aphrodite. She asks the goddess to 'breathe desire on our bosoms and thighs, and engender rigid pleasure and hard-ons in our husbands, so that we will, I think, be called Lysimaches throughout Greece' (ἵμερον ἡμῶν κατὰ τῶν κόλπων καὶ τῶν μηρῶν καταπνεύσῃ, / κᾀτ' ἐντέξῃ τέτανον τερπνὸν τοῖς ἀνδράσι καὶ ῥοπαλισμούς, / οἶμαί ποτε Λυσιμάχας ἡμᾶς ἐν τοῖς Ἕλλησι καλεῖσθαι, 552–4; translation mine). This graphic description of the remainder of her plan and the indication of her intentions refocuses our vision on her character as female. Any holes in the illusion of femininity are repaired. This is necessary for the plot to continue. The play is not literally about transvestite men; it is about women who use their femininity to accomplish a plan, and the audience needs to believe in what happens on stage.

Still, a close look reveals that Aristophanes uses this scene to deconstruct, as it were, the male actor playing a female role. We are forced to recall the actor-as-female character, for in fact, Lysistrata *is* a man underneath the costume. Why is Lysistrata a woman? Because she cannot be a man and propose a return to the regular *oikos* and peace. She cannot be a woman and speak out against the war and public policy either, however. So Aristophanes confuses her gender to let the play go on. In the end, he confirms male power by emphasizing the artificiality of her character.[35] Yet for the bulk of the play, Lysistrata's identifiable identity is fluid rather than static – like a woman's.

Her final stroke entails rendering the Proboulos completely powerless. Lysistrata adorns him as a dead wife, mentioning a grave, a honey-cake, and a wreath (600–4). The powers of costuming are highlighted in this scene. With just a few accessories, a man goes from being a blustering magistrate to being a silent wife to being a corpse, a change of gender identity and a change in physical condition. Lysistrata mocks him the entire time; we are not to believe that the man actually becomes a wife, alive or dead. This scene runs upon theatrical motifs, however, and these motifs all emphasize the same issue of representation: how do you play the part of a man or a woman? Representing a woman is particularly difficult because of this inability to pin down anything stable in woman besides instability.

REPRESENTING THE TOTAL WOMAN

The second half of *Lysistrata* plays out in a clearly self-conscious, theatrical manner. First, the wives occupying the Acropolis display some weakening of their resolve. Their confrontation with Lysistrata takes the form of an almost burlesque comedy act, with one clown after another proposing, to an unconvinced straight man, some outlandish excuse for returning home. The episode ends up mocking women and reinforcing comic stereotypes.

It seems right to back up a bit first, though. Lysistrata herself introduces this scene and tells its internal audience, the chorus, what has happened, and what will happen. Lysistrata says that she is pacing because of the actions and the 'female mind' of the women (708–9).[36] Her overdetermined oxymoron there – 'female mind' – calls to attention her own ambiguous gender; we must assume that she does not possess such a 'female mind'. Even more telling is her famous short but sweet description of the situation. The chorus leader asks Lysistrata not to hide the crisis from her. Lysistrata reveals the secret, saying: 'We must screw' (βινητιῶμεν, 715). This is a shocking moment. The otherwise discreet heroine uses clearly blunt and obscene language; she also suddenly allies herself (through the use of the first person plural 'we') with the group. Without pressing the point too strongly, this might be another instance of Lysistrata speaking in a more identifiably male rather than female voice. Instead of echoing the ridiculous but discreet excuses for going home for sex that the other women concoct, she foreshadows the straightforward demands that Kinesias will soon make. She also uses the verb κινεῖν, which bears the obscene meaning 'to screw', in the active voice rather than the passive, which is the more common masculine usage (Henderson 1975: 151–2).[37] Lysistrata then recounts some attempts by the women to escape, to go home and satisfy their sexual desires (717–27). The skit finally begins with a woman trying to escape. Her excuse is to spread her wool out on the bed. Another appears, wanting to go home and work with the flax. A third appears, claiming that she is in labor. A fourth says that the owls sacred to Athena keep her awake at night. No one, not Lysistrata nor the audience, is fooled by these excuses. We know that this is a set routine, with the women displaying their clever obscene *double entendres*. It complements the metatheatricality of the first half of the play by showing the wives putting on acts, playing with language, and designing costumes, literally and linguistically, to deceive. Lysistrata's response is ingenious. As the master actor/actress of the play, she produces a document that will satisfy the wives' desires, at least for the moment. She reads to them an oracle predicting their victory through solidarity (770–3, 774–6). Scholars have noted the demagogic allusion here: politicians circulated false prophecies and oracles widely during the war (Thucydides 2. 8. 2; see also Henderson 1987b: 168). Lysistrata creates a new fiction for an appropriately gullible audience. She is completely in control of language and the actors in her play.[38]

After a pugilistic choral interlude, we finally see the sex strike in action. This scene, well known for its teasing suggestiveness, is framed by theatrical suggestions as well. Lysistrata spots a man approaching the citadel and, after locating his wife, gives her instructions just as a director might guide an actor: 'You've got to light his fire, get him hot, [love him but don't make love,] do everything that turns him on, except the thing that you're under oath not to' (σὸν ἔργον ἤδη τοῦτον ὀπτᾶν καὶ στρέφειν / κἀξηπεροπεύειν καὶ φιλεῖν καὶ μὴ φιλεῖν / καὶ πάνθ' ὑπέχειν πλὴν ὧν σύνοιδεν ἡ κύλιξ, 839–41). The principle behind the male-actor-as-female-character is at work here also: she is to do everything *but* make love with him, which makes the sex conspicuous by its absence. Myrrhine exits and Lysistrata remains, elevated and looking over the top of the wall, to begin the tantalizing of Kinesias. Lysistrata functions as an intermediary spectator (between the audience and the two characters) for the introduction of this little play-within-the-play. Even though she leaves her perch to fetch Myrrhine, the frame she has set up remains.

We see in Myrrhine, then, an actor playing a woman who plays being a seductress, and in Kinesias, an actor playing a man playing a man. The audience is in on the joke; it knows that Myrrhine will not give in to Kinesias' demands and that her apparent capitulation is only an act. Her femininity is, then, quite clearly a false construct and Kinesias' tumescent masculinity commands our attention. The scene is representative of male and female sexuality: even the names of the participants are symbolic.[39] The encounter parodies seduction scenes in which women are the aggressors.[40] In a seduction scene which involves a female aggressor, a female makes herself attractive, with specific reference to Aphrodite and the Graces (*Hymn to Aph.* 61–5), and then positions herself as an object of the male gaze. There is a suggestion or promise of sex or marriage (ibid. 45–6; 53–8). The male audience is smitten with desire (ibid. 91; 144–54). An element of trickery and also some feat may be present, especially if the encounter includes a divinity (see Forsyth 1979: 109).

Myrrhine plays at becoming the woman Kinesias desires, and she does so by turning the tables on both him and on the audience. The seduction is cut short and the seducer's object of desire is left high and dry, without satisfaction. The seduction starts out as a joke, of course – Myrrhine's absence rather than her sudden and sexy appearance has inspired Kinesias' desire – but the traditional elements are present. Lysistrata acts as the catalyst for Myrrhine's actions (841). There are invocations of Aphrodite and other goddesses of desire (831–4). While Myrrhine does not really need to adorn herself (she seems quite attractive to Kinesias already, 885–6) and her name imbues her with desirability, she reverses the usual element of dress by beginning to take her clothes off instead of putting them on (931; 950–1). She also adorns the site of their sexual encounter with a bed, blanket, and pillow (929–33), and her husband with perfume (938–45). Their encounter does not end in sexual activity; Myrrhine leaves Kinesias in sexual desperation (952–8).

In this scene, then, it becomes necessary that Myrrhine, more specifically the actor as Myrrhine, appear as feminine as possible. Myrrhine says that she needs all sorts of accoutrements before she can go to bed with Kinesias. The comedy lies in her exploitation of the image of a sexy woman and the audience's knowledge that Kinesias will not get what he wants. In fact, most of Myrrhine's needs involve the bed (κλινίδιον, bed, 916; ψίαθος, mattress, 921; προσκεφάλαιον, pillow, 926; σισύραν, blanket, 933). She avoids the sexual encounter by setting up an elaborate stage and an image put together for his specific gaze and to elicit a certain type of response. Kinesias, his masculinity overdetermined by the costume phallos and by his single-minded remarks, apparently requires no further props nor costumes. In fact, Kinesias becomes the ideal audience for this act. His vision is not completely clear: through her absence or through his desire, Myrrhine appears to have grown younger since he saw her last (885–6). Her hard-to-get act also excites him (887–8). Her act works. Myrrhine's ultra-feminine teasing makes Kinesias' masculinity all the more obvious. Just as her femininity is staged for him, his masculinity is staged here for the audience.

Should Myrrhine be thought of as completely female in this scene?[41] Certainly the scene enacts, ostensibly, the possibility of married, heterosexual sex, and intimations of homosexuality seem inappropriate. Theatrically, however, Myrrhine's very striptease could threaten the illusion of a wife seductively teasing her husband. Myrrhine says she is taking off her breastband (τὸ στρόφιον, 931) and her shoes (ὑπολύομαι γοῦν, 950). These two items alone do not completely compromise her feminine identity. Neither the audience nor Kinesias knows, however, how much more she might remove. This scene, by calling attention to masculinity and femininity, to naked bodies and to the removal of clothes, and to images of desire and the effect of desire on sight, at least offers great potential for some ambiguous gender play.

REPRESENTING THE SYMBOLIC FEMALE

After Kinesias sings with the chorus a paratragic lament at not being able to relieve his sexual needs (954–79), he meets a Spartan in similar distress. When both men discover that women all over Greece have conspired in this strike to stop the war, they agree to progress toward a reconciliation. As the play draws to a close, Lysistrata summons in Diallage, Reconciliation, the physical embodiment of the pleasures and benefits of peace (1115). By sharing Diallage, the Spartans and Athenians will reunite and stop the war. Diallage is conceived as a female figure, and represented by a male actor dressed as a nude girl.[42] Her appearance is neither unique nor surprising; similar female figures appear at the end of five of the six extant Aristophanic comedies dated before 411 BCE (*Ach.* 989–99, 1198–221; *Kn.* 1388–95; *Peace* 525, 842–908, 1329–57; *Wasps* 1341–81; *Birds* 1706–65; see also Newiger 1967: 106–8). The tableau on stage must have been remarkable, however. The exaggeratedly masculine bodies of the Spartan and Athenian ambassadors flank either side of this artificially female icon, as 'she' holds them by their extended phalloi (1119).[43] The ostensibly female (yet gender-ambiguous) figure of Lysistrata looks on. She may even stand obliquely in front of Diallage to become a visual reduplication of Reconciliation herself: at 1122–3, she orders the Spartan ambassador to stand on her left and the Athenian on her right.

The scene's beginning is also marked by Lysistrata's gender-ambiguity. The ambassadors have agreed to negotiate, and the Athenian ambassador expresses a need to call Lysistrata for the arbitration. The Spartan ambassador says, 'Lysístratos, Lysístrata, whoever' (ναὶ τὼ σιώ, καὶ λῆτε, τὸν Λυΐστρατον, 1105). He does not care whether the arbitrator is male or female, clearly.[44] However, his remark underlines the transparency of Lysistrata's sex.

The theme is immediately picked up by the chorus. As Lysistrata enters, they hail her as 'the most manly woman of all' (χαῖρ', ὦ πασῶν ἀνδρειοτάτη, 1108; my translation). She was called this earlier (at 559), after she vanquished the Proboulos by dressing him as a woman and then as a corpse. At that time, Lysistrata gained the upper hand through that manipulation and her gender identity was quite unclear. Here the appellation is most ironic. Surrounded by these men with enlarged phalloi and associated with the feminine Diallage on stage, Lysistrata would appear the least masculine that she ever has.

The chorus continues its greeting with some advice. Lysistrata must balance her talents to succeed in the arbitration: 'Now you must be more besides: firm but soft, high-class but lowbrow, strict but lenient, versatile' (δεῖ δὴ νυνί δὲ γενέσθαι / δεινὴν ⟨μαλακήν,⟩ ἀγαθὴν φαύλην, σεμνὴν ἀγανήν, πολύπειρον, 1108–9). These terms, none of them specifically male or female, nevertheless work to draw Lysistrata as a nobler-than-life figure. Certainly, none of the women involved in the strike could sustain such an attitude. Here they give her directorial suggestions for her presentation to the audience gathered for arbitration.

Lysistrata begins the arbitration with the programmatic rhetorical effort to establish credibility. Quite boldly, she does so by declaring and calling attention to her sex: 'I'm female, yes, but still I've got a brain. I'm not so badly off for judgment, either. My father and some other elders, too, have given me a first-rate education' (ἐγὼ γυνὴ μέν εἰμι, νοῦς δ' ἔνεστί μοι. / αὐτὴ δ' ἐμαυτῆς οὐ κακῶς γνώμης ἔχω, / τοὺς δ' ἐκ πατρός τε καὶ γεραιτέρων λόγους / πολλοὺς ἀκούσασ' οὐ μεμούσωμαι κακῶς, 1124–7). Her credentials confront a comic oxymoron reminiscent of the one at 708–9. She also quotes a line from Euripides' *Melanippe the Wise* (fr. 483): 'I am a woman, but still I have a brain'.[45] Aside from establishing some masculine, even paternal, credibility with this description of her education, Lysistrata also makes yet another transparent reference to her own ambiguous gender identity. She does, as her own explanation makes clear, seem like a strange combination of male and female: a woman with an idea, a woman with a brain, is a woman whose teachers are men, and who perhaps is a man disguised as a woman. She is also rewriting tragedy again, as a comic hero may.

The final moments of the play present two final problems. The first is the dividing up of Diallage between the Spartan and Athenian ambassadors. Lysistrata's aim is to bring together these two men, representatives of the two central warring cities, and to reproach them for fighting each other. After she describes the expulsion of tyranny from Athens in terms of the Spartan reclothing of Greece in democratic attire, she turns the ambassadors' attention to Diallage. They envision her as a map of Greece, and they claim their respective territories. The Athenian ambassador lays claim to the Malian Gulf between Diallage's legs; the Spartan ambassador wants the promontory behind (see Henderson 1987b: 204–5). That they share Reconciliation sexually, as symbolic of peace, seems unsurprising. The strangeness of the scene is surprising, however. The men are brought together as brothers by a masculine woman by means of a clearly artificial, naked woman. Femininity has not reconciled Greece. Creatures who play to the male gaze have caused that gaze to refocus upon masculine desire. In addition, woman has been put back in one of her rightful places, as a silent token of exchange between men.

Second, it is unclear in what capacity Lysistrata herself appears at the end of the play. She exits at 1189 into the Propylaea with the ambassadors. She may or may not return; if she returns, she may or may not speak.[46] It seems strangely inadequate to modern readers, perhaps, that Lysistrata, the designer of the dual plan and the arbitrator who reunites Greece, should not appear and not speak at the very moment of her success. Ideologically, however, Aristophanes' choice makes some sense. Lysistrata is clearly not an ordinary woman. Within the world of the play, she is an amalgam of Athena and Aphrodite, educated by men, not necessarily a wife (and so not necessarily a part of the sex strike itself). Once Athens and Sparta, and their respective husbands and wives, have been reunited, she has served her purpose. Once marriage has been restored, there is no place for her. She has a place in this world only as long as the war continues and men and women inhabit separate spheres, since only then is there a middle space for her to bridge.

In the world of theater, the male-actor-as-female-character has served to disturb the illusion of 'woman' on stage, to remind us that what appears to be female is an imitation and that the admirable qualities of the main character are in fact part of an authentic male interior. *Lysistrata* ends with remarriages and celebration; while it is festive, it is also serious. Lysistrata, whose character has served to undermine the integrity of gender identity, does not belong there. If she returns to the stage as part of the background chorus, now mute, then she truly reduplicates the figure of Diallage and her revolutionary portrayal of 'woman' in comedy retreats back into a more traditional image.

CONCLUSIONS: ATHENS IN 411 BCE

As a conclusion to this analysis, I would like to offer some thoughts on what conditions in Athens late in 412 and early in 411 BCE may have inspired the innovations of *Lysistrata*.[47] The aftermath of the disastrous Sicilian expedition had taken hold in Athens. The deaths of so many young and middle-aged men must have caused a shift in the daily reality of all Athenians. The population was, in fact, quite clearly different: by 411, all the events of the war had reduced the male citizen population by about one-third (Kagan 1987: 110). When Lysistrata complains about a dearth of lovers (107), Aristophanes reacts comically to a very serious loss of male population. Undoubtedly, this shortage of men resulted in the impression that there was a surplus of women in the city. Such an impression could, quite simply, have inspired Aristophanes' creativity here.

Furthermore, such a great loss of men could have affected the overwhelming male-oriented self-definition of Athens terribly. I have tried to show that *Lysistrata* is not simply 'about' women and women's concerns in war, but rather that it focuses upon the representation of women by men for men and upon masculine desire. Above all, it focuses quite clearly on the phallos, a part of costume and male identity unmistakably present on stage from Lysistrata's opening remarks. How appropriate for Aristophanes to write for a severely wounded city a peace play that seeks to heal with a celebration of masculinity and a return to traditional values.[48]

In summary, then, I offer here a sort of feminist revisionist reading of this play, one that takes into consideration as much as we can know about performance practice at the time of *Lysistrata*'s production, as much as we can know about social conditions in Athens and Greece, and some very modern literary theories about interpreting representation. Such an approach reveals a layer of the play as yet undiscovered. Recalling that male actors played all the female roles in this play elicits some further explanation of Lysistrata's ambiguous gender identity. She is not simply masculine because she takes on a male role or because she resembles Athena. She is masculine at times because that masculinity is part of her identity as a 'woman' on the Athenian comic stage and part of the joke is that she is not a woman at all. A recognition of the interaction between performance conventions and comic texts forces us to re-evaluate our understanding of both gender definitions in ancient Greece and the image of women in ancient Greek literature. If, on the comic stage, female figures highlight not the authenticity of female experience but rather the absence of real women, the inauthenticity and artificiality of femininity, and the presence of men, then we may say in a new way that the definition of gender in ancient Greece ran along the lines of male/not male, real/artificial, normal/not normal, inimitable/easily imitated. Women in Aristophanic comedy, then, become jokes in and of themselves, figures who may be the ultimate tricksters, for their images are artificial. Finally, we must recognize that Aristophanes' *Lysistrata* is not 'the world's first and indeed still the world's greatest feminist drama'. Indeed, it is a play inspired by the absence of men that highlights the inauthenticity of women and reasserts the power of masculinity.

3
MEN AS WOMEN: *THESMOPHORIAZUSAE*

Thesmophoriazusae, known literally as *Women at the Thesmophoria* (Barrett 1964) or sometimes more descriptively as *The Poet and The Women* (Fitts 1957), continues Aristophanes' apparent interest in the characterization of women on the comic stage. Probably produced just a few months after *Lysistrata*, at the City Dionysia in 411 BCE, *Thesmophoriazusae* works some changes on the comic idea of 'women on top'.[1] The tragic poet Euripides and his representations of women in tragedy inform the ostensible center of the plot. About to be tried by the women of Athens for portraying women badly in his plays, Euripides sends a relative, dressed as a woman, to infiltrate the proceedings of his trial, which will take place on the middle day of a religious festival for women only, the Thesmophoria, and to defend him against their charges.[2] The Relative is eventually discovered and held hostage; at the end of the play, Euripides is reconciled with the women and helps the Relative escape by fooling the Relative's guard with parodies of his own plays, some of the same plays at issue in his trial, and also with some old-fashioned comic strategies. In the scholarly record, the topic of the representation of women in comedy is often obscured somewhat by the play's focus on Euripides and his tragic women. In fact, all the representations of women and men impersonating women in this play are undertaken in a comic, rather than tragic, spirit, and the convention of male actors playing female roles is not only explicit but also showcases the inauthenticity of the 'real' women who hold Euripides responsible for their bad reputations.

Unlike *Lysistrata*, in which women secretly infiltrate a traditionally male public space and male public roles to carry out a plan of social change, in *Thesmophoriazusae* women openly occupy the Thesmophorion near the Acropolis as part of a civic religious festival in honor of Demeter and Persephone. Men do the infiltrating here, imposing themselves on places and gatherings from which they are usually excluded.[3] Yet the play itself is a fiction performed near the Acropolis also, as part of the civic religious festival in honor of Dionysus, the City Dionysia. The Thesmophoria took place for three days during the early to middle part (the 11th, 12th, and 13th) of the month Pyanopsion, which corresponds roughly to late October or early November (see Mikalson 1975: 71–3). The legal wives of Athenian citizens, apparently along with some female servants and attendants, left their regular lives to celebrate this festival, and they set up tents or some other form of temporary shelter at the sanctuary (the Thesmophorion) under the auspices of the civic religion (see Detienne 1979: 196–7). Since what went on at the festival was kept secret, we can only piece together assorted bits of information about the proceedings.[4]

On the first day, called Anodos, 'the way up', the women proceeded up the slope of the Acropolis to the sanctuary, which was situated near the Pnyx, carrying their equipment and supplies. In the evening they would perform a sacrifice of piglets, which they tossed into pits in the ground. These sacrifices are thought to have been representative of the rape of Kore by Hades; the piglets are symbolically swallowed up by the earth just as Kore was (Burkert 1985: 243). The second day was called Nesteia, 'the day of fasting', and activity was correspondingly subdued. The third and final day, Kalligeneia, 'the beautiful birth', led to an evening celebration accompanied by the opening of the sacrificial pits, perhaps the removal of the remains of the piglets in a ritual symbolic of renewal and rebirth, and the invocation of a divinity who represents beautiful birth. The festival was clearly allied with agricultural as well as civic and spiritual fertility.

The time of the play, on the second day of the Thesmophoria, does quite simply, give the women a logical opportunity to carry out the scheme Aristophanes has cooked up for them; only at a festival like this are the women alone and at some leisure together. The women in *Ecclesiazusae* appear to have come up with their plan at the Skira, another festival for women only (*Eccl.* 58–60). Finally, this festival constitutes one of the most widespread forms of the worship of Demeter and Persephone (Burkert 1985: 242). As others do, it requires some gender role reversal. Women leave their homes, families, and husbands, and move in a group to an area near places of male public domain: the Acropolis and the Pnyx, areas from which they are usually, both literally and symbolically, excluded (except in the performance of certain religious rites; e.g. the Panathenaia).

Consequently, the Thesmophoria contains the implicit threat of social revolution:

> At the core of the festival there remains the dissolution of the family, the separation of the sexes, and the constitution of a society of women; once in the year at least, the women demonstrate their independence, their responsibility, and importance for the fertility of the community and the land.
>
> (Burkert 1985: 245)

Yet the ritual is finite, and Burkert also writes: 'The Greeks finally interpreted Demeter *thesmophoros* as the bringer of order, the order of marriage, civilization, and of life itself, and in this they were not entirely mistaken' (1985: 246).[5] It is this return to order that *Thesmophoriazusae* advocates. Feminist performance criticism and literary theory highlight a facet of the play that sets the spirit of Dionysus, god of theater and transformation, against the spirit of Demeter, goddess of fertility and rebirth; at the end, Dionysus triumphs.[6] Masculine power over representation on stage is reaffirmed, as is the innately comic representation of women by men.

It has become a recent scholarly *topos* to remark upon the relative lack of serious critical attention paid to *Thesmophoriazusae* and upon the delegation of the play to the shadows of Aristophanic studies. The play has often been declared of lesser importance through a judgement about its lack of overt political references and its obsession with parody and other allegedly purely theatrical issues. Yet the play does contain some political satire, both broad (e.g. the parody of the *ecclesia*) and specific (e.g. the caricature of Kleisthenes).[7] Additionally, the theatrical issues at its core are hardly frivolous; in fact, they are essential to the health of the *polis*, especially if misunderstood or misemployed.

Rather than begin at the beginning, I shall start this discussion of *Thesmophoriazusae* at the center of the play. About two-thirds of the way through, the chorus performs what functions as a parabasis.[8] They speak about male attitudes towards women and attempt to establish the general superiority of women to men. Many of their comments, appropriately enough, recall the themes of role-playing and gender identity. The first section of the parabasis (785–803) discusses the 'bad thing' (τὸ κακόν: 786, 787, 789, 791, 794, 796, 797, 799) that a woman is to a man, and it points out the absurdity of male attempts to control women and to keep them invisible, especially when men really want to see women in the first place (788–91; 797–9).[9] The argument then

MEN AS WOMEN: *THESMOPHORIAZUSAE*

attempts to establish feminine superiority by comparing women's names to men's names and women's honorable behavior to men's dishonorable behavior (804–18). The accoutrements of feminine and masculine identity are discussed:

> And we in domestic economy too
> Are thriftier, shiftier, wiser than you.
> For the loom which our mothers employed with such skill,
> With its Shafts and its Thongs, – we are working it still,
> And the ancient umbrella by no means is done,
> We are wielding it yet, as our Shield from the Sun.
> But O for the Shafts, and the Thong of the Shield,
> Which your Fathers in fight were accustomed to wield,
> Where are they to-day? Ye have cast them away
> As ye raced, in hot haste, and disgraced, from the fray!

> καὶ μὲν δήπου καὶ τὰ πατρῷά γε
> χείρους ἡμῶν εἰσὶν σῴζειν·
> ἡμῖν μὲν γὰρ σῶν ἔτι καὶ νῦν
> τἀντίον, ὁ κανών, οἱ καλαθίσκοι,
>   τὸ σκιάδειον·
> τοῖς δ' ἡμετέροις ἀνδράσι τούτοις
> ἀπόλωλεν μὲν πολλοῖς ὁ κανὼν
> ἐκ τῶν οἴκων αὐτῇ λόγχῃ,
>   πολλοῖς δ' ἑτέροις
> ἀπὸ τῶν ὤμων ἐν ταῖς στρατιαῖς
> ἔρριπται τὸ σκιάδειον.

(819–29)[10]

A typically Aristophanic analogy recalls the simile in *Lysistrata* in which Lysistrata likens straightening out the city to the women's task of cleaning, beating, plucking, carding, spinning, and weaving wool (567–86): women are better at their traditional tasks of spinning and weaving than men are at their traditional tasks of running the city and fighting (see Moulton 1981: 49–58). Aristophanes inserts some comic tension into the speech with this traditional division of labor based on sex by having the women claim superiority so ineffectively. In addition, the punning double meaning of the words ὁ κανών (loom-rod, 822; spear-shaft, 825) and τὸ σκιάδειον (sunshade, 823; shield, 829) perhaps plays upon the idea that both men and women are easily imitable – the various accessories that mark each gender are described with identical terminology. Unless you know which one is being referred to, the gender identity of the referent is unclear. This image of the potential ambiguity of costume elements, dress, walk, behavior, and accessories does, as Moulton suggests, lie at the heart of the play (see Moulton 1981: 131; Zeitlin 1981: 185).

Yet the parabasis does not completely succeed in concretely establishing this topsy-turvy view of gender roles, the solid superiority and nobility of women over the hypocritical inconsistency and corruption of men, that it appears to seek.[11] Rather, the motifs of the play – transvestism, mimesis, parody, poetic ingenuity – combine to cast a veil of doubt and illusion over this moment when the chorus addresses the audience directly. A feminist interpretation may thus argue that Aristophanes uses the image of woman here to criticize the behavior of men rather than to exculpate the comic stereotype of woman, and that all the trappings of theater aid him in exposing the tricks of men. Like *Lysistrata*, *Thesmophoriazusae* is less about real women than it is about comic images of women; unlike *Lysistrata*, *Thesmophoriazusae* offers a more oblique analysis of gender roles in public life.

I shall begin with a consideration of the opening scenes in order to investigate the themes of spectatorship and desire introduced by the characters of Euripides, Agathon, and, in particular, Euripides' Relative. Present in nearly every scene of the play, the Relative functions throughout as an intermediary through whom the audience's gaze is filtered. He also functions as an object of vision himself, as a self-conscious actor on stage. I shall then go on to discuss the Relative's impersonation of woman and his interaction with the 'real' women of the Thesmophoria and with Kleisthenes. Finally, I will discuss the imitation of Euripidean drama that Euripides and his Relative carry out. The chapter will conclude with some thoughts about the historical context of the play and how the play fits into a theory about the construction of the comic female in Aristophanes. This examination will show how masculinity in this play cannot be completely disguised; its power will always reveal itself through any costume, even on stage.[12] *Thesmophoriazusae* succeeds no more than *Lysistrata* in presenting successful representations of women on the comic stage. It works, in fact, to misrepresent women and to make a joke of male actors' attempts to portray female figures in tragedy and comedy.

MEN AS WOMEN: *THESMOPHORIAZUSAE*
IMITATING WOMEN

When the play begins, two men, eventually revealed to us as Euripides and his unnamed relative, are seen heading towards the home of Agathon, another tragic poet. As they approach it, they begin a sort of play-within-the-play. Their enigmatic banter about what the Relative is about to see and hear, or what he is not going to see and not going to hear, establishes this Relative as a naïve but witty spectator and Euripides as a riddling sophist, and initiates the play's overwhelming preoccupation with the position of the spectator. The Relative does not understand what Euripides says to him (6–12) as Euripides tries, in a roundabout way, to teach the Relative how to be a secretive spectator about to witness a mystery (when they approach Agathon's house, he tells the Relative to look (ὁρᾷς, 26), to be quiet (σιώπα νυν, 27), to listen (ἄκου', 28), and to step aside (ἀλλ' ἐκποδὼν πτήξωμεν, 36); see Muecke 1982b: 42). The Relative is also a joker: in his opening remarks, he parodies tragedy, apparently without guile (1–2). While he appears to share the paratragic talents of Dikaiopolis and Trygaeus, he does not at first share their inventiveness. Euripides invents the initial situation; later on, in the style of previous Aristophanic male heroes, the Relative will invent plays for himself. For now, the audience watches as Euripides and the Relative observe the door to Agathon's house. A servant emerges to announce the entrance of the mysterious Agathon.[13]

The ensuing discussion of Agathon precipitates the introduction of the motifs of body image and gender identification (see Moulton 1981: 110–23; 167). Interest focuses upon Agathon's appearance:

RELATIVE. Dark, brawny fellow?
EURIPIDES. O no, quite different; don't you know him really?
RELATIVE. Big-whiskered fellow?
EURIPIDES. Don't you know him really?
RELATIVE. No. (*Thinks again.*) No, I don't; at least I don't remember.
EURIPIDES. (*severely*) I fear there's much you don't remember, sir. [*Lit.*
Well, you may have screwed him, but still you may not know him.]

    MN.[14] μῶν ὁ μέλας, ὁ καρτερός;
    EUR. οὔκ, ἀλλ' ἕτερός τις· οὐχ ἑόρακας πώποτε;
    MN. μῶν ὁ δασυπώγων;
    EUR. οὐχ ἑόρακας πώποτε;
    MN. μὰ τὸν Δί' οὔτοι γ', ὥστε κἀμέ γ' εἰδέναι.
    EUR. καὶ μὴν βεβίνηκας σύ γ', ἀλλ' οὐκ οἶσθ' ἴσως.
                                    (31–5)

This ironic banter centers on Agathon's lack of a beard, on his lack of physical strength, and, finally, upon his role as the passive partner in homosexual relationships; all these traits identify him, before he even appears on stage, as an effeminate.[15] It also emphasizes the Relative's role as spectator, specifically as one who will gaze upon both women and men dressed as women.[16] Agathon is his first object of vision and, as it turns out, desire. In addition, the Relative opens this new play-within-the-play by spying upon Agathon, and spying becomes a significant motif later on.

When the two men are discovered, we finally learn the purpose of their mission. Euripides explains what the women are planning at the Thesmophoria, although the Relative agrees that Euripides does say bad things about women (85–6). In fact, the Relative characterizes Euripides quite clearly as a trickster when he asks if Euripides has a trick (μηχανή) for escaping this fate (87; 93–4). Euripides does, of course, and so he anticipates another play-within-the-play: Euripides wants Agathon to go in secret, dressed as a woman, and to speak on his behalf in the women's assembly. He uses language reminiscent of theater (λάθρᾳ, στολὴν γυναικὸς ἠμφιεσμένον, 92) to describe his plan for Agathon's costume.[17]

Agathon's entrance creates a spectacle, appropriately enough, even though he is not meant to be seen and does not know that he has an audience. Wheeled out on the *ekkyklema* (96) and dressed in women's clothes, he is singing the parts of his new composition – both the chorus' and the actor's parts – and they are both female.[18] Agathon himself also seems confused about the gender logic of his chorus. They sing of 'queen Leto, and the famous lyre, mother of hymns, with a masculine shout' (Λατώ τ' ἄνασσαν, / κίθαρίν τε ματέρ' ὕμνων, / ἄρσενι βοᾷ δόκιμον, 124–5; translation mine).[19] The scene provides an opportunity for an analysis of the spectator's gaze and the semiotics of theater, for the Relative sees the man underneath Agathon's female costume and jokes about thinking, at first, that he was seeing the prostitute Cyrene (97–8).

Although the Relative immediately praises Agathon's song, he also wonders in mock-tragic diction about the singer's gender:

> Whence art thou, what thy country, what thy garb?
> Why all this wondrous medley? Lyre and silks,
> A minstrel's lute, a maiden's netted hair,
> Girdle and wrestler's oil! a strange conjunction.
> How comes a sword beside a looking-glass?
> What art thou, man or woman? If a man,

MEN AS WOMEN: *THESMOPHORIAZUSAE*

Where are his clothes? [lit. Where is his penis? his
cloak?] his red Laconian shoes?
If woman, 'tis not like a woman's shape. [lit. Where
are her breasts?]
What art thou, speak; or if thou tell me not,
Myself must guess thy gender from thy song.

ποδαπὸς ὁ γύννις; τίς πάτρα; τίς ἡ στολή;
τίς ἡ τάραξις τοῦ βίου; τί βάρβιτος
λαλεῖ κροκωτῷ; τί δὲ λύρα κεκρυφάλῳ;
τί λήκυθος καὶ στρόφιον; ὡς οὐ ξύμφορον.
τίς δαὶ κατόπτρου καὶ ξίφους κοινωνία;
τίς δ' αὐτός, ὦ παῖ; πότερον ὡς ἀνὴρ τρέφει;
καὶ ποῦ πέος; ποῦ χλαῖνα; ποῦ Λακωνικαί;
ἀλλ' ὡς γυνὴ δῆτ'· εἶτα ποῦ τὰ τιτθία;
τί φής; τί σιγᾷς; ἀλλὰ δῆτ' ἐκ τοῦ μέλους
ζητῶ σ', ἐπειδή γ' αὐτὸς οὐ βούλει φράσαι;

(136–45)

The Relative is perplexed; he does not know how to interpret the figure he sees, and he does not know how to react to it. He mentions all the obvious visual aspects of theatrical masculine gender identity: the phallos, cloak, and Laconian shoes (142). Agathon appears to be missing these attributes, and that fuels the Relative's confusion. Instead of traditional masculine garb, Agathon wears a woman's costume (στολή, 136; κροκωτός, 138; κεκρύφαλος, 138; στρόφιον, 139), and he carries the emblem of feminine vanity and interest in appearances, a mirror (κατόπτρος, 140). The Relative's search for incontrovertible evidence, the phallos (τὸ πέος, 142), is even more amusing than his confusion, for it calls attention to the male under Agathon's costume while it highlights the apparent absence of Agathon's badge of masculinity. It also provides a thematic foreshadowing of the women's search for the Relative's own phallos later on (644–8). Moreover, Agathon's figure has no breasts (143), so he is not clearly either female or male. This appears reasonably strange to the Relative, for false breasts would seem to be the most clearly necessary piece of theatrical equipment that an actor portraying a woman might need. On the one hand, the construction of Agathon's image here recalls the gender ambiguity of some of the women played by male actors in *Lysistrata*. Yet Agathon does not mean to portray a woman on stage convincingly; he only dresses as a woman (incompletely) in order to compose the verses that a real actor will eventually perform (148–51). At this point, the spectacle of Agathon on stage is a puzzle to be deciphered. Indeed, the Relative twice calls Agathon an enigma (τάραξις, 137; ξύμφορον, 139). Since Agathon appears in such a confused form, with theatrical markers of gender mixed up all around him, a naïve spectator might in fact need some interpretive help.

The audience knows that Agathon really is male, no matter what his gender identity in public might appear to be. Perhaps he even resembles the effeminate god Dionysus.[20] It is our, as well as his, first lesson in how to look at male actors playing women. Here we are treated to a mistaken reading by a comic buffoon who mixes genres when he is confused about genders. Agathon displays a mix of genders, sexes, and genres. We know he is a man, yet he dresses as a woman; we know he is a tragedian, yet here he performs in a comedy; he is male, yet his sexuality is allied with female sexuality: these incongruities are comic in themselves.

The usual critical evaluation of this scene is nonetheless accurate: Aristophanes does mock contemporary, effeminate tragedians like Agathon here (see Muecke 1982b *passim*; Zeitlin 1981: 178). He asks figuratively, 'What sort of perverse tragedies can we expect from men who dress as women in order to compose verses and who carry that "art" of dressing (and performing) as women into their private lives?' Yet tragedy and transvestites are not the only objects of ridicule here. A tendentious joke about male desire also lurks in this scene. The spectacle of Agathon dressed and speaking like a woman, no matter how confused or incomplete the pretense of femininity, has aroused the Relative's desires and he, as an aggressive and masculine comic figure, voices them. When Agathon explains his theory of poetic composition, that the poet must attempt to resemble the character whom he wishes to compose (148–52, 154–6), the Relative responds with sexual advances: 'Well, whenever you make satyrs [i.e., write a satyr play], call me, and I'll get right behind you with my hard-on and make [it] with you' (ὅταν σατύρους τοίνυν ποιῇς, καλεῖν ἐμέ, / ἵνα συμποιῶ σοὔπισθεν ἐστυκὼς ἐγώ, 157–8).[21] The Relative had been aroused by the sight of Agathon's servant earlier and displayed the same sort of aggressive sexual attitude toward that particular object of vision (50, 57). The Relative's attitude toward spectatorship is clear: objects of vision become objects of desire. It makes sense, then, that Whitman called Agathon's song 'an aphrodisiac' (1964: 221). There is no question of whether he should or should not be aroused by the effeminate images of the servant or Agathon, or whether or not it is

MEN AS WOMEN: *THESMOPHORIAZUSAE*

wrong for the male spectator to be aroused by another man. As the effeminate, and thus passive, partner, Agathon bears the burden of homosexuality. He is the bugger (κατάπυγον, 200) and he is the 'wide-ass' (εὐρύπρωκτος, 200).[22] The Relative thus acts as an interior audience between us and Agathon, who is seen in a contrived but private moment. It is possible to imagine that male spectators might consider male actors playing women's roles on stage as objects of desire even while they were aware that they were men and not women.[23] The Relative has made that quite clear (e.g., 97–8).

In making his case to Agathon, Euripides compares his own aging masculine physique to Agathon's youthful, feminine beauty: 'And I am gray, you see, and bearded too, But you've a baby face, a treble voice, A fair complexion, pretty, smooth, and soft [Lit. feminine, delicate, and beautiful to look at]' (ἔπειτα πολιός εἰμι καὶ πώγων' ἔχω, / σὺ δ' εὐπρόσωπος, λευκός, ἐξυρημένος, / γυναικόφωνος, ἁπαλός, εὐπρεπὴς ἰδεῖν, 190–2). Euripides' remark that Agathon's feminine appearance is constructed to be looked at, and looked at with pleasure, reinforces one of the theatrical presuppositions behind *Thesmophoriazusae* as a whole: that women are creatures whose appearances, and even personalities, are carefully designed for being viewed by men. Agathon knows this, not only because of his method of composition but also because of his own personal life. He dresses, as a woman does, to be an object of vision and desire. This ability and desire to use costume, to live more as a woman than as a man, differentiates the effeminate Agathon from the masculine Euripides. Agathon does retain some masculine self-authority: he is a poet and is allowed a voice in public affairs by virtue of his natural sex. His femininity is a mask he dons to carry out his profession, much as an actor does. In addition, the feminine persona he affects facilitates his relationships with other men.

Agathon refuses Euripides' request with a clever excuse: 'I'm too much like a woman, and they'd think that I was come to poach on their preserves' (δοκῶν γυναικῶν ἔργα νυκτερείσια / κλέπτειν, ὑφαρπάζειν τε θήλειαν Κύπριν, 204–5). This implies a great deal for an analysis of gender representation in theater. Euripides is too much of a man to pull off the plan (190), yet Agathon is too much of a woman.[24] In fact, Agathon is afraid that he makes a better woman than the women themselves.

After Agathon declines to help Euripides, the Relative abruptly and spontaneously offers to do whatever he can to help. Euripides seizes the opportunity and immediately enjoins the Relative to take off his *himation* and have his facial hair shaved. In other words, the palpable, physical aspects of his masculine gender identity must be removed before he can imitate a woman. He will learn how to disguise his voice and his speech later.[25] First, the two men acquire a razor from Agathon, who always has one ready (218–19). One of the costume accessories that distinguishes women from men, a razor is woman's equipment.[26] In an instance of comic overdetermination, not only does effeminate Agathon own a razor (he does not participate in the masculinity of hairiness), he carries an entire case of them (ξυροφορεῖς, 218; ξυροδόκης, 220).[27] For the Relative, the shaving is traumatic: as soon as the razor touches his skin, he screams (222). He then swears by the Eumenides and Demeter (224–6). These are women's goddesses, and perhaps a sign that the transformation of the Relative into a feminine figure is taking hold already.

The Relative also becomes an official buffoon, physically as well as spiritually. Now that his face is half-shaved, Euripides declares that the Relative is ridiculous, significantly using the theatrical word for comic figures (καταγέλαστος, 226).[28] The Relative is halfway between male and female at this point, and there is a pause in his transformation to allow us to ponder and enjoy the process. He is also called εὐπρεπής, an adjective reserved in comedy for women and effeminate men (192; *Lysistrata* 1713; *Ecclesiazusae* 427; see Ussher 1973: 135 *ad* 427–30).

After the shave is completed, the Relative admires himself in a mirror (234).[29] Euripides wants the Relative to regard himself (θεᾶσθαι) as a woman might, and he encourages the Relative to see himself as an object of desire.[30] He transforms the Relative from a gazing spectator to an object of vision, an actor to be gazed at. Appropriately, the Relative looks in the mirror and sees the effeminate Kleisthenes, who will appear himself later on. This is an Aristophanic tease: the Relative has no idea how much he really does resemble Kleisthenes. At this point the resistance that the Relative has put up against the transformation into a woman bears significance. He is not overly pleased with either the process or the result, and his resistance to the woman's role facilitates his double position as both a spectator and an object of vision. Spectators in the audience may identify with him as a man reluctant to be 'feminized'.[31] Thus the 'real' identity of the Relative underneath his female costume can never be fully hidden.

After his pubic hair is singed (236–48), the Relative is finally ready for clothes.[32] Euripides borrows a cloak (ἱμάτιον, 250) and a breastband (στρόφιον, 251) from Agathon for him, as though he were dressing the Relative in Agathon's (or Dionysus') image (see Rogers 1920: 28 *ad* 249). The Relative ties the band (στρόφιον), which functions as a kind of supporting undergarment, around his chest.³³ He also puts on the little yellow dress (κροκωτός, 253), a garment usually associated with seductive women.³⁴ He wears his cloak (ἱμάτιον) over one shoulder and probably brings it around the back of the head to form a hood.³⁵ The Relative also wears a veil in addition to the hood formed by the cloak. The resemblance of Agathon to the theatrical image of Dionysus has been noted (H. Hansen 1976: 174; Muecke 1982b: 42; Saïd 1987: 230; Zeitlin 1981: 196). Yet since the Relative dresses up with Agathon's clothes, he too comes to resemble Dionysus, however imperfectly: a man in women's clothes, among women, present at a women's festival, indulging in theatrical games, and attempting to defend a ritual celebration of Dionysus (Euripides' plays) against charges made in the celebration of Demeter. He is, of course, a comic Dionysus, more suggestive than literal. With his mirror instead of a thyrsus and veil instead of an ivy crown, he resembles a woman conscious of her status as an object of vision (just as Dionysus does, whose rites depend on vision and spectacle).

Thus, with the Relative, Euripides constructs a theatrical and comic woman on stage right in front of the audience. In this play, 'woman' is an image quite easily constructed through physical and linguistic disguises, as if 'woman' were a creature waiting to be created by men. Ferris writes:

> Aristophanes' comedy tells us how easy it is to be a woman, a metonymic piece of skirt: Agathon, the poet, has merely to costume himself as a woman in order to write about women in his tragic poems; Euripides puts on the mask and, *voila!*, the manners make the woman! Mnesilochus' disguise as a woman is a more complicated dramatic re-invention... But Euripides' dressing of Mnesilochus is an ideal lesson in the male creation of 'woman'... And what is this woman? She is a yellow gown, a wig, a head band, a girdle, with smooth, hairless skin, shoes, shawl – a list of items, of props.
>
> (Ferris 1989: 28)

At this point, we might also hypothesize that Aristophanes begins to exploit on-stage femininity as a powerful comic tool and to claim the power of 'femininity' for comedy. By making Euripides, the tragic playwright, the author of a comic female figure and the director of a male actor in a comic female role, Aristophanes puts his favorite target for humor in the role of the comic playwright. The rivalry between genres comes to the fore.

Still, the convention of male actors as women on stage has been baldly exposed. As the play moves into its next section, we are given a model in the Relative by which to measure the performance of the real male actors as comic women and vice versa. There is no longer any reason for us to believe that they are women. We must now actively suppress our knowledge of theatrical conventions. We have spied on one of the secrets of the theater, of the worship of Dionysus.

Unlike that of the women in *Ecclesiazusae* (e.g. 155–60), the Relative's language immediately displays a certain generic femininity. He swears by Aphrodite and admires the fabric of his dress (254). He becomes more and more involved in the transformation, expressing concern about the straightening of his hem (256), the look of his headdress (260), and the fit of his slippers (263). When the Relative is fully dressed and Agathon has returned to the interior of his house, Euripides admires his latest creation and pronounces the physical disguise complete, although the Relative needs to work on his voice: 'There then, the man's a regular woman now, At least to look at; and if you've to speak, Put on a feminine mincing voice' (ἀνὴρ μὲν ἡμῖν οὑτοσὶ καὶ δὴ γυνὴ / τό γ' εἶδος· ἢν λαλῇς δ', ὅπως τῷ φθέγματι / γυναικιεῖς εὖ καὶ πιθανῶς, 267–9). The Relative will have to speak, so he will have to disguise his voice. Euripides uses λαλεῖν (used for women's talk) to describe what the Relative will do when he talks.[36] The scene is reminiscent of a director giving instructions to an actor. The actor (the Relative) has been costumed and transformed; now he receives his lessons so that his performance might be effective (πιθανῶς, 269). He will not be an object of vision and desire in the same way that Agathon is. Although he has been presented as the one whose gaze we should scrutinize and perhaps identify with, now that he is costumed as a woman it is difficult for him to become an object of desire as Agathon did. We have seen what goes into the costume of this male actor in a female role, and we have seen how he resists the role.

When Euripides dismisses him to go on to the festival, the Relative immediately speaks up, but in his masculine voice, and he swears by Apollo (269), thus confounding the image of actor and costume. The assembly of the Thesmophoria is about to begin and Euripides exits, leaving his Relative to begin yet another play-within-the-play. Spectatorship is complicated here. We are at one and the same time to identify with the gaze of the Relative and also to make him an object of our gaze (as he performs his female impersonation). But making him an object of desire is impossible, because we have been exposed to the secrets and the components of his costume and its construction. We have also witnessed the aggressive and potent nature of his masculinity. A feminist reader may interpret this scene as frustrating the illusion.

AMONG WOMEN

The Relative makes his ascent to the Thesmophoria as an actor opening an Aristophanic play might. In a monologue spoken in his woman's voice, he describes what he sees and what is happening. Just as an actor in any opening monologue might, he sets the stage for the beginning of this next new play, the true 'Women at the Thesmophoria' for which we have all been waiting. The opening of this new play-within-the-play also resembles the opening of *Lysistrata*. Although the solitary figure on stage does not complain about the tardiness of the other women (they are filtering onto the stage), she nevertheless appears alone and on her way to a specific destination where women will meet by themselves. She has been revealed as a man underneath her costume; Lysistrata eventually proves to be a masculine woman.

The Relative displays the same trouble maintaining his new linguistic gender identity that other Aristophanic characters in some gender disguise do (see, for example, *Ecclesiazusae*). He tries hard to speak correctly as a woman, and for the most part he succeeds. For example, at 285 he uses a feminine participle (λαβοῦσα), appropriately, to refer to himself. He knows which deities to offer sacrifices to (Demeter and Persephone, 286–7). Yet he also uses an expression that is more commonly found in the masculine singular (θύειν ἔχουσιν), a slip which may serve to break or blur the illusion of accurate gender representation (see also *Thesm*. 853, 1151; *Clouds* 509; *Birds* 341; *Lysistrata* 945; *Frogs* 202, 512, 524; Rogers 1920: 33 *ad* 288). The Relative also makes some veiled references to his fears of being discovered, references that the audience can 'read' through to remember the man underneath the costume (e.g. 283–4, his prayer for a safe return and good luck; 288, his prayer for escape). Then he utters a 'woman's' prayer for a rich, yet stupid, husband for her daughter – and the daughter is given an obscene joke name, Choirion.[37] The Relative is well aware of the characterization of women as tricksters, which makes sense since he is trying to be both a woman and a trickster as well.

However much an object of the spectator's gaze he may be at this point, the Relative still wants and needs to be a spectator himself again, and he searches for a good place from which to hear the women's speeches (292–3). His position as a voyeur and as an object of vision is clear. So far the layers of theatricality and spectatorship on stage have been remarkable: we, the audience, have watched Euripides and the Relative; Euripides and the Relative have watched Agathon and his servant; Euripides is on trial for his theatrical representations of women and searches for a substitute to represent him at the Thesmophoria; he sought that substitute in a man who composes theatrical representations of women and who also himself resembles a woman physically (even though he says it is only for inspiration, details indicate that it is his personal preference as well); the Relative has agreed to substitute for Euripides and to represent a woman in order to represent Euripides, and we have witnessed the process of creating his representation of woman. Now the Relative acts as a woman with some strange gender equivocation in his language; he is quite clearly performing an imitation. Finally, the Relative sets himself up as, alternately, actor and spectator in and at the festival.

When the women's assembly of the Thesmophoria opens, the pretense of women represented on stage begins in earnest. Up until now, we have seen male actors representing older and younger men, a man who dresses as women, and a man who has disguised himself as a woman (but whose disguise has been constructed openly on stage and so is transparent to us). Now we finally see male actors portraying women whom we are supposed to believe are really women (and not necessarily men dressed as women). A certain symmetry marks these role reversals: as the Relative dresses and acts like a woman at the Thesmophoria, so the 'women' proceed to act as men might in the *ecclesia*.[38]

The scene opens with a gender-modified announcement of the assembly meeting.[39] There are some technical deviations from the regular (male) *ecclesia*, but the format of the assembly meeting is duly adapted to its present context. The women's identification of themselves as women is, in contrast to the Relative's methods of self-identification, quite accurate. They make no mistakes in linguistic identity (306–9). It is clear now that this is not so much a play about the women at the Thesmophoria as a play about the 'women' (the Relative and Euripides) at the *ecclesia* of the Thesmophoria. Any voyeuristic curiosity that may have been sparked in the spectators, who look forward (like the Relative, perhaps) to seeing what goes on in secret women's meetings like the Thesmophoria, is now disappointed. This council meeting, with its speeches and formalities, resembles the meeting of any *ecclesia*. What we watch and wait for is the performance of the Relative as a woman among other comic actors playing women. Woman A puts on the speakers' garland in preparation for speaking (380; cf. *Ecclesiazusae* 131–2). The herald calls the speakers orators (οἱ ῥήτορες, 382), because Woman A coughs and clears her throat just like the speakers in the regular Athenian assembly. The pretense of her feminine gender identity is not in question, and she shares in the ability to imitate. In this case, she imitates male ways of speaking in the assembly, a trait that Lysistrata exhibited in her play and for which her gender identity was regularly in question. Here, however, the ability to speak in ways that might reveal a male identity is not the primary issue – the problem of gender identity and representation is graphically illustrated in this play by Agathon, the Relative, and Kleisthenes – but rather the content of the women's words calls attention to the issue of gender representation on stage. We are, after all, focused upon the Relative, and these 'real' women act as foils to his 'imitation' woman. In fact, we do not yet forget that these women are women: they make no slips in their linguistic gender identity. For example, at 384, Woman A addresses the women accurately as women (ὦ γυναῖκες). The Relative is the one we watch for slips of the tongue. There are really two distinct images of women here. The first is of women with serious charges and ideas, the 'real' women, and this is a paratragic construction. Women in tragedy often complain of their treatment by men; these complaints are also often trenchant and sympathetic (e.g. Euripides' *Medea* 230–51; Sophocles, *Tereus* fr. 583 Radt (Procne)).[40] Here they complain of unfair dramatic representations and they plan a tragic end for the playwright (as women in tragedy sometimes plan disastrous ends for their male enemies: again e.g. Euripides' *Medea* and Sophocles' Procne). Their reason is not, however, that Euripides misrepresents them; rather, it turns out that he has been telling the truth. The representation of 'woman' by the Relative does not follow this pattern. In masculine style, 'she' tells the truth, and that representation identifies 'her' as an unsuccessful trickster, for women are usually good at lying. This is a comic representation; a woman is a man in drag, we might say.

In her speech, Woman A alleges how Euripides represents women: as secretive (μυχοτρόπους), sex-crazed (τὰς ἀνδρεραστίας καλῶν), tipplers (τὰς οἰνοπότιδας), traitors (τὰς προδότιδας), gossips (τὰς λάλους), unclean (τὰς οὐδὲν ὑγιὲς), and a great evil for men (τὰς μέγ' ἀνδράσιν κακόν, 392–4). This list, however, proves to be fairly accurate according to Aristophanic, but not Euripidean, standards;

both this play and *Lysistrata* construct women in this very image. She also complains that theater has affected life. Whatever men see represented in the theater, they believe, and they go home from the theater angry (ὑποβλέπουσ') at their wives and looking (σκοποῦνται) for illicit lovers (395–7). The men have gazed upon theatrical representations of women just as (ideal) male spectators are supposed to.[41]

After this indictment of Euripides, she turns to a revelation of the truth about women. At line 398, she complains that ordinary tasks have become difficult under the suspicion aroused by Euripides' plays. Later, she admits that women's deceptions, such as passing off other women's babies as their own or marrying old men and ordering them around, are in fact what women do best (407–13). Because of Euripides, she says, women are locked up and their access to the usual little goodies (grain, oil, wine) cut off (414–21). She closes with a proposal to kill Euripides (428–31). In short, her speech has revealed that Euripides actually tells the truth about women.

When the Relative steps up to speak (467–573), the linguistic dimensions of his remarks offer a respectable imitation of female gender identity. He begins by identifying himself with the women and their complaints (467–70). He also swears by Artemis, a woman's oath (517; see Rogers 1920: 58 *ad* 517).[42] However, the unsubtle and unironic content of his speech does not conform to the feminine ways of Women A and B. The message of the speech is rather markedly male. As long as they are alone, he says (which we know is not true, since he is deceiving them, and the audience is spying also), they should admit that Euripides' characterization of women is true (472). He describes a female trick – sneaking off with a lover as a husband sleeps – that even Euripides does not know about (477–89). He lists other things as well: hiding a lover under a shawl, having sex with anyone, chewing garlic to hide wine on the breath, and harboring false children. In order to convince the women that they should let Euripides be, he elaborates on details of women's behavior that, he says, Euripides does not reveal. Here his characterization of 'woman' grows more transparent, for his syntactical accuracy never slips (as does the women's in *Ecclesiazusae*), but the content of the speech reveals his gender. When women are in disguise, gender identity becomes muddled, as in *Lysistrata* and *Ecclesiazusae*. Here, a man is in disguise who cannot hide his gender, even though the exterior details of his disguise may be technically flawless. His identity becomes suspect rather through the themes of his commentary. His physical presence altogether undermines the 'serious' representations of women played by the other actors. The mincing, high-voiced, accusatory part played by the Relative (whom we know to be a hirsute and masculine figure) diminishes and exposes the truth about women.

The chorus now expresses a problematic self-blame. They claim: 'O, nothing, nothing in the world so hateful will you find As shameless women, save of course the rest of womankind' (ἀλλ' οὐ γάρ ἐστι τῶν ἀναισχύντων φύσει γυναικῶν / οὐδὲν κάκιον εἰς ἅπαντα πλὴν ἄρ' εἰ γυναῖκες, 531–2). As they quote from Euripides' now lost *Melanippe Desmotis*, the chorus signals to the audience that they are men underneath.[43] This discloses the big joke, then, for there are no women on stage and Aristophanes is having fun at the expense of both Euripides and women. The Relative reveals the convention of men acting as women here, and shows that they are just as Euripides says they are. In many ways, this line is the center of the play. As Ferris writes:

> What is interesting in this single line is its quality of intrigue and conspiracy with the audience – an audience who, it is assumed, will agree wholeheartedly with such sentiment. Indeed, the entire play conspires with its audience against the women it has dramatically stereotyped; first, by allowing the audience to take part in the secret rituals of the women's festival; secondly, by allowing a man disguised as a woman easily to enter the festival, and to subvert with equal ease the women's purpose in relation to Euripides; and lastly, by allowing the audience to witness the 'creation' of a stereotypical woman twice over.
>
> (Ferris 1989: 23)

Ferris also proposes, not altogether inaccurately, that we are meant to understand this passage as a conspiratorial aside to the audience, who here would understand that the voice of the actor playing the woman would come through (ibid.).

Woman A now swears by Agraulus (533), identifying herself linguistically as a woman and thus restoring the pretense of gender representation on stage.[44] Then she proposes that they torture the traitor. Her plans for this torture are ironic: she proposes singeing the woman's genitals with a hot poker (536–9). This serves to call attention to the absence of any real χοῖροι on stage, to reinforce the revelations of the previous scene, and to remind the audience of the Relative's real gender identity: after all, we have already seen his genitals singed with a hot poker.

The arrival of Kleisthenes ushers in yet another layer of transvestite joking. He mirrors once more the male transvestism that forms the emblem for this play. Probably wearing an effeminate style of dress, he even calls the women 'kindred to my shape' (ξυγγενεῖς τοὐμοῦ τρόπου, 574), when the truth is actually the other way around (he is kindred to their shape). Although he is mistaken for a woman at first (571), it is not clear whether Kleisthenes cross-dresses completely, as Agathon does, and so he probably does not. He feels kinship with women, but functions in the world of men.[45] Kleisthenes is male biologically, but his gender identity is female. The Relative is also male, both in his biological identity and in his true gender identity; he is, however, disguised as a female and is having trouble hiding his masculinity. The women are biologically female, and their gender identity is unequivocally female, even though Aristophanes plays little jokes to remind us that they are imitations and female only for the performance of this play.

Kleisthenes' theatrical and spiritual bisexuality is perhaps the trait that Aristophanes plays upon here. He is mentioned twice in *Lysistrata*, in fact, as a possible mediator between men and women (621) and as a last-resort sexual substitute for a woman (1092). His body resembles a woman's body almost naturally. For example, his smooth cheeks are proof of his femininity (575, 583), but a razor is never mentioned (as it is in the case of the apparently artificially smooth-skinned Agathon). He clearly identifies with women spiritually, and surprisingly he likes them (574–6). He is 'mad about women' (γυναικομανῶ) and functions as their advocate (576), representing them in male company, such as in the real assembly, in the same way that the Relative represents Euripides in this setting. The difference is that Kleisthenes represents 'the other' on behalf of 'the other' (women) and for an audience of men; the Relative represents 'normal' (men, and specifically Euripides) on behalf of 'normal' and for an audience of women. Kleisthenes provides another substitution, another man who speaks for women and who takes their place in a different sort of theater, in the *ecclesia*.

Kleisthenes tells the women to be on their guard and to look out for 'the terrible and big thing' (σκοπῆτε καὶ τηρῆτε καὶ μὴ προσπέσῃ / ὑμῖν ἀφράκτοις πρᾶγμα δεινὸν καὶ μέγα, 580). His choice of words is significant. First, he uses σκοπῆτε, which recalls the theme of spectatorship and hints that they should be looking for an actor and a costume (cf. 396). He also reveals that Euripides has sent a spy (κατάσκοπος, 588). With 'the terrible and big thing' (πρᾶγμα δεινὸν

MEN AS WOMEN: *THESMOPHORIAZUSAE*

καὶ μέγα), he not-so-subtly hints that what they should look for is a phallos (cf. *Lysistrata* 23–4). He reveals that the women have been the victims of a Euripidean trick which has taken the form of a play, for his description of the process of the Relative's disguise borrows a term used often of men dressing as women (ἐσκεύασεν, 591; cf. Hdt. 1. 60, 5. 20).

The chorus sets out to find the spy, using that significant word σκοπεῖν again (599), and they ask Kleisthenes to help (601–2). He interviews Woman A, who provocatively admits that she is Kleonymus' wife (605).[46] Woman A is, however, safely vouched for. Having Kleisthenes perform this task of interviewing the women to find the man lurking underneath the disguise is rather provocative as well, and perhaps more revealing of the problems of representing femininity on the comic stage.

Kleisthenes' encounter with the Relative serves to reveal these problems once and for all. First, Kleisthenes' inquisition must wait until the Relative relieves his bladder (he is both nervous and stalling for time). This brings his phallos into view (in the imagination). The women, and Kleisthenes, strip the Relative of his female clothes (636) and loosen his sash (638). Underneath the disguise, they discover a masculine body. He appears strong (στιβαρά, καρτερά, 639) and not at all feminine (he has no breasts, 640). Despite his attempts to justify this physique (637, 641), his phallos appears (643) and reveals the truth once and for all. Kleisthenes notices it first, and leads the women in a chase for it around his body (644–8). While the women hold the Relative prisoner, Kleisthenes departs to announce the event in the meeting of the regular assembly, where he will act as the women's advocate among the Prytaneis, those men assigned to keep order in the *ecclesia*, so that they may obtain official help (654). This is an important moment in the play, since now the Relative has been 'deconstructed' on stage by two other representations of female figures. His body has been objectified and viewed as a map may be (647–8; cf. the treatment of Diallage in *Lysistrata*), for Kleisthenes remarks that the Relative's phallos goes back and forth between his legs like a ship through the Gulf of Corinth. In fact, his phallos has been the center of attention from the moment when it was hidden to the moment when it was revealed.[47]

Now the chorus sings in accompaniment of its search for other male intruders, and its song continues the theme of mixed gender, although the integrity of representation on stage has been restored once again. The chorus members clearly represent women now, for they use feminine words to describe themselves accurately. Yet they also make a point of girding up their tunics 'in male fashion' (ἀνδρείως, 656), a gesture that makes their attire somewhat ironic. They are looking for men, yet they look everywhere except at themselves. They interact with the audience, perhaps, as they search 'through the tents and the gangways, and up by the tiers and the rows' (τὴν πύκνα, τὰς σκηνὰς καὶ τὰς διόδους, 658). In another joke on gender identity, they find no men, when it is clear that many men have in fact infiltrated this secret meeting and the men are just where you might expect to find them, too: in the audience.

In the middle section of *Thesmophoriazusae*, Aristophanes explores and has fun with the illusion of men acting as women on stage. He plays with both successful and unsuccessful impersonation, with both intentional and unintentional imitation, and with imitation for several different reasons. Agathon imitates women for artistic (and perhaps personal) reasons, Kleisthenes for personal reasons (and perhaps physical – his thin or missing beard is constant source of effeminacy), and the Relative out of necessity. None of these men is able to mask his masculinity completely. While each may don the outward physical and linguistic properties of a woman, he cannot represent a woman seamlessly. Consequently, we are reminded of the play as play and the representation of 'real' women is undermined.

PLAYING THE WOMAN'S PART

The first of the Relative's escape plans involves the use of a strategy taken from Euripides' play *Telephus*. The scheme also enables the Relative to parody *Telephus* at the same time as he makes use of it.[48] This *Telephus* parody is related to the general shape of *Thesmophoriazusae* as a whole, as it inverts the gender roles of the story of Telephus.

In Euripides' *Telephus*, the Mysian king Telephus infiltrates Mycenae and the palace of Agamemnon in the disguise of a beggar. He has been wounded by Achilles and told that the wound can only be healed by the one who inflicted it, so Telephus is searching for that Achaean hero. In this disguise, he argues in front of the king and his court a defense of Telephus, and the disguise is revealed by Achilles himself. In desperation, Telephus seizes the baby Orestes and threatens to sacrifice it if his wound is not cured. A settlement is reached at the play's end and the baby's life spared. In *Thesmophoriazusae*, the Relative (who has infiltrated a meeting in disguise, delivered a defense speech, and been unmasked) seizes the baby that belongs to Woman A and threatens to sacrifice it (688–91). Instead of a male baby, the child is referred to as female (as befits the feminine context of the Thesmophoria). This 'child' eventually turns out to be a wineskin rather than a human infant, however, and it is eventually 'sacrificed' (drunk) by the Relative. The Relative, no longer playing his female role as the representative of Euripides, chooses an alternative role, that of Telephus, which nevertheless does not correspond with his costume (see Zeitlin 1981: 184; also Miller 1948: 182–3). The pattern of the Telephus story – disguise, infiltration, defense, exposure, sacrifice (or attempted sacrifice) – clearly recalls the structure of *Thesmophoriazusae*, and also recalls the earlier invocation of Aristophanes' parody of *Telephus* in *Acharnians* (39–70), thus tying the ends of the play together. The disjunction of costume and character not only facilitates the parody (the Relative performs a Euripidean male role in drag), but once again explicitly points out the convention of male actors in a female role, perhaps even the technical necessity for ancient actors to play more than one role and sometimes both genders in the same play.

When the chorus of women return from their fruitless search for other spies, the play's focus shifts from the imitation of women to the imitation of Euripidean plays, for all of the Relative's subsequent schemes to escape from his bonds revolve around imitations of Euripidean dramas. Aristophanes dispenses, in fact, with the metaphorical and suggested 'play-within-the-play' format, and stages actual 'plays-within-the play' to make his point about Euripides and female roles on the stage. There is no fooling the audience in the theater: they know that what they are watching is an imitation of an imitation (Muecke 1977: 64). In the three Euripidean imitations that follow the *Telephus* episode, the issue of gender representation becomes more apparent and increasingly complicated.

Next the Relative decides to imitate (μιμήσομαι, 850) Euripides' *Helen* – after all, he says, he has the correct costume (850).[49] The play he chooses represents an alternative story about Helen: she has been held prisoner in the palace of Proteus in Egypt and remained faithful to Menelaus throughout the war; the Helen who appeared at Troy was merely an *eidolon* (insubstantial image). In Euripides' play, which was produced in Athens in 412 BCE, shortly before both *Lysistrata* and *Thesmophoriazusae*, Menelaus arrives at Proteus' palace and undergoes an elaborate recognition scene with the estranged Helen; they escape Egypt and sail for home. What is significant in the *Helen* imitation here, in addition to its parody of the romantic, alternative Helen story, is the development of its performance as a play in front of an 'internal' audience, the Relative's guard Krytilla. She is the second female audience to whom the Relative has played. He was quite unsuccessful with the first, the women at the Thesmophoria, and Krytilla appears to share in their skeptical spectatorship. Her identity is undeniably female (she swears by Hekate at 858, and by the 'two goddesses' at 897 and 916).[50] Just as with the other women, we are to believe in the pretense of her representation by a male actor, although the specter of the male actor underneath her costume is never absent. In addition, her role as the prison guard reflects the gender-role reversals of the Thesmophoria appropriately. If we remember that both she and the Relative are men playing women's parts, although one (Krytilla) plays the man's role and the other (the Relative) plays the woman's role, then they appear to mirror each other theatrically for a moment.

By line 855, the Relative is speaking as if he were Helen (855–7). His costume and voice are meant to convince his audience of the validity of his representation, to draw her in her gaze as a spectator-participant and to facilitate his release. Yet Krytilla does not participate appropriately as a spectator; she does not appear to know how (Muecke 1977: 67; Zeitlin 1981: 187). She cannot develop a way of looking that will enable her to identify with either Helen or Menelaus, to suspend her disbelief, to let her imagination be transported to the world of this new play and to allow the Relative/Helen to depart with Euripides/Menelaus. Too literal-minded (they cannot even involve her in playing a role, 875), she provides extra comic depth to the theme of *mimesis*. She watches the performance without illusions (861–2) and remembers the proper venue for theater, knowing that where they are, the Thesmophorion, is not it (879–80). Krytilla may not be terribly cooperative as a theatrical audience, but she is not altogether dull: she calls both the Relative and Euripides πανοῦργος (899, 920). It is quite clear that Aristophanes does not consider the female gaze as one conducive to theatrical manipulation. Women create and facilitate theater; they are actors, not spectators.

In the meantime, a policeman enters, accompanied by a Scythian archer, looking for the πανοῦργος of whom Kleisthenes spoke in the assembly (929–30). Krytilla warns the policeman about Euripides' attempt to help the Relative escape: 'Aye, one came but now Spinning his yarns, and all but got him off' (νὴ Δί' ὡς νῦν δὴ γ' ἀνὴρ / ὀλίγου μ' ἀφείλετ' αὐτὸν ἱστιορράφος, 934–5).[51] The Relative asks the policeman to have the archer strip him (939) before putting him on the execution block so that he does not die in a humiliating fashion, in women's clothes (ἐν κροκωτοῖς καὶ μίτραις, 941–2).⁵² He is assured that this will not happen: everyone should see that he is a πανοῦργος (943–4). Self-consciously, the Relative curses his κροκώτος (945), the emblem of the female that has led both him and Euripides into so much trouble.

After a choral ode (947–1000) to which I shall return, Euripides and the Relative reappear and attempt a performance of Euripides' *Andromeda*. This play, also produced in 412 BCE, concerns the rescue of Andromeda from her chains and from the threats of a sea serpent by the hero Perseus.⁵³ The Relative, still in female dress (although it must be in more disarray by now), is in the pillory, which not only gives him a believable motivation for the bound Andromeda, but also literally sets him in his own little stage on stage. The metatheatricality here is not subtle.

The humor in this representation lies in the extended and exaggerated contrast between the role of Andromeda, the princess in distress and in need of rescue, and the actor playing her, the old, masculine Relative in parodic female dress. The audience has changed, too: now the Relative is being guarded by the Scythian archer. With the exit of Krytilla (946), power of punishing the Relative and Euripides for their transgressions has passed to the regular, male authority of the *polis* and the regular *ecclesia*. This Scythian archer is not, however, any better a spectator than Krytilla was. He does not even understand what is happening when, as Echo, Euripides teases him (1083–97).⁵⁴

In their performances, both the Relative and Euripides display remarkable acting ability, and each moves fluidly from one voice to another, the Relative from Andromeda to himself and back (1015–55, although he makes one error at 1022–3), Euripides from Echo to Perseus (1056–132). For example, as Andromeda the Relative mentions his own situation, especially his costume: 'First with razor keen he hacks me, Next in yellow silks he packs me, Sends me then to dangerous dome, Where the women prowl and roam' (ὃς ἔμ' ἀπεξύρησε πρῶτον, / ὃς ἐμὲ κροκόεν εἶτ' ἐνέδυσεν / ἐπὶ δὲ τοῖσδ', ἐς τόδ' ἀνέπεμψεν ἱερὸν, ἔνθα γυναῖκες, 1043–5). Euripides enters as Echo at 1056; he finally imitates a woman himself.⁵⁵ 'She' mentions the play and gives the Relative directions on playing his part (1059–63). Euripides physically enters as Perseus at 1098. At 1108, the Scythian asks the Relative, who is still acting as Andromeda, to be quiet, using the feminine verb λαλεῖν (1108, 1109). Unlike Krytilla, he must believe in 'her' to some extent, even though he tells Euripides shortly after that 'she' is not a woman (1111–12).[56] This stratagem fails, too, however; it may be too subtle for the Scythian, who is a rather difficult spectator, to place himself correctly within the dramatic paradigm.

The control that both the Relative and Euripides display over the power of representation in the *Andromeda* episode is notable, even withstanding the Relative's slight slip-up at 1077, where he calls upon Echo/Euripides by uttering the masculine ὢγάθ' ('dear'; see Rogers 1920: 117 *ad* 1077, who wonders if the Relative is thinking of Euripides or of the actor). Yet the dramatic validity of their representation is never strong: they are always viewed as men acting as women. They are comic, and they become comic actors in this version of *Andromeda*. Here Aristophanes claims once and for all for comedy the image of the male actor in a female role. The metatheatricality of this phenomenon cannot, he implies, be the focus of a successful romantic tragedy. It is just too comic. Zeitlin writes that

> Echo as the embodiment (more properly, disembodiment) of mimesis is also the focal point for the concept of the feminine which can never be grasped as primary and original, but only as the one who is imitated or the one who imitates and yet as such, is therefore also empowered as the mistress of imitation.
>
> (Zeitlin 1981: 192)

There is one more point, however. Men make the voice of Echo heard on the stage. Woman, with Echo as her essentialized disembodiment, may be the one who imitates and is imitated, but she is always made visible and audible, given a stage body and a stage voice, by a male actor. *Thesmophoriazusae* makes that quite clear.

Aristophanes' choice of plays to parody has been peculiar. Most notably, he does not stage parodies of the plays to which the women at the Thesmophoria object. Rather, he chooses a series of escape dramas, only two of which require female impersonation. This suggests, first and foremost, that the women's complaints are not Aristophanes' own objections to Euripidean drama, and that they form the pretext for mocking Euripides. Rather, I would suggest that Aristophanes objects to the Euripidean plays of disguise and trickery, those which tread most clearly on the territory of comedy. The outrageousness of each parody increases in *Thesmophoriazusae*, just as the presence of feminine figures becomes more prominent in each parody. Aristophanes objects to Euripides' adoption of the essential features of Aristophanic humor: escape, trickery, and femininity.

Placed between these travesties of Euripidean tragedy are two choral songs. After the *Helen* episode, the chorus sings a hymn in honor of the gods (947–1000). They celebrate being women at the Thesmophoria (947–8) and, appropriately, remark upon the need for vigilance against intruders (959). Even though these women are attending a festival in honor of Demeter, they praise Apollo, Artemis, Hera, Hermes, Pan, and the Nymphs as well. Their song ends with an extended tribute to Dionysus (985–1000). As they change the style of their song and the pattern of their dancing steps (985–6), they also shift the focus of their (and our) attention away from Demeter and towards Dionysus. It would be most appropriate to invoke Dionysus here: Dionysus presides over the festival that the women, as comic figures, have been created for, and so he makes possible their appearance and their speech in the first place.[57] He is also the god of transformation and sexual ambiguity, an appropriately metatheatrical god.

After the *Andromeda* parody, the chorus invokes Athena (1136–47) and identifies itself as female (1145). Although the conventions and trappings of theater, even the necessities of comic theater, have been exposed, we are now asked to believe once more in the pretense of the chorus's disguise. They also sing to the Thesmophorian goddesses (1148) and mention that no men should be there (1150) to look upon the rites. The ode seems naïve and ironic accordingly. This rule has been violated right in front of the audience at another festival. Through the medium of Dionysus, Demeter has been exposed and forced to take second place, just as through the medium of Aristophanes, Euripides has been exposed and forced to take second place.

Wrapping up the final scene of the play, Euripides thinks of yet another scheme for rescuing the Relative and offers the women an ultimatum: if they let the Relative go, he will not abuse them in his plays; if not, he will tell their husbands what they really do at home in secret (1165–9). The chorus agrees, as long as Euripides is able to trick the Scythian and free the Relative by himself. After all, they are not responsible for the Scythian guard; the Prytaneis are. Dressing himself as an old woman (her name is later revealed as Artemisia, 1200), Euripides has a nude flute girl parade in front of the Scythian, all the time quite conscious of the effect his actress will have on her intended audience (1178). He gives her provocative directions, as the blatantly comic director that he now is (1181–3, 1189–90). The scene is a stroke of comic genius: Aristophanes makes Euripides produce a comedy with a woman in her traditional comic role, and claims the innovation of women in central roles for himself. An actor dressed as a nude flute or dancing girl, a false woman created for the male spectator's gaze, decorates the ending of most Aristophanic comedies (even *Lysistrata*). This is the right kind of theater for the Scythian, for he runs after her.[58] Aristophanes triumphs, making humor of men dressed as women and of men falling for the comic ploy that manipulates the spectator's gaze and plays with the comic convention of male actors in female roles. Perhaps Aristophanes cannot help it: the male actor in the comic female role is so clearly false and theatrical that the jokes become easy. Dionysus, the god of theater and transformation through costume, triumphs with him.

CONCLUSIONS

Consideration of the male gaze elucidates *Thesmophoriazusae* as a series of variations upon the theme of the comic construction of woman by the male actor. The play presents many alternatives for gender representation alongside the motifs of gender identification and construction through costume and language, spying and watching, ritual and role-playing. The Relative cuts an unambiguously masculine figure; for him, the representation of a woman is an impossible and futile task. Agathon chooses to play the woman for poetic and personal reasons; his representations are quite accurate, both physically and linguistically. Kleisthenes remains male, but he represents the woman's voice within the male assembly. His body shares some feminine tendencies naturally (he is clean-shaven) and he sympathizes with the women, yet he is neither a transvestite nor a poet like Agathon, nor a deceiver and an actor like the Relative. Euripides' presence is diminished somewhat by his role as the impresario of the several dramas presented on stage; he costumes and directs the Relative's female impersonation. At the very end of the play, however, he too becomes implicated in the impersonation of women as he dresses as an old woman and emancipates the Relative by means of a traditional comic strategy. Finally, the 'real' women of the Thesmophoria provide a backdrop for the female impersonations of the other male characters. None of the male characters who borrow the female figure or female language succeed in creating the illusion of women. By contrast, the 'real' women of the Thesmophoria cannot be seen as completely successful either. The joke is that male actors as women always remain male actors as women; they cannot be viewed seamlessly as women *per se* at all. The image of a man in women's clothes, speaking in a woman's voice, is, from *Lysistrata* on, fundamentally comic.

MEN AS WOMEN: *THESMOPHORIAZUSAE*

The date of *Thesmophoriazusae* can be fixed at either 411 or 410 BCE, but cannot be known for certain. Scholars remain divided upon the date, with as many supporting the one as the other. On the basis of literary evidence, however, it is possible to imagine the possibility that the performance of *Thesmophoriazusae* followed *Lysistrata* by a few months at the City Dionysia of 411. As I have shown in the previous chapter, the strikingly innovative *Lysistrata* wears the comic representation of women as its outer garment. In an equally striking literary maneuver, by presenting *Thesmophoriazusae* in some conjunction with *Lysistrata*, Aristophanes produces another play almost exclusively concerned with the theatrical representation of women by men, only this time at the expense of his favorite literary target, Euripides.[59] Surely more literary than political, *Thesmophoriazusae* unites male Athenian spectators with their allies in a vision of male control over representation and power. Instead of suggesting that role-playing is a strategy for survival, *Thesmophoriazusae* suggests that playing a woman is the prerogative of men.[60] If the play suggests anything at all by way of survival strategy, it is that even tragic poets can harness the inherently comic image of woman to fool the other 'other', the barbarian spectator, as long as they adhere to comedy. In other words, even the female can help us, for she is male underneath her gown.

Finally, the function such extreme play with and manipulation of comic transvestism may have performed at the City Dionysia of 411 BCE can only be suggested, for the truth of such things remains forever elusive. I suggest, however, that the identification of men in the roles of women, taking control over representation and drama, would nourish a social bond between men that theater has always been thought to support and which might have been called for in the days before the oligarchic coup. Zeitlin has written that in tragedy,

> *functionally* women are never an end in themselves, and nothing changes for them once they have lived out their drama on stage. Rather, they play the roles of catalysts, agents, instruments, blockers, spoilers, destroyers, and sometimes helpers or saviors for the masculine characters. When elaborately represented, they may serve as antimodels as well as hidden models for that masculine self.
>
> (Zeitlin 1985: 69)

In comedy, and specifically in this comedy, Aristophanes uses the image of woman to serve as a common bond between all the figures on stage and those in the audience. Women provide no model for any masculine behavior in *Thesmophoriazusae*. Rather, they challenge Euripides' presentation of them. Aristophanes does not exonerate Euripides. The action of the play implies that manipulation of the representation of women belongs to Aristophanes, to comedy, and to the comic actor who plays the woman. Thus the scholarly equation of tragedy with femininity and comedy with masculinity need not be absolute. Comedy must have femininity to exist. In addition, comedy needs the overlapping of gender that the male actor in female dress provides.

4
WOMEN AS MEN: *ECCLESIAZUSAE*

Ecclesiazusae (392 or 391 BCE) combines Aristophanes' interest in female protagonists with his use of gender disguise and role reversal as comic devices, themes he explored twenty years earlier, albeit in different ways, in both *Lysistrata* and *Thesmophoriazusae*. In *Ecclesiazusae* the women of Athens, tired of conditions in the city, dress themselves as men, pack the assembly, and propose that a new government run by women be established.[1] The measure passes, and the women set up a communal government in which everyone shares ownership of everything and all needs are provided for. The manipulation of costume and role makes theatricality a central motif of *Ecclesiazusae*. Women in particular receive special dramatic treatment. As its main characters, they assume most of the play's action. The characterization of women here follows the trends of female characters in Aristophanes' earlier plays. Although they are in control of the plot and eventually of civic power, women reveal their theatrical ability to deceive by appearing in guises other than female; at the same time, their disguises also reveal their true natures.

This chapter will argue that in *Ecclesiazusae* the traditional division of authority, based on sexual difference, no longer functions normally and that the play presents an evanescent illusion of gender that exists in a rapidly changing Athens. An analysis of both the physical and the linguistic costumes of the women in *Ecclesiazusae* will show that gender definitions and representations can be constructed and taken apart quite easily. Aristophanes links the cultural definition of male and female directly to the health of the state. The manipulation of costume and disguise also links the workings of theater directly to the workings of government. Finally, our knowledge of social and political conditions in Athens in the early fourth century leads to the conclusion that the time was right for this comic fantasy.

RENDERING THE MALE BODY

Ecclesiazusae opens with a visual trick on costume and identity. A figure enters dressed in men's clothing, a *himation* draped in the masculine style and Laconian shoes, and carrying a walking-stick (βακτηρία; 73–5).[2] She is identified later as Praxagora, the head of the conspiracy. At first, however, her appearance suggests the uneasiness and humorous incongruity that cross-gender dressing generally provokes. Although the actor wears a woman's white mask, for his character is female, he also wears men's clothing. Stone conjectures, reasonably, that 'the actors' female costumes must be realistic, while the male disguises are unconvincing and transparent. The poet relies on the rigid conventions of mask color, which provide a much needed point of reference' (Stone 1980: 410–11). In other words, the audience is never meant to believe the disguise of this woman as a man. Vase illustrations show, however, that even the conventions of mask color themselves tend to underscore the artifice of dramatic representation (for example, see again Figure 1, p. 6). While real upper-class women's skin may indeed have been lighter than that of women and men exposed to the sun, surely it was not as chalky white as the masks and vase-paintings indicate. Yet, if a woman wore make-up to enhance the whiteness of her skin, as the old women at the end of *Ecclesiazusae* do, then the mask imitates that sort of artificial skin color. The figure at the opening of the play most likely wears a light-colored female mask. Its exaggerated color reminds us that it is a mask, and perhaps that there is a male underneath playing the part of a woman.[3] The artificiality of the representation establishes the difference between what might appear to be a real woman and what might appear to be an artificial woman.

True-to-life representation seems not to have been the central aim of comic costumes and masks, however. The mask offered a somewhat believable convention for the portrayal of females by male actors. A female mask worn by a padded actor in woman's clothes emphasizes, in fact, the theatrical nature of the imitation. The vase illustrations also show padded actors playing women; the pads are as rigid a convention of drama as the colored masks are (see Figure 2, p. 7). Underneath the feminine clothing they wear to present themselves as women, the comic actors here may well be wearing the exaggerated padding and adjustable phallos. There is no way to determine the actual nature of the costumes for *Ecclesiazusae*, but speculation on the possibilities is not entirely useless. If the actors wore pads and the phallos protruded from these supposedly feminine bodies once in a while, the comic and metatheatrical effects would be hilarious. The audience may see actors, identified as comedians by their stylized padded uniforms, consciously playing women.[4] The audience may choose to suspend their disbelief and accept the fiction of seeing women on stage. At times Aristophanes requires that suspension; the audience should occasionally see women mocking men. When the male actors acting the parts of women put on their masculine costumes, they play women playing men; both sexes are mocked simultaneously. The phallos may be hidden or displayed. As long as the audience knows it is there, it is aware of the illusory nature of the stage representation the entire time, accepting it as part of the dramatic experience. If the phallos is not worn, then these effects can only be suggested or imagined.

One other aspect of Praxagora's costume blurs the visual and auditory distinction between an actor self-consciously representing a woman and the representation of a real woman on stage: her voice. Whether or not ancient Greek actors who played women spoke in falsetto is unclear.[5] If the actor here hopes to make Praxagora even just the least bit convincing, however, he must give her a plausible feminine voice; a deeper masculine falsetto may be saved for the assembly rehearsal. Praxagora is dressed in men's clothing at the start, and should not present a convincing male figure now. An incongruent feminine voice would help her do so.

The prologue of *Ecclesiazusae* announces all of the play's important themes. This as yet unnamed transvestite figure addresses a little oil-lamp:

> O bright eye of this lamp turned on the potter's wheel, invented beautifully by the clever artisans – for we shall reveal your birth and fortune – set in motion by the potter's whirl, you possess the bright honors of the sun in your nostrils – the starting-point, the agreed-upon signal of fire. We reveal [things] to you alone, naturally, when quite often you stand beside us when we are trying out the positions of sexual love [lit. the twists and turns of Aphrodite] in our bedchambers, the guard of arched bodies, and no one in the house awakens from your eye. You alone shine in the corners of the thighs that are not to be spoken about, singeing the blooming hair, and you stand with us when, in secret, we open the storehouses full both of grain and of the spring of Bacchus [wine]. And, being a companion in these actions, you don't babble about it to others.

> Ὦ λαμπρὸν ὄμμα τοῦ τροχηλάτου λύχνου
> κάλλιστ' ἐν εὐστόχοισιν ἐξηυρημένον –

γονάς τε γὰρ σὰς καὶ τύχας δηλώσομεν·
τροχῷ γὰρ ἐλαθεὶς κεραμικῆς ῥύμης ἄπο
μυκτῆρσι λαμπρὰς ἡλίου τιμὰς ἔχεις –
ὅρμα φλογὸς σημεῖα τὰ ξυγκείμενα.
σοὶ γὰρ μόνῳ δηλοῦμεν εἰκότως, ἐπεὶ
κἀν τοῖσι δωματίοισιν 'Αφροδίτης τρόπων
πειρωμέναισι πλησίον παραστατεῖς,
λορδουμένων τε σωμάτων ἐπιστάτην
ὀφθαλμὸν οὐδεὶς τὸν σὸν ἐξείργει δόμων.
μόνος δὲ μηρῶν εἰς ἀπορρήτους μυχοὺς
λάμπεις ἀφεύων τὴν ἐπανθοῦσαν τρίχα·
στοάς τε καρποῦ Βακχίου τε νάματος
πλήρεις ὑποιγνύσαισι συμπαραστατεῖς·
καὶ ταῦτα συνδρῶν οὐ λαλεῖς τοῖς πλησίον.

(1–16)[6]

The most obvious quality of this monologue is its tone. The speaker's elaborate diction parodies tragedy, and this description of a lowly little oil lamp becomes more and more absurd. By means of paratragic apostrophe, the speaker turns the lamp into another comic actor: it wears a mask and its 'nose' illuminates the scene. Here Aristophanes employs one of his standard comic techniques, borrowing postures from tragedy to aid his protagonist.[7] The monologue is a joke on the audience as well. Since the audience is expecting a comedy, its naïve expectations may be disappointed for a moment. If we recall that this is an Aristophanic comedy, and remember to expect paratragedy, then everything fits into place (cf. the paratragic openings of *Lysistrata* and *Thesmophoriazusae*, for example). The speaker takes words from one type of dramatic situation and makes them comic by recasting and reclothing them. The speaker is clever, albeit overly dramatic. Finally, the lines emphasize that the play opens at night, the time for trickery and secrecy.

This light is not for practical illumination alone, however. It is, first, a signal (σημεῖα, 6) for the speaker's companions. The speaker also has a more intimate relationship with the lamp, one intimate enough to say melodramatically that she knows – and will reveal – its birth and its fortune (3). Her choice of verb (δηλόω) emphasizes her own identity as one who knows and reveals secrets. Throughout this play almost every character will cover up or reveal something true or something false. When she invokes Aphrodite (8–9), the speaker gives us the first syntactical indication of her actual sex: she uses a feminine participle (πειρωμέναισι, 9).

The nature of her intimacy with the lamp is clear: it has shone on the secret parts of her body (12–13).[8] These secret places are not found on a man and this particular method of depilation is feminine. Although the women will later admit to discarding their razors in order to encourage a hairy masculine appearance, razors do not remove hair in these private places. Finally, the lamp has witnessed actions typical of women in some comic situations: their presence at and theft of the stores of grain and wine (14–15).[9] The lamp is an ideal confidante for women, since it witnesses secrets but does not babble about them in public. Later on, Praxagora will claim the same qualities for women (442–4). Since the lamp has seen such behavior, and since the speaker reveals the behavior to the audience, the stereotype of woman here is reinforced. Speaking as a woman, Praxagora accepts not only the image but also the aggression that it expresses.

Praxagora addresses the lamp respectfully and her posture suggests a mocking attitude towards men. Spoken at night, her words parody an invocation of the sun and remind us that night is women's time for action. Daylight is the time for men to act (the *ecclesia* meets at dawn). The lamp shines for women just as the sun shines for men. It watches over them (ἐπιστάτην, 10), but also takes part in their activities by watching and not stopping them (παραστατεῖς, 9; συμπαραστατεῖς, 15). Praxagora will get away with what she can under men's eyes as easily as she does under the eyes of the lamp, which seems to be an appropriate feminine substitute for the sun.

Praxagora's monologue also sets the women's entrance to the *ecclesia* in a theatrical context. She recalls an actor's control, or lack of control, over language by referring to one actor's legendary mistake:

> Yet it is near dawn and the *ecclesia* will meet quite soon. Then it is necessary for us to take our seats (*hedras*) and, upon settling our limbs, to escape detection as the *hetairai* (*hetairas*), whom Phyromachos mentioned, if you still remember that.
>
> καίτοι πρὸς ὄρθρον γ' ἐστίν, ἡ δ' ἐκκλησία
> αὐτίκα μάλ' ἔσται· καταλαβεῖν δ' ἡμᾶς ἕδρας
> δεῖ τὰς ἑταίρας κῶλά θ' ἱζομένας λαθεῖν,
> ἃς Φυρόμαχός ποτ' εἶπεν, εἰ μέμνησθ' ἔτι.[10]
> (20–3)

Ussher writes: 'The concluding words permit a moment for her hearers to recollect the context of *hetairas*: an actor's *lapsus linguae*' (1973: 75 *ad* 21–3). When the audience remembers an actor well known for his slips of the tongue, it may remember that the women will be acting in the assembly and should avoid slips of the tongue also. Later Praxagora will rehearse the women to avoid just that, and the chorus will remind itself to avoid errors (295a). Slips of the tongue become of crucial importance to the women; just one could ruin the entire plan. If there were *hetairai* in the assembly, as Phyromachos indicated (most likely mistakenly), then the women's plan could be in jeopardy should other women – or, worse yet, men – read through their male disguises. Finally, she emphasizes the special time for the *ecclesia*. All of this hints that the proceedings in the assembly are structured along the lines of a theatrical performance.

The women need costumes, and Praxagora discusses them here as well: 'What could it be? Don't they have the stitched beards, which it was ordered that they have? Or was it difficult to escape detection in stealing their husbands' cloaks?' (τί δῆτ' ἂν εἴη; πότερον οὐκ ἐρραμμένους / ἔχουσι τοὺς πώγωνας, οὓς εἴρητ' ἔχειν; / ἢ θαἰμάτια τἀνδρεῖα κλεψάσαις λαθεῖν / ἦν χαλεπὸν αὐταῖς; 24–7). Ἐρραμμένους ('stitched') is the perfect passive participle of ῥάπτειν, to sew or stitch together. 'Ράπτειν also carries a metaphorical meaning: to devise, contrive, plot.[11] The beards are stitched, but they are also deceptive and part of a plot. Ἐρραμμένους ('stitched') underlines the deceptive costume theme and the involvement of women in a plot which requires costumes, for women sew and, like Penelope, could stitch or weave a deception easily. The prologue has mentioned and begun to develop the significant motifs in *Ecclesiazusae*: secrecy, inversion, gender-related behaviors and accessories, signs and apparent meanings, revelation and deception, acting and performance, and costumes. The parodic element of the prologue complements its emphasis on secrecy, disguise, and theatricality by being a kind of disguise also: tragedy disguised as comedy. This teasing comic disappointment is a standard feature of Aristophanic comedy.

The opening of *Ecclesiazusae* shares several structural features with *Lysistrata* and *Thesmophoriazusae*. Its structural similarity to *Lysistrata* in particular may serve to remind the audience of past Aristophanic triumphs and also to provide an example of self-imitation and self-reference. *Lysistrata* opens at dawn with one woman on stage, and that central female figure also waits for more women to join her before she reveals her identity and her scheme. Both Lysistrata and Praxagora perform tasks unusual for females, calling other women together for a meeting rather than a festival, possessing a certain amount of willpower, and formulating ideas. Although not as similar to *Ecclesiazusae*

WOMEN AS MEN: *ECCLESIAZUSAE*

as *Lysistrata* is, *Thesmophoriazusae* does present some of the same motifs, which is not surprising in a play centered on a man who dresses as a woman to carry out a secret plan, and a playwright who must stage parodies of his own plays with an ineffective actor and eventually play the part of a woman himself (see Henderson 1980: 169–70; Moulton 1981: 111–22; also MacMathúna 1971: 161). Unlike *Ecclesiazusae*, however, the women in *Thesmophoriazusae* do not plan to benefit the city, and the play's focus is rather on the male characters of the Relative and Euripides and their invasion of the women's usual sphere of operation.

Some readers of *Ecclesiazusae* would argue that the light at its opening foreshadows a positive outcome for Praxagora's plan, that she brings illumination and sunlight to a dark and ill-fated city with her new policies (see, for example, MacMathúna 1971: 179–81). The lamp enjoys too many feminine qualities to bring only benefit to the city, however. The inversion of normality in Aristophanes, and in this play in particular, is never altogether positive. Although the scheme may seem wonderful at first, the idea of rule by women is never wholly successful in practice. *Lysistrata* ends on a positive note exactly because the status quo is reinstated. In *Ecclesiazusae*, women gain permanent control of the city, change everything, and make sure that nothing will ever be the same. The second half of the play promises darker things to come for an Athens ruled in this fashion.

After Praxagora's compatriots arrive on stage, she inquires whether they have done what was decided at the Skira (58–60). The Skira was, like the Thesmophoria, a festival of Demeter celebrated by women.[12] More details of their costumes are divulged and a formula for sexual differentiation laid out. In preparation for the disguise, Woman A has let the hair underneath her arms grow and has acquired a suntan when her husband was out of the house (60–4). While all the female characters wear white masks, even when they are disguised as men, perhaps this woman wears a different sort of mask from the other women. Woman B has done the same (κἄγωγε, 65) and has also thrown her razor out of the house, a particularly symbolic gesture. She has discarded an object closely associated with the appearance of femininity. In order to look like a man and appear different from what she is, she must get rid of what helps her look like a woman. Her comment is significant: 'so I might not resemble a woman at all' (μηδὲν εἴην ἔτι γυναικὶ προσφερής, 67). Lack of body hair is a sign of femininity. Facial hair, by contrast, is a marker of masculine identity; the women bring false beards with them (69).[13] The women acquire three other items for their impersonations: Laconian shoes, walking sticks, and men's cloaks (74–5).[14] In addition to emphasizing the outward signs of masculinity and femininity, this passage highlights the special value attached to certain objects basic to theater.

Praxagora first emphasizes the physical aspect of the women's impersonation. She chastises Woman B for carding wool in the midst of their rehearsal:

> Look at you carding, when it was necessary not to reveal any part of your body to those already sitting down. We would suffer fine things then, if all the people happened to be there and then someone, climbing over with her cloak pulled up, were to show her *Phormisios*.
>
> ἰδού γέ σε ξαίνουσαν, ἣν τοῦ σώματος
> οὐδὲν παραφῆναι τοῖς καθημένοις ἔδει.
> οὐκοῦν καλά γ' ἂν πάθοιμεν, εἰ πλήρης τύχοι
> ὁ δῆμος ὢν κἄπειθ' ὑπερβαίνουσασά τις
> ἀναβαλλομένη δείξειε τὸν Φορμίσιον.
>
> (93–7)

This image suggests that the women's carefully planned sexual disguise could be easily disrupted. Phormisios was famous for his hairiness.[15] Praxagora facetiously imagines a scenario in which the plan might be spoiled by the abrupt display of female genitalia, in public, underneath male clothing. The use of the term *Phormisios* is strange, however. She describes the sexual marker of femaleness with the name of a man known for his excessive physical masculinity. The simple logic behind this posits that women are not so different from men; they have beards in a different place. Her comments emphasize the fragility of an actor's disguise. Praxagora elaborates her picture of men in the assembly by telling the women how to sit: in front, bearded, with their cloaks gathered around them. She then encourages her friends, asking, 'who, upon seeing us, wouldn't think that we were men?' (τίς οὐκ ἂν ἡμᾶς ἄνδρας ἡγήσαιθ' ὁρῶν; 101). There are clearly certain rules for behavior in the assembly, just as there are rules for behavior as an actor, and carding wool is not allowed. The women need to learn, and practice, these behaviors.

The women mean also to gain political power, and the acquisition of power in Athens seems to be related to the appearance of masculinity. Woman A comments on the effeminate Agyrrhios: 'Agyrrhios certainly escaped notice wearing the beard of Pronomos, although he once was a woman. At this very moment, you see, he does the greatest things in the city' ('Αγύρριος γοῦν τὸν Προνόμου πώγων' ἔχων / λέληθε· καίτοι πρότερον ἦν οὗτος γυνή· / νυνὶ δ', ὁρᾷς, πράττει τὰ μέγιστ' ἐν τῇ πόλει, 102–4). It is not clear what Woman A means when she describes Agyrrhios as wearing the beard of Pronomos. The ancient sources describe Agyrrhios as a prominent public figure.[16] Yet the phrase suggests that Agyrrhios has a relationship with Pronomos which has, in some way (perhaps sexual), masculinized him. If Agyrrhios gained power with some sort of disguise, literal or metaphorical, these women can too. At this point, I suggest that the male actor himself offers the ultimate confirmation of the sexualization of power in the city: it apparently takes masculinity to rule, and these 'women' have real masculinity under, as well as over, their costumes. As long as someone appears masculine, even if he 'once was a woman', like Agyrrhios, he may be able to acquire political power. The security of gender identity is no longer certain. The lines of gender difference are blurred while they seem to be made distinct. Like Agyrrhios, the women 'become men' by putting on false beards (121). The absurdity of this moment of transformation does not escape Woman B's notice: the women look ridiculous (καταγέλαστον, 125). Her self-consciousness calls even more attention to the costume. It is clear by now that, since there is a special time, a special place, special rules, special objects, and no material result of their actions, the women will rehearse and perform a 'play' for the *ecclesia*.

In her final remarks, Praxagora reviews the components of the women's costumes in an almost ritualistic sequence:

Come now, gird up your tunics. Put on the Laconian slippers as quickly as possible, just as you have seen your husband do, each time he is about to go to the *ecclesia* or out the door. Then when you have all these things right, put on the beards. And when you've got them fitted on accurately, then throw on your husbands' cloaks, which you stole, and proceed, leaning on the walking-sticks, singing the old man's song, imitating the manner of farmers.

> ἄγε νυν ἀναστέλλεσθ' ἄνω τὰ χιτώνια·
> ὑποδεῖσθε δ' ὡς τάχιστα τὰς Λακωνικάς,
> ὥσπερ τὸν ἄνδρ' ἐθεᾶσθ', ὅτ' εἰς ἐκκλησίαν
> μέλλοι βαδίζειν ἢ θύραζ' ἑκάστοτε.
> ἔπειτ' ἐπειδὰν ταῦτα πάντ' ἔχῃ καλῶς,
> περιδεῖσθε τοὺς πώγωνας. ἡνίκ' ἂν δέ γε
> τούτους ἀκριβώσητε περιηρμοσμέναι,

καὶ θαἰμάτια τἀνδρεῖ' ἅπερ γ' ἐκλέψατε
ἐπαναβάλησθε, κᾇτα ταῖς βακτηρίαις
ἐπερειδόμεναι βαδίζετ' ᾄδουσαι μέλος
πρεσβυτικόν τι, τὸν τρόπον μιμούμεναι
τὸν τῶν ἀγροίκων. (268–79)

All the signs for representing men are given: the correct clothes, facial hair, voice, and a specific style of gait. By imitating farmers, perhaps the women will disguise their interests even further; they will not appear to be urbanites manipulated by a demagogue (it is interesting to note, however, that to the citizen Khremes the women appear to be shoemakers rather than farmers: 385). At the outset, however, Praxagora warns the women to hike up their tunics, which men do not wear, and hide them under their costumes. Still women underneath, their real identities are in danger of being revealed at any time. This advice seems to hold for actors portraying women as well. Again, the vase illustrations should be remembered here. The figures discussed above show the illusoriness of any actor's costume, especially the costume that makes an actor resemble a woman.

As the women depart for the assembly, their song complements the reversals of the play. It begins with a cleverly twisted statement: 'It is time for us, men, to proceed' (ὥρα προβαίνειν ὦνδρες ἡμῖν ἐστι, 285). The chorus urges its members on into the main stage action as if this were a *parodos*. This chorus goes off-stage, however, into action that we will not see. They remind themselves to maintain the linguistic disguise so as not to expose their femininity: 'It is necessary for us to remember always to say this [i.e. "men"] so that it doesn't slip from the memory' (τοῦτο γὰρ χρὴ / μεμνημένας ἀεὶ λέγειν, ὡς μήποτ' ἐξολίσθῃ, / ἡμᾶς, 285–7). The chorus reinforces the lessons of the previous scene. Both the actor and the audience are always aware of the actor's identity under his costume and the actor always has to be on guard lest it be revealed.

The chorus' syntax does, however, let femininity slip through. They refer to themselves with feminine words (μεμνημένας, 286; ἡμᾶς, 287) while reminding themselves to call each other men. They mention voting – which requires that they raise their hands in an unfamiliar, masculine way (χειροτονῶμεν, 297) – to help their female friends (τὰς ἡμετέρας φίλας, 299). Having struck a wrong note (295a), they correct themselves in the usual fashion of exposing the joke that exposes, by self-consciously changing the gender of the noun and drawing attention to the mistake: 'O, what am I saying? For it is necessary for me to name *male* friends' (καίτοι τί λέγω; φίλους γὰρ χρῆν μ' ὀνομάζειν, 299).

The chorus also advocates a certain kind of mass action. Each member should acquire a token (σύμβολον), sit down in the assembly, and vote. By possessing σύμβολα, not only do these women acquire tickets for entrance to the meeting, to which only men are entitled, but they also gain figurative phalloi, another attribute central to the impersonation of men.[17] It is impossible to determine whether the women's costumes really added phalloi at this point. If the actors wore comic costumes with phalloi underneath their feminine costumes, they could simply display them here. We would then remember that they *are* entitled to enter the *ecclesia* and that we are watching a play, a fiction that could not really happen. The costume might be funnier with the phallos, since then not only would the women be making fun of men but they would also mock comic costume in a comedy, creating another ironic Aristophanic self-parody (see Pickard-Cambridge 1968: 220–1). We would also be forced to recognize that this is a highly stylized imitation of women.

When Praxagora meets her husband, her stage persona is restored to that of a stereotypically comic woman. She constructs this image of herself to justify wearing his cloak and shoes and walking-stick (539–46). Although she is the most successful at impersonating a man, she easily returns to her original gender when the theatrics are over. It was just artifice after all. Blepyrus' entrance in Praxagora's clothes provides an almost perfect visual counterpart to the masculine women of the choral exit. Underneath the little yellow dress (ἡμιδιπλοίδιον, 318; κροκωτίδιον, 332) and the Persian slippers (Περσικάς, 319), he probably wears the pads, mask, and phallos of the comic buffoon.[18] His lengthy description of the search for clothes and of his troubled bowels makes a farcical comment on the public construction of gender. He is more ridiculous than the men half-dressed as women on vase-paintings. Women can wear men's clothes and hope to be taken seriously; the appearance of masculinity connotes a certain amount of public power. Men in women's clothes embody a mockery of femininity and become symbolically stripped of their public power. The only way for a cross-dressed actor, on stage or in real life, to restore his integrity and his identity is by exposing the masculinity under his disguise.[19] Blepyrus' travesty of women's clothes and the experience of wearing them underscore the devaluation of femininity in *Ecclesiazusae*.

While the audience does not see the actual event in the *ecclesia*, it does hear about it firsthand from Khremes, a friend of Blepyrus, who enters at line 372. He describes the crowd at the assembly as quite large (383) but odd: it seems, according to Khremes, that there were a lot of men with white skin present (λευκοπληθής, 387) and that he thought that they must be shoemakers (385–7). He figures that they must all practice their trades indoors, which is what has kept their skin so pale. This account of the women's appearance recalls both their disguise and their displacement of the men. Despite this blatant flaw in their disguise (not all the women tried to become tanned like Woman A), they succeed in their plot. Instead of looking like normal men, however, one of their most obvious physical features is conspicuous – and indeed it may have been so on stage, since the actors playing women could hardly have changed masks on stage.

When the women return from their triumph, a wonderful event happens on stage: they remove their male costumes in a ritual as elaborate as the previous ritual of putting them on. As if this were now the *parodos* (they entered one by one originally, rather than in a group), the chorus of women enters suspicious of any man who might be watching: 'Guard yourself keenly, lest someone somehow behind us watches our gait, for there are many clever men' (φύλαττε σαυτὴν ἀσφαλῶς, πολλοὶ γὰρ οἱ πανοῦργοι, / μή πού τις ἐκ τοὔπισθεν ὢν τὸ σχῆμα καταφυλάξῃ, 481–2). Their physical self-consciousness prevails even after the assembly has met (they also warn each other to be extra vigilant and wrap up their cloaks tightly, 486–8). The women certainly fear the gaze of anyone clever or crafty (πανοῦργος), any rival in comic deception who might therefore see through their disguises. If such a one were to detect femininity in their gait, he might figure out the entire conspiracy. Just so, an actor might feel that his physical conduct as a woman might not be convincing enough for an audience. These 'women' understand the power of dress. The chorus closes its song with a few more remarks about the beard, the one item most representative of the entire plan: 'But take heed everyone and hate having that coarse beard on your chin; for in fact they [the chins] for a long time have worn this disguise against their will' (ἀλλ' ἐπείγου / ἅπασα καὶ μίσει σάκον πρὸς τοῖν γναθοῖν ἔχουσα· / χαὖται γὰρ ἄκουσαι πάλαι τὸ σχῆμα τοῦτ' ἔχουσιν, 501–3).[20] The beard, the manner in which they walk, and the way in which they must stand leaning upon their walking-sticks all combine to make up the complete masculine disguise. For now, beards will be only on the chins of men, giving them the disguise (τὸ σχῆμα) that they need to be called men.

Praxagora arrives and encourages the women to remove their disguises. Her orders reverse the dressing ritual:

WOMEN AS MEN: *ECCLESIAZUSAE*

Now, as quickly as possible, before any man sees, throw off the woollen cloaks, let the shoes go out of the way – loosen their fastened Laconian reins – throw away the walking-sticks. Then put them all back in their proper order again.

> ἀλλ' ὡς τάχιστα, πρίν τιν' ἀνθρώπων ἰδεῖν,
> ῥιπτεῖτε χλαίνας, ἐμβὰς ἐκποδὼν ἴτω –
> χάλα συναπτοὺς ἡνίας Λακωνικάς –
> βακτηρίας ἄφεσθε. καὶ μέντοι σὺ μὲν
> ταύτας κατευτρέπιζ'.
>
> (506–10)

The women must keep the secrets of successful disguise hidden; no man must see the transition. Aside from any man jeopardizing the plan by seeing the women disrobe, the audience should not necessarily see an actor as he puts on his costume; it might ruin the illusion. The men in the assembly were as much of an audience for the women acting as men as the people in the theater are for men acting as women. Some of the magic of a theatrical performance comes from the initial introduction of a character when he first appears on stage in costume. At that point we are able to suspend our disbelief and invest our faith in the illusion of the actor as his character. Aristophanes, however, makes us watch the moment that the women return to their original characters to show clearly that role-playing is role-playing, whether it is in the theater or in the *ecclesia*. Praxagora and the chorus try to preserve some of the illusion by claiming to dress and undress in the dark (496–7). Unfortunately, they only preserve the illusion of costume and character for themselves, since they also blatantly manipulate their dress in full view of the audience. It remains to be seen, however, how well a city can be run by such crafty women, even though costumes and gestures rendered these women 'most manly' (ἀνδρειόταται, 519) in the assembly.

RENDERING THE MALE VOICE

In addition to physical disguise, linguistic disguise plays a key role in the women's plan. In their rehearsal, it is at times not clear who is speaking. The women fall in and out of masculine voice often. Do we hear the woman character's voice, that of the male role she plays, or that of the actor underneath the two layers of costume? Just as clothes create and disguise gender identity, so language creates and disguises gender identity. Like the disruption of physical trickery and disguise, the exposure of linguistic trickery and disguise takes several forms.

For example, one of the women immediately displays a certain awareness of her male character's identity. Upon meeting Praxagora at the play's opening, she refers to herself and her companions with a masculine participle, ἡμῶν προσιόντων (31).[21] This is the first in a string of references the women make to themselves as men. The dramatization of the rehearsal allows the audience to witness a facet of theatrical practice usually out of sight. We see the women move in and out of their new personae and we are reminded that the actors are men underneath the costumes.

When Praxagora asks if anyone has practiced speaking, Woman A answers, 'Who of us does not know how to gossip?' (τίς δ' ὦ μέλ' ἡμῶν οὐ λαλεῖν ἐπίσταται; 120). In this play, only women use the masculine appellation ὦ μέλ', blurring the identification of gender slightly (see Ussher 1973: 91 *ad* 120, 124–5). The verb λαλεῖν implies not just speaking but gossiping or babbling; it often characterizes women as creatures who, among other things, talk incessantly. Woman A identifies herself with the accepted male representation of comic women.[22] Does the male actor underneath the costume speak here and allow his character to make this joke, or does the male costume on top of the female costume imbue the character with enough masculinity to make the joke, or does the female character conceive of herself in just this way? The image λαλεῖν provokes is stereotypical. The joke gains its humor at female expense; its view is male.

Following this, Praxagora has the women put on their beards and garlands in preparation for speaking (121–3). The garlands remind the women of ritual preparations for festivals and banquets, and thus they expect to drink. When men put on garlands, they perform a ritual preparation for public speaking. This double referent for men and women lets us see that the costume never fully changes the person in it. The women never really become men, even for the fictional *ecclesia*, for they cannot separate their own view of things from the male view. By analogy, we may imagine a male face under the female mask or phallos under the costume; the actor himself never completely becomes a woman, not in his own eyes nor in the audience's. The vase-paintings bear this out (see Figures 3–4, p. 8).

Some women make improper references and oaths. For instance, Woman B has several problems with her linguistic masculinity. She begins her speech well but stumbles when she tries to speak with more conviction. Stereotypically protesting innkeepers who keep water in their storage pits instead of wine, she says:

WOMEN AS MEN: *ECCLESIAZUSAE*

WOMAN B. This doesn't seem right to me, by the two goddesses.
PRAXAGORA. 'By the two goddesses'? Wretch, where is your mind?
WOMAN B. What is it? For I certainly did not ask you for a drink.
PRAXAGORA. By Zeus, being a man you swore by the two goddesses, although you said everything else correctly.
WOMAN B. Oh, then 'by Apollo'.

Γυ.ᵝ   ἐμοὶ μὲν οὐ δοκεῖ, μὰ τὼ θεώ.
Πρ.   μὰ τὼ θεώ; τάλαινα, ποῦ τὸν νοῦν ἔχεις;
Γυ.ᵝ   τί δ' ἔστιν; οὐ γὰρ δὴ πιεῖν γ' ᾔτησά σε.
Πρ.   μὰ Δί' ἀλλ' ἀνὴρ ὢν τὼ θεὼ κατώμοσας,
       καίτοι τά γ' ἄλλ' εἰποῦσα δεξιώτατα.
Γυ.ᵝ   ὢ νὴ τὸν Ἀπόλλω.

(155–60)

Although there are some gods by whom anyone may take an oath, there are others identified specifically with either men or women. Woman B's oath, by Demeter and Persephone ('the two goddesses'), is a woman's oath. Apollo is a more appropriate god for men and speechmakers.[23] Earlier, Woman A swore by Hekate when Praxagora asked about the availability of beards (70). Hekate was often, if not exclusively, invoked by women. When Praxagora and Woman B argued over carding in the *ecclesia* (90), Woman B swore by Artemis. Woman A swore by Artemis also, after mentioning drinking wine in the *ecclesia*. After a woman says something that reveals her female identity, she responds to Praxagora's rebuke with 'by Artemis'. Such an oath reinforces the speaker's femininity and does not correct the slip of the tongue.[24]

The women betray their identities through complicated syntactical combinations. Praxagora exhibits some tricky linguistic maneuvers. In reference to Woman B's error, she first uses the masculine participle (ὤν) instead of the feminine (οὖσα). In her next reference, she uses the feminine (εἰποῦσα). The genders are doubly reversed: Praxagora addresses Woman B as a man about what she said in a feminine way, and as a woman about what she said in a masculine fashion. Finally, Praxagora reproaches women who make linguistic errors with τάλαινα (90, 156, and 190). She uses the feminine form and does not keep the illusion of the male voice, the very thing which angered her. These quick switches between masculine and feminine words for the same people establish a distinction between the rehearsal, Praxagora's editorial comments, and the various voices that the women assume. The joke is still on Praxagora and her buddies: she contradicts her own edicts.²⁵ Annoyed with the women's mistakes now, Praxagora reminds them that they are to practice acting like men (160–2). Woman B still is not accustomed to speaking like a man, and she starts her speech by addressing the women: 'For to me, women seated here' (ἐμοὶ γάρ, ὦ γυναῖκες αἱ καθήμεναι, 165). Praxagora interrupts the woman's error: 'Ill-fated one, you call men *women*?' (γυναῖκας αὖ, δύστηνε, τοὺς ἄνδρας λέγεις; 166). If her invocation refers to her friends, then Woman A has a flaw in her disguise. If Woman A is addressing the audience in the theater, then Praxagora's retort could be mocking the audience with a gesture that refers to them.²⁶ Praxagora could also be having fun with a fellow actor: she calls the men on stage dressed as women 'women', which is appropriate for the illusion created by the play, but inappropriate for both the actors' true identities and the pretense of the plot. As a final reinforcement of the confusion, Woman B claims that she was led astray by seeing an effeminate man in the audience: Epigonos made her think she was addressing women (167–8; cf. *Clouds* 355).²⁷ If just the visual suggestion of femininity causes a slip in her diction, then Woman B will probably not be a uniform public speaker. She also draws the audience into the comic play on stage.

Although the other women have trouble maintaining the linguistic aspects of their masculinity, Praxagora succeeds. She sustains what has been defined as the masculine way of speaking: composing a speech in the traditional manner, discussing the proper topics, swearing by the appropriate gods, remembering the male perspective on things, and maintaining an awareness of the audience. The first section of her speech (173–88) has a serious tone; she seems to be an experienced speaker. She expresses her feelings about the city: 'To me just as to you there is an equal share of the land. I also grieve and bear all the deeds of the city heavily' (ἐμοὶ δ' ἴσον μὲν τῆσδε τῆς χώρας μέτα / ὅσονπερ ὑμῖν; ἄχθομαι δὲ καὶ φέρω / τὰ τῆς πόλεως ἅπαντα βαρέως πράγματα, 173–4). Her claims are ironic, for women do not have an equal share in the city. Praxagora deceives with rhetoric here; only her male persona can claim such things. As the one woman in this group who might successfully impersonate male speech, she seems the most threatening to the established social order.²⁸

After Praxagora has outlined the city's problems and the crafty nature of public officials, Woman A interrupts her with another linguistic exposure of her sex. Although Woman A means to praise Praxagora, she is not in costume linguistically as a man:

WOMAN A. By Aphrodite, you say these things quite well.
PRAXAGORA. Wretch, you swear by Aphrodite? You would do nicely, if you said that in the *ecclesia*.
WOMAN A. But I won't say it.
PRAXAGORA. Then don't get used to saying it now.

Γυ.ᵃ νὴ τὴν 'Αφροδίτην εὖ γε ταυταγὶ λέγεις.
Πρ. τάλαιν' 'Αφροδίτην ὤμοσας; χαρίεντά γ' ἂν ἔδρασες, εἰ τοῦτ' εἶπας ἐν τἠκκλησίᾳ.
Γυ.ᵃ ἀλλ' οὐκ ἂν εἶπον.
Πρ. μηδ' ἐθίζου νῦν λέγειν.

(189–92)

A typical oath that reinforces the comic stereotype of woman, a creature preoccupied with sexuality, the oath to Aphrodite would certainly disclose Woman A's identity. Just in case Praxagora's speaking ability fooled us or set us on edge, Woman A's remark brings us back to the rehearsal. Woman A's error jars our perceptions, making blatant the difference between a smart woman who can speak like a man, a dumb woman who cannot succeed at the imitation, and the differences between men and women. Men speak consistently and about civic issues; women babble, drink, and ramble on about other topics.

Praxagora's speech, with its detailed awareness of masculine speaking style, tone, and voice, now convinces Woman A of Praxagora's assumption of masculinity, if not her own as well. She praises Praxagora: 'Such a shrewd man!' (ὡς ξυνετὸς ἀνήρ, 204). Praxagora is pleased, both by her own speech and by the woman's ability to utter the correct phrase, and she praises Woman A, exclaiming 'Now you praise well' (νῦν καλῶς ἐπήνεσας, 204). Finally, Praxagora states her plan for saving the city: 'If you trust in me, you will be saved yet. I say that it is necessary for us to turn the city over to the women. Indeed, in our houses we make good use of them as managers and stewards' (ἢν οὖν ἐμοὶ πείθησθε, σωθήσεσθ' ἔτι. / ταῖς γὰρ γυναιξὶ φημὶ χρῆναι τὴν πόλιν / ἡμᾶς παραδοῦναι. καὶ γὰρ ἐν ταῖς οἰκίαις / ταύταις ἐπιτρόποις καὶ ταμίαισι χρώμεθα, 209–12). The announcement does not cause the women to reveal themselves. They follow her words with general applause and affirmation (213) and address her as a man (ὦγαθέ, 213). Between Woman A's correct praise of Praxagora at 204 and this remark, the women have learned to be overtly masculine.

Praxagora opens her speech rationally enough, with some comments on the traditional female tasks of weaving and dying wool (215–

18). You will never find a woman trying something new, she says, criticizing a male tendency for novel solutions and supporting the women's offer to solve the city's problems through tradition. Her emphasis on women's avoidance of novelty strikes an ironic note: although a woman, she speaks as a man and advises a novel solution. Praxagora employs rhetorical trickery again. The female Praxagora uses what she learned by observation while living on the Pnyx.[29] Her male persona, however, speaks in character. That Praxagora can do this at all casts suspicion upon her actual gender identity.

Praxagora accounts for all applicable positive feminine traits with more irony. She lists a few of woman's affirmative attributes but ends with a traditional characterization of women: creatures with a taste for gluttony, wine, and sex (224–8). She still speaks from a traditional male point of view.[30] She appeals to the men in the assembly and tells them what they want to hear. She also affirms the stereotype for herself and her comrades while reminding us of the values upon which a *gynaikokratia* might be based. Her characterization of female priorities and interests turns out to be true: the women's gluttony and bibulousness is recalled at the play's end.[31]

Praxagora converses with the others, but she does not chastise them for speaking as women, and the women elect her their general (στρατηγός, 245–7). At the beginning of the play, Praxagora called the women out to battle (6). Now her band of comrades grants her an appropriate masculine title for her masculine persona.[32] In response to their questions, Praxagora offers her friends an aggressive male attitude that recalls wrestling in the *palaestra*, a distinctly masculine activity and skill (258–60; cf. 8–9).

Although the other women have trouble sustaining the linguistic aspects of their masculine costumes, Praxagora succeeds in the trick. She is able to achieve what she has defined as the masculine way to speak: composing the speech in the traditional manner, discussing the proper topics, swearing by the appropriate gods, remembering her voice as a man, and maintaining an awareness of the audience. Praxagora still retains her crafty feminine personality, especially since she holds to male views of women both in her speech and in her treatment of friends, and so presents a dangerous capacity for deception through language. She has designed, costumed, rehearsed, and will perform the trick successfully.

Praxagora's linguistic abilities prove formidable later on when she meets Blepyrus after the assembly meeting. Through language she creates an extremely feminine image of herself that will deceive her husband and conceal her recent escapade. She manipulates her ability to behave and speak in a traditional feminine fashion while hiding the truth of her activities. When she left her bed and took his cloak, says Blepyrus, she spread her cloak out over him, as though he were a corpse laid out for burial, missing only a garland and a little bottle of oil (536–8).[33] In response, Praxagora sketches a feminine justification for her transvestism:

PRAXAGORA: It was cold and I am thin and weak. Then, in order to be warm I put on this cloak. I left you lying in the wool and blankets, husband.
BLEPYRUS: My Laconian shoes and walking stick came with you for what purpose?
PRAXAGORA: So that I might protect your overcoat, I changed my shoes, imitating you and stamping with my feet and beating the stones with the stick.

Πρ. ψύχος γὰρ ἦν, ἐγὼ δὲ λεπτὴ κἀσθενής·
    ἔπειθ' ἵν' ἀλεαίνοιμι τοῦτ' ἠμπεσχόμην.
    σὲ δ' ἐν ἀλέᾳ καταμείμενον καὶ στρώμασιν
    κατέλιπον, ὦνερ.
Βλ. αἱ δὲ δὴ Λακωνικαὶ
    ᾤχοντο μετὰ σοῦ κατὰ τί χὴ βακτηρία;
Πρ. ἵνα θοἰμάτιον σώσαιμι, μεθυπεδησάμην
    μιμουμένη σε καὶ κτυποῦσα τοῖν ποδοῖν
    καὶ τοὺς λίθους παίουσα τῇ βακτηρίᾳ.
                                    (539–46)

She draws a picture of a frail, vulnerable, feminine creature. The shoes were necessary to keep the cloak clean, and the walking-stick to help her on her way. She did it all, she seems to say, out of necessity because of her sex. She tells the truth, of sorts: she did put on the cloak because she is feminine, and she did imitate him by wearing his clothes and stamping her feet. Praxagora tricks Blepyrus with her presentation of the truth, however. She does not tell him the real reason why, but she did need all the parts of the costume to make her impersonation complete.

In explaining the new government to Blepyrus, Praxagora still follows linguistic patterns that distinguish her speech as feminine (she swears by Aphrodite at 558, for example), but she is forthright in her suggestions for instituting social reform. When they discuss the new order in the city, in fact, Praxagora uses the language of the theater:

'Trust that I will teach you the most useful things. This is what I fear most: that the audience will not want to open a new vein and will want to go over the customs and old things too much' (καὶ μὴν ὅτι μὲν χρηστὰ διδάξω πιστεύω· τοὺς δὲ θεατάς, / εἰ καινοτομεῖν ἐθελήσοισιν καὶ μὴ τοῖς ἤθάσι λίαν / τοῖς τ' ἀρχαίοις ἐνδιατρίβειν, τοῦτ' ἔσθ' ὃ μάλιστα δέδοικα, 583–5). The verb for 'teach', διδάξω, sometimes refers to play production, and she also acknowledges the audience's presence.[34] Praxagora produced and directed her own little play inside the first half of *Ecclesiazusae*; now she will outline her plans for its second half. She suggests that it is time for new things in the theater as well as the government, although she fears the audience's reaction. Indeed, after she describes her plans for the new government, we see three vignettes of life under her rule, staged, presumably, with innovation in mind.

In practice with comic incongruity, Praxagora seems at first to contradict her claim that women will rely on old traditions to save the city (215–18, for instance). There is reason to suspect an Aristophanic joke on both the audience and on Praxagora here: Aristophanes makes us ask whether a woman can be consistent in her words and actions or whether the playwright must determine her constancy. By trying an innovative governmental form, Praxagora does what she said men do. From a woman's point of view, however, the idea is not so innovative; Praxagora's government follows the pattern of household management that women have always followed. The *gynaikokratia* runs on female tradition. It is only new to those who have not thought of it, namely men (See Foley 1977: 15).[35] Praxagora herself probably sees no contradiction in these statements, although it is implied for the audience. Innovation and cleverness lie in the ambiguity of Praxagora's speech. They apply to her designs for Athens and for the theater. They may contradict or affirm her previous statements, depending upon their point of view. They expose Aristophanes' experimentation with various theatrical effects and make us wonder whether or not to take the *gynaikokratia* seriously at all.

At Blepyrus' request, Praxagora reviews the details of her new government, but she does so with a strange self-reference. Listen to the speaker, she says, using a masculine participle to refer to herself (τοῦ φράζοντος, 589). Although she does not speak in the guise of a man as she did in the assembly, perhaps she identifies the innovative aspects of her plan as masculine enough to warrant the participle for herself.[36] She also speaks against gender expectations with an oath to Apollo (631), an oath identified with men in this play.[37] Aristophanes sneaks these masculine linguistic habits into Praxagora's speech in order to undercut the femininity of her *gynaikokratia* and to shed some suspicion onto her character. After all, she is a man underneath the costume.

RENDERING FEMININITY

As Praxagora's regime takes hold, we see a citizen turning over his goods while also trying to figure out a way to keep them (728–876), and then three hideous old women who attempt to enact the new law designed to provide equity of sexual pleasure: young men must sleep with old ugly women before courting young women, and young women must sleep with old ugly men before choosing a young male partner themselves (877–1111). The episode involving the hags, the maiden, and the young man illustrates not only the value of clothing but the powers of language. It is without a doubt one of the strangest scenes in the Aristophanic corpus. It has been called a 'randy, boisterous, grotesque triumph of comic energy' (Konstan and Dillon 1981: 382), a '*reductio* (or *exaggeratio*) *ad absurdum* of the motive scheme' (Henderson 1987a: 119), and 'hilarious rather than pathetic, with the young man's distaste and horror arousing mirth rather than agreement' (McLeish 1980: 155). Perhaps the most salient remark about its structure and form has been that the scene illustrates 'a reversal of the standard seduction scene' (ibid. 99). Closer investigation shows that the scene parodies rather than reverses literary representations of seduction in which women are the aggressors.[38]

Aristophanes worked most of these elements into the mocking seduction of Kinesias by Myrrhine in *Lysistrata* (829–953). The erotic taunting of Kinesias by Myrrhine shows that Aristophanes is aware of a literary tradition in the representation of allurement or sexual manipulation of men by women. In *Lysistrata* he mocks sexual desire rather than the literary tradition, simply by exaggerating that desire and thwarting its release. Unlike the accommodation of the literary representation of seduction in *Lysistrata*, the seduction scene in *Ecclesiazusae* mocks tradition by inverting the usual elements of sexual allurement. In this parodic seduction there is grotesque adornment, ineffective trickery, suggestions of sterility and incest, and threats of death. The outcome is comic, grotesque, and not erotic. The episode breaks down into three parts: a dialogue between an old woman and a young woman (877–937), a love duet sung by the young woman and a youth, perhaps named Epigenes, who arrives to court her, interrupted at intervals by the old woman (938–1044), and a series of advances and threats made by the youth, the old woman, and two of her friends (1045–111).[39]

The old woman begins by describing her plight (877–83). In the stereotypically female approach toward attracting men, she has dressed up and adorned herself with cosmetics. She puts on white paint (καταπεπλασμένη ψιμυθίῳ, 878) to enhance her feminine pallor.[40] She wears the saffron-colored robe (κροκωτός) that young women usually wear for special, often seductive, occasions.[41] Dressed to play the seductress, this old woman tries to disguise her true nature. However, she entices no one. With the body and mind of an old hag, she appears all the more distorted in these cosmetics and items of clothing. She is transformed into a strange sort of monster.

By plucking hairs and rubbing paint on her skin, says the young women, the hag has not become an object of sexual desire but rather 'a little darling for death' (904–5). Adorning herself with make-up to entice a man, she reveals more of her actual physical condition. Trying to rejuvenate herself, she comes nearer to death.[42] Costume and disguise are ineffective here; they reveal the truth instead of hiding it. Now the powers of cosmetic deception have the opposite effect from the one planned, neither inspiring sexual desire as they do in other seduction scenes nor bringing success as they did at the beginning of the play. Under Praxagora's new rule, such attempts will not work. Just as feminine attire rendered Blepyrus ineffective and foolish, so does it mock these old women.

The old woman reminds the young woman that no man is allowed to court her until he courts an older woman first (925). The older woman asks the younger if her age is bothersome. No, the maiden answers, the rouge and white paint are (929). Again the young woman points out the problem of the older woman's appearance. If her application of cosmetics is bad, or if cosmetics are unnatural for a woman of her age, then this new law causes an unnatural change in the social order. All the usual powers for altering or enhancing appearances, successful so far in this play, are in jeopardy. The implications are far-reaching: is drama possible in a society in which make-up and costumes have little validity? The answer may be that the special provinces of ritual theater are no longer exclusive to theater at all, that once the techniques of theater – which audiences are aware of all along – become popular techniques of demagogues and others who use them to move into the realm of politics, society changes. Aristophanes' last plays bear this out: *Wealth*, and according to some scholars *Ecclesiazusae*, mark a change in

Aristophanes' comic sensibility, and *Frogs* sends Dionysus on a quest to retrieve a playwright from the depths of Hades. There is even some social change present that implies potential danger when theater moves outside the Theater of Dionysus: women here signal danger that is only contained by the absurdity and grotesque nature of this scene.

Meanwhile, the women continue to bicker. The young woman claims that no one could be dearer to the old woman than Geres, an old man (932), and she calls the old woman 'the deadly one' (ὤλεθρε, 934), reinforcing the relationship between old age, unsuccessful and inappropriate deception, and death. She then reveals to the audience a deception of her own: she plans to speak to her lover outside alone, while the old woman thinks that she is inside the house (949–51). She initiates the duet that follows.[43] The song twists the traditional language of love poetry into an obscene series of *double entendres*.[44] The images of love whirling and wearing away the lover and the beloved are popular, given a parodic spin.[45]

The old woman then steps up her aggressive pursuit of the young man and even threatens to drag him off against his will (1001). She swears three oaths by Aphrodite (981, 999–1000, 1008) and marks herself as a traditional seductress. That the old woman does so is extremely ironic: even Aphrodite could not possibly help in this case. Aristophanes thus mocks the presentation of an older woman in the role of seductress.[46]

The young man has a legal argument with the old woman (982–93), and at 991 he compares her to a flour-sieve (κρησέρα). The comment is another in the series of jokes about her made-up face. Both she and a flour-sieve are covered with powder, in one case flour, in the other a cosmetic powder, like the κιναχύρα and the κανηφόρος (730–3). In addition, the woman's complexion probably resembles the texture and pattern of a sieve. The young man is not at all smitten with sexual passion, as he should be were this a standard allurement scene. To mock the tradition, the seductress becomes a common kitchen utensil.

The youth is reluctant to kiss the older woman because he fears her lover (993–4), the one who is the best of painters (τὸν τῶν γραφέων ἄριστον, 995). Such a man proves to be an appropriate choice, for the woman is an expert in painting herself: she paints over her face every day in order to look younger. This artist lover, however, brings her closer to death. The young man explains that the best of painters is 'the one who paints from life the jars for the dead' (ὃς τοῖς νεκροῖσι ζωγραφεῖ τὰς ληκύθους, 996). In other words, the woman resembles a model for the pictures of dead people on funeral vases.[47] This old woman has become so allied with paint and the two-dimensional image on a vase that she could only have death, or one who fashions images of death, as a lover.[48] Again we are shown that she paints herself to cover up her age and condition, and that these efforts expose her age and condition instead.

The youth continues to describe the old woman with images of death and burial (1028–33). She turns his words into images of marriage, reminding him to provide a garland of flowers (1034). He agrees to provide a wax wreath for her grave (1035–6). The suggestion of marriage central to a traditional allurement scene is perverted further by the comments of the young woman. She fears that the union between the older woman and the youth will set an unnatural and tragic precedent, filling the land with Oedipuses (1041–2). Her statement is straightforward, although tellingly metatheatrical, and clarifies the misguided nature of the old woman's seduction: she is old enough to be the youth's mother, not his wife (1038–40). True to form, the young woman puts a theatrical spin on the moment by recalling the well-known tragic scenario of the young man who finds himself married to his mother.

Just as the youth is about to be dragged away by the first old woman, another crone enters. The youth sees her a bit differently than she imagines also: as 'some monster clothed in a blister of blood' (ἀλλ' Ἔμπουσά τις, / ἐξ αἵματος φλύκταιναν ἠμφιεσμένη, 1056–7).[49] The youth describes the woman in terms of her costume, which seems to be a far cry from a sexy saffron-colored robe. Resembling a blood-blister, she becomes an enigmatic monster, an ἔμπουσα. This particularly disgusting metaphor is also particularly revealing: once again we see a character identified and indeed characterized by her outward appearance. Praxagora's regime causes some women to look (and perhaps act) like monsters. The scene also functions as a foil to the earlier scene of younger women dressing as men; there the women were feminine, funny, and successful. Here old women, near death and with little femininity left, try to dress as their opposites, as attractive young women. They nearly destroy themselves and their intended lover instead. The play eventually displays three travesties: young women as men, men as young women, and aged women as young women.

The youth describes the third hag in terms of her cosmetics also: 'Is she a monkey filled up with white paint or a hag having come up from the many [the dead]?' (πότερον πίθηκος ἀνάπλεως ψιμυθίου, / ἢ γραῦς ἀνεστηκυῖα παρὰ τῶν πλειόνων; 1072–3).[50] She is no longer a human being; her image is either disguised or dead. The youth closes the scene with a final monologue. He laments his fate and once again turns the women into hideous creatures with his words. He calls the third woman a Phryne with an oil-bottle between her jaws (1100).[51] Finally, he closes the scene by wishing her a painful death:

> Still, if I die, as is probable, sailing there with these two whores, bury me at the very mouth of the harbor, and this one here, from the top of her body, pouring tar into her, living, and then pouring molten lead in a circle around her ankles, put her on top as the representative for a *lekythos*.

> ὅμως δ' ἐάν τι πολλὰ πολλάκις πάθω
> ὑπὸ τοῖνδε τοῖν κασαλβάδοιν δεῦρ' ἐσπλέων,
> θάψαι μ' ἐπ' αὐτῷ τῷ στόματι τῆς ἐσβολῆς,
> καὶ τήνδ' ἄνωθεν ἐπιπολῆς τοῦ σήματος
> ζῶσαν καταπιττώσαντες εἶτα τὼ πόδε
> μολυβδοχοήσαντες κύκλῳ περὶ τὰ σφυρὰ
> ἄνω 'πιθεῖναι πρόφασιν ἀντὶ ληκύθου.
>
> (1105–11)

This woman, who has such a predilection for make-up and trying to look like something other than what she is, gets a permanent disguise (πρόφασις). She will not just have a *lekythos* in honor of her death, but she will also become one herself. For her seductive efforts she gets this horrible death instead of sexual pleasure.

The crones' attempt at seduction fails. They employ all the correct elements, but perversely. Their trickery relies upon make-up and dresses that do not allure. Their sexual liaison turns out to be with death. They resemble monsters instead of goddesses, and they have no erotic persuasion, only legalistic maneuvers and distorted love lyrics. The scene also plays up the link between women and drama, for it highlights the unsuccessful attempts of the hags to present themselves as desirable objects of the male gaze.

The final ironic aspect of this scene involves the old women's interpretation of the decree that gives them the right to demand sexual favors from the young man. Aristophanes presents the decree in a way that makes the hags exhibit an eagerness for arbitrary interpretation and throws a negative light on the legal stability of the new government. The first hag presents the decree, whose wording parodies traditional Athenian decrees (1015–20).[52] Old Woman B, however, argues over interpretation. According to her, Old Woman A has transgressed the law and she should have the youth herself first (1049–51, 1077). That the interpretation of the decree should be left up to these women is frightening in itself, but the women in charge have adapted traditional legal forms for their laws first. Women's values have been disguised in legalistic jargon and do not remain stable even then, for more women argue over how to read them. The *gynaikokratia* may foster such things in the future, since women have shown themselves to be masters at rhetorical trickery.

Both festive and ironic interpretations of *Ecclesiazusae* might look at this episode as a parody of traditional literary treatments of seduction. On the one hand, Aristophanes frequently parodies literary tradition for comic effect. To a festival audience primed for laughs, seeing and understanding such an exaggerated representation of sexuality, aggression, and desperate avoidance could indeed be hilarious. The youth is in a humorously unpleasant and unenviable position. While being the object of a woman's attempted seduction could be desirable, being seduced by these women is definitely not. The youth seems to be the victim of a practical joke brought on by Praxagora's absurd government.[53]

On the other hand, an audience with a taste for comic irony sees that Aristophanes mocks the fantasy of seduction controlled by women. His seductress is not Aphrodite herself or Hera or Penelope; instead he has chosen three old women usually defined as being beyond sexual activity. Their attempts at rejuvenation and sexuality become grotesque, ineffective, and ugly. They approach death rather than marriage or sexual union. Their intended sexual partner does all he can to get away from them, instead of all he can to get closer. Aristophanes' sharp literary parody here must support the latter view. The concerns of lovers, often kept apart by legal obstacles or intervening guardians, would later become a standard theme of New Comedy. This scene presages such sentimental themes with Aristophanes' customary ironic, obscene, and often grotesque sensibility.

For the play's finale, a servant-girl arrives on stage and announces that dinner is ready. She describes her feminine attire, reveals her tipsy condition, and asks the chorus where her owner's husband is (1125–6). The servant-girl coins a new term here: ἡ κεκτημένη, feminine for the usual term for owner, ὁ κεκτημένος, for men usually own property. When a man (perhaps Blepyrus) arrives, she recognizes him and invites him to the feast.[54] Then she turns to the audience and addresses the judges, inviting them to join the meal (1141–3) and blurring the boundaries between the audience in the play and the citizens of Praxagora's city.

This man agrees to attend the dinner on one condition, that no one neglects the children and the older people (1144–5). He urges the servant-girl to invite more people, although technically only men: 'But like a free-born citizen, you invite the old men, the young men, and the boys' (ἀλλ' ἐλευθέρως / καλεῖς γέροντα, μειράκιον, παιδίσον, 1145–6). There is no 'linguistic feminism' for him.[55] The dinner song is sung and the play ends with no satisfactory resolution. The chorus sings about a strange concoction of fish dishes, and chaos marks the banquet and the end of the play.[56] None of the sexual rejuvenation and festivity common to an Aristophanic *exodos* are present here; such things are veiled by disorder and disturbance.

This ending poses a problem for both an audience and a reader; it is almost as if Aristophanes himself did not know what to do next. Nevertheless, we can say that the important themes of the first half of the play are used in the second half to investigate the nature of dramatic performances and to undermine the strength of a *gynaikokratia* founded upon role-playing. Aristophanes sets up a government of women and knocks it down with the same principles from which it was constructed, namely that appearance brings power. Aristophanes also sets up a dramatic fiction and uses the components of theatrical performance to dismantle it. We see how actors act, how characters develop, and how both costume and language define character. We also witness the interplay, vulnerability, and ephemerality that exist between the actor and his role.

CONCLUSIONS: COMIC DRAMA AND EARLY FOURTH-CENTURY ATHENS

Both physical and linguistic trickery have a dual value in this play. Sometimes they are comic and harmless, as when women who try to imitate men make mistakes when they practice. Sometimes they are dangerous and lead to serious changes, as when Praxagora indulges in the masculine disguise.[57] Aristophanes makes explicit connections between gender and proper government through costumes and language as well as through the plot. The use of costume inherent to the action of *Ecclesiazusae* ties the main plot (women taking over the city) to its subtext (acting is a phenomenon at work outside the theater). In this conclusion, I will discuss some of the implications that may be drawn from my reading of *Ecclesiazusae*. Scholars have argued in the past that, in reality, women had little to do with government and the economy in ancient Athens, and so the plot of *Ecclesiazusae* is simply part of a silly dream.

Counter to this traditional interpretation runs the fact that gender roles were so clearly delineated in Athenian ideology that metaphors of gender were often used to illustrate power relations. Thus, a playwright might often use gender disguise to highlight social problems. Aeschylus' *Oresteia* and Aristophanes' own *Lysistrata*, to name just two, have been accepted as documents which reveal a careful structure of male dominance (see Foley 1977; Zeitlin 1978). A good example in *Ecclesiazusae* of the linking of gender to political power through sexual relations is Woman A's comment about Agyrrhios (102–4). Agyrrhios 'once was a woman' because he played the passive role in a homosexual union. When he 'wears the beard of Pronomos', he is able to attain political power. The manliness of Athenian statesmen and their preferred roles in sexual relationships certainly affected their images and hence their ability to gain power among the people (see Winkler 1990: 55–64). My first point is, then, that the centrality of gender to *Ecclesiazusae* cannot be dismissed as just a circumstance of comic fantasy.

My second conclusion is that, since gender is brought to the fore most obviously by the plot of *Ecclesiazusae*, the convention of male actors in female parts must be of significance. The illustrations of actors in female dress on vases show that, for whatever reason, male actors were not regularly depicted in performance as women without an indication that the representation of woman was just that, a representation of woman. Male actors playing women are represented with a reminder of their sex displayed in some way or as wearing grotesque and distorted female masks. I suggest that, while he might want to commemorate his performance of a female part, a male actor might not want to indicate that he actually became a woman. By analogy, we are forced to remember that the female characters in *Ecclesiazusae* never really become men, although they do a fairly successful imitation. Praxagora, the center of our attention, is not clearly all woman, however, as her speech to the women assembled in the *ecclesia* shows. The same illusion of gender disguise at work in the vase-paintings is at work in *Ecclesiazusae*.

Historians have long used *Ecclesiazusae* to discuss late fifth-century and early fourth-century history and political philosophy. Mossé writes that Praxagora's communal plan reflects the inequality of life in post-war Athens: 'This total communism is intended to bring to an end the shameful inequality of fortunes and the destitution of the majority' (1973: 13). After the Peloponnesian War, from the end of the fifth century through the early fourth century, Athens experienced political, economic, social, religious, and moral crises. Athens became involved in the Corinthian War soon after the Peloponnesian War ended. Poverty ran wild throughout the city. Aristophanes reacted to the social and political effect of this poverty in *Wealth* (388 BCE).[58]

After the war, Athens' population suffered greatly. Its decrease lead to perhaps the most tangible and marked social changes in the city. The adult male population before the war was over 40,000 (*c.*434 BCE); after the war, the number of adult male Athenian citizens dropped to between 14,000 and 16,250, a 60 per cent loss (B. Strauss 1987: 81).[59] Thus traditional gender roles must have been in transition. In a city where men were scarce and where women's roles were changing, Aristophanes seizes upon a comic idea appropriate for its time. *Ecclesiazusae* examines the nature of being a woman and of being a man, but in the end restores the old and established gender order. Women dress as men, appropriating male costume and language, in a comic vision of what Aristophanes perhaps saw happening in real life.[60] Aristophanes' comic vision of a *gynaikokratia* may have been informed by the disproportionate number of women in Athens at the time. In his fantasy, women take the places of the absent men, wearing men's tunics and beards, and threaten to change the city entirely.

Men are not wholly safe from ridicule, however. Disgruntled at what he sees in the *ecclesia*, Aristophanes uses the social situation to lampoon the political leaders of the early fourth century. Now the men in power are those who, like Agyrrhios, appear masculine but who are really feminine underneath. There are no real men any more. There are men who look like men but act like women, and there are women who act like men. Both are theater; both are representations but not effective reality. Both actor and politician wear costumes that hide their true natures, and both deliver lines designed to persuade their respective judges, either those of the dramatic festival or those of the *demos*. Because of the varying attendance in the Athenian *ecclesia*, it was probably possible, with the proper costumes and the appropriate numbers of men, to carry out any number of political dramas. In effect, Aristophanes demonstrates that there is little difference between the *ecclesia* and the theater.

It is instructive to compare the circumstances of the production of *Ecclesiazusae* with plays produced during a time of equivalent social change in America, from 1890 to 1920. *Ecclesiazusae* resembles the plays that Stephens has said 'adhered to the conventional belief in the moral superiority of females while simultaneously addressing issues arising from women's changing position in society', and so like these plays it 'can be newly appreciated as a site of struggle over the meaning of gender' (Stephens 1990: 283). In her essay, Stephens aims to show 'how drama, as cultural practice, can both challenge and reinforce dominant gender ideology in periods of social change' (ibid.). Her findings shed light on *Ecclesiazusae*. The plays she discusses arise from reaction to feminist thought that, as Praxagora and Lysistrata do, 'argued that women could weed out corruption and ultimately reform society if given the chance to extend their housecleaning and sanctifying talents into the public arena' (ibid. 284). What the plays actually do, Stephens points out, is adopt this language to reinforce the status quo and the traditional norm of women in the home. The plays she selects are characterized by a dominant morally superior female hero who must make a moral decision on which her future rests. The decision is seen to call for a return to traditional gender-role behavior. Just so in *Ecclesiazusae*, Praxagora chooses to change society, but by inventing a large *oikos* in which all women are mothers, wives, and lovers. While she is a skilled *rhêtor*, she does not advocate the introduction of women into the traditional male political arena. It is not even clear whether she will exercise this skill any longer once the play is over. *Lysistrata* dramatizes this paradigm even more clearly. Lysistrata only speaks out in order to call for a return to silence, the home, and traditional marriage and gender-role behavior.

In investigating the equation of performance in the theater and in the assembly, Aristophanes mocks current trends in Athens – perhaps women voicing opinions more than before or during the war, perhaps the growing economic and political instability – then reaffirms traditional gender roles and traditional values by making Praxagora's *gynaikokratia* selfish and ineffectual. His serious statements to the citizens of Athens are that imposters can rule if allowed, that costumes change only appearances, and that political power can be won with the same persuasive tactics of illusion and artifice employed by actors. The consequences of his message are manifest in his disassembly of Praxagora, her companions, and her horrific society: it is impossible to consider this *gynaikokratia*, as it has been revealed to us, as a wholly positive solution. *Ecclesiazusae* presents us with a comic fantasy, yet not a simple one. It is, in fact, as complex a series of role-playings as can be found.

Ecclesiazusae examines the disruption of gender-role differences in post-war Athens. Established boundaries between the genders, once the stable basis of Athenian society, where men were men and women were silent and invisible, are being crossed both in the play and in real life. Aristophanes makes these boundaries clear through the semiotics of dress and language. His comedy of female rule becomes a disturbing vision where no system of difference is stable. *Ecclesiazusae* is not a subversive fiction, however. While cross-dressing itself may have a subversive aspect, challenging the fixity of gender identity and so the shape of society, the restoration of proper dress and language relieves that tension. At the end of *Ecclesiazusae*, Athens is one big *oikos* with the women in charge, a pleasurable, albeit thought-provoking, comic utopia. As twentieth-century readers, we should interpret *Ecclesiazusae* as a play which represents a comic stereotype of woman in order to reaffirm the male power base of Athenian society.

5

THE LEGACY OF ARISTOPHANES' WOMEN

Two other extant Aristophanic comedies, *Frogs* and *Ploutos* (*Wealth*), remain. Produced between *Thesmophoriazusae* and *Ecclesiazusae*, *Frogs* was performed in 405 BCE at the Lenaea, where it won first prize. Aristophanes' final play, *Ploutos*, can be dated to 388 BCE.[1] Both of these plays display a marked change in Aristophanes' treatment of female figures, a change even from the trends of *Ecclesiazusae*, although some similarities do occur between that play and *Ploutos*. An analysis of these plays with regard to gender reveals the extent to which Aristophanic comedy, and perhaps Old Comedy in general, changed over time and toward the end of the fifth century.

FROGS

Frogs concerns a quest by the god Dionysus to find a worthy tragic poet and to return him to Athens. Accompanied by his slave Xanthias, Dionysus descends to Hades in search of the shades of Aeschylus and the recently deceased Sophocles and Euripides. Only three female figures appear in this play, and their undistinctive roles are relatively minor. Perhaps when Dionysus himself appears in a comedy, there is no need for the gender play precipitated by a female figure. Dionysus, the god of theater, controls the power and privilege of establishing the theatricality of this play. In fact, *Frogs* opens with a metatheatrical joke on Dionysus himself. Dionysus and Xanthias are discussing the kinds of jokes that Xanthias will be allowed to make during their trip. Xanthias prefers to rely on vulgar jokes that always get laughs (1–2) and that he finds amusing (5); Dionysus objects (4), but nevertheless utters such jokes himself (3, 5, 8).[2] Later on, he exhibits the same vulgar behavior that he has refused to even mention, for example farting (267–8) and defecating (308; 479–91).

Dionysus wears the lion-skin and carries the club iconographic of Heracles, for Heracles successfully returned from Hades when he went to steal Cerberus; Dionysus hopes to benefit from Heracles' luck with this costume. Myths of descent and return from the underworld undertaken in order to steal or retrieve something or someone provide the mythic structure for the plot of *Frogs*. Heracles, a favorite character of Euripides, has perhaps been selected for ridicule here not only because of his theft of Cerberus but also because of his retrieval of Alcestis in the Euripidean play of that name.[3] For instance, Dionysus mockingly explains to Heracles that his effeminate dress has something to do with Kleisthenes (48) before he admits that he is imitating Heracles himself.

After his discussion with Heracles, Dionysus arrives at the house of Hades and Persephone. Aiakos answers the door. Thinking that Dionysus really is Heracles, and still angry over Heracles' theft of Cerberus, he slams the door in Dionysus/Heracles' face with threats of torture (465–78). Xanthias and Dionysus then exchange clothing and Xanthias tries the door again. This time, a maid responds and, with the expected comic irony, welcomes Xanthias/Heracles into the house with tempting offers of food, drink, and dancing girls (503–18). We never see these dancing girls, however.[4] The maid's role is perfunctory. She carries out her official function as a servant, answering the door and offering guests some appropriate hospitality. She also becomes allied with food, wine, and sexuality through her enthusiastic and extravagant welcome of Xanthias/Heracles. Yet her character displays no distinct prevarication or theatrical awareness. Again, these are the tasks of Dionysus and Xanthias, who compete to play the role of Heracles. In their own ways, both are successful actors.

Shortly after Dionysus has been re-costumed as Heracles, two other women enter. They are food merchants whom Heracles neglected to pay during his last trip to Hades. Recognizing their delinquent client, they try to settle his bill now, and eventually run off stage to seek legal assistance in their claim (549–78). These women emerge from the stock comic mold of the angry market woman (cf. e.g. Myrtia in *Wasps*). Like Persephone's maid, however, they display little of the theatrical awareness usually found accompanying female figures in other Aristophanic comedies. As also with the maid, there is no mention of their physical appearance, nor do they actively play tricks or refer to other plays. Their function is to continue the reversal-of-fortune gag involving a master (the god Dionysus) and a slave (the clever

Xanthias). They participate in a transparent comic situation, albeit without any specific ironic flavor on their parts.

In addition, all the female figures in *Frogs*, with the exception perhaps of the chorus of initiates, appear within the play's first 600 lines.[5] The play continues with a competition between Aeschylus and Euripides and closes with Dionysus' decision to return to Athens with Aeschylus. There is no marriage, no rejuvenation of the comic hero, no mass invitation to a celebratory feast (although Hades does invite Dionysus to supper, 1479–80). Above all, no nude female figure appears. The figures of rejuvenation here are male: Aeschylus, who will revivify the dying art of tragedy, and Dionysus, who sponsors the festival.

PLOUTOS

Almost never included in the category of Old Comedy, as *Frogs* often is, *Ploutos* is usually described as a work of Middle Comedy. Its plot, form, and characters do depart from the usual Aristophanic style.[6] *Ploutos* revolves around the fortunes of Khremylos, who has been told by the Delphic Oracle to befriend the first man he meets on his way home from the sanctuary. Accompanied by his slave Karion, Khremylos encounters an old, blind man who eventually reveals himself to be the god Ploutos (Wealth), blinded by Zeus so as to make no distinction between good and bad men when bestowing his blessings. Khremylos determines to restore Ploutos' sight and thus to return his blessings to those worthy of them. Two women appear in this play, Khremylos' wife and an old woman who, once Ploutos can see again, loses her money and thus the hold she has on her young lover. The abstract concept of Penia (Poverty) also appears in female form.

Like the women's roles in *Frogs*, the role of Khremylos' wife reveals little of what we have come to expect of an Aristophanic female. She appears only briefly (641–770, 788–801), and then mostly to listen to Karion's account of the events at Delphi.[7] In her first appearance, she makes up the audience for Karion's story and her lines consist primarily of responses and prompts. In her second appearance, she welcomes the god Ploutos into her house with generous hospitality. It is only in this second appearance that she assists the character of Ploutos in creating a metatheatrical moment. Ploutos rejects her offers of food and drink and announces that he will provide guest-gifts (790–3). He suggests going inside, however, to avoid the kind of scene Aristophanes dislikes, one in which sweets are thrown to the audience in order to get a laugh (οὐ γὰρ πρεπῶδές ἐστι τῷ διδασκάλῳ / ἰσχάδια καὶ τρωγάλια τοῖς θεωμένοις / προβαλόντ' ἐπὶ τούτοις εἶτ' ἀναγκάζειν γελᾶν, 797–9). The wife responds that this is a good idea, for she can see that Dexinikos, in the audience, is already standing up and in position to grab for figs (εὖ πάνυ λέγεις· ὡς Δεξίνικός γ' οὑτοσὶ / ἀνίσταθ' ὡς ἁρπασόμενος τὰς ἰσχάδας, 800–1). Still, she is neither mute, nude, and symbolic of rejuvenation, nor an expert with costumes, trickery, or tragic parody; rather, encouraged by another character, she simply breaks the 'fourth wall' of the stage and recognizes the audience.

Near the end of the play, an old woman appears and complains that her young lover has deserted her, now that she no longer has money since Ploutos' blindness has been cured. At the end of her scene, she is described as a grotesque creation of costume and make-up, for there she becomes an object of ridicule for her ugliness (1047–65). Reminiscent of the hag scene in *Ecclesiazusae*, this episode also emphasizes the creation of the woman through cosmetics and of the old, desirous woman as a false and horrible creature.

The most unusual feature of this play that attention to the treatment of gender reveals is the personification of Wealth as an old man and of Poverty as a woman. According to the usual logic of both the ancient Greek, as well as the Aristophanic, imagination, we might expect that riches and wealth would appear in female form, for these concepts imply the happiness, fertility, and abundance that is usually associated with femininity.[8] Accordingly, we might also expect Poverty to be personified as an old man, for it implies harshness, impotence, and lack. Yet the characterizations here seem traditional and linguistically determined. In *Theogony*, Hesiod personifies Ploutos as a man (969), while proverbs make him blind, and so Aristophanes appears to have hit upon a nevertheless traditional and linguistic gender determination for his divinities.[9] Since this play lacks any of the conventional treatment of female figures in previous comedies, with the exception of parts of *Ecclesiazusae*, it appears to do away with the need for an element of the feminine even more than *Frogs* does (after all, *Frogs* has Dionysus, who contains feminine elements within his character). *Ploutos* gives us a comedy without the slippery Aristophanic humor that femininity provides.

The conventionally and comically feminine tendencies to change shape and to inspire fertility both become masculine here. Not only does Ploutos regain his sight and become transformed into the god that he is, but he also transforms Khremylos' ordinary material goods into gold, silver, and ivory. While Ploutos' name may suggest ties to death and the underworld rather than to life, he is a deity equally allied with agricultural riches. Femininity, on the other hand, is represented by the sophistic goddess Poverty, who has the aspect of an ugly old hag and who belongs in a tragedy rather than a comedy (423–4). Like the old woman later in the play and the three hags in *Ecclesiazusae*, she receives abusive comments about the falseness of her cosmetics (602).

The play ends on a strange note, with the arrival at Khremylos' house of Hermes and a priest, who, like the embassy of gods in *Birds*, are both famished because there have been no sacrifices since Ploutos regained his sight. Accompanied by a procession, Ploutos finds a permanent place on the Acropolis. The complete absence of any feminine principle, and thus the much smaller element of play with costume, parody, and metatheater, only enhances the estrangement of *Ploutos* from the rest of the Aristophanic corpus. Perhaps influenced by the defeat of Athens in the Peloponnesian War and the subsequent internal political and economic struggles in Athens, or perhaps led to change his comic style through age and experience, Aristophanes has in any case made a clear break with the past. *Ploutos* must herald a different sort of comedy from his previous plays, for whatever aspects of femininity essential to the basic Aristophanic comic spirit that it does not eradicate, this play completely replaces with masculine forms.

CONCLUSIONS

The preceding chapters of this book have argued that a traditional Greek view of femininity and gender roles, along with the theatrical convention of male actors playing female roles, informs the portrayal, construction, and meaning of female figures in Aristophanic comedy. Aristophanes' early plays display an incipient interest in the relationship between traditional feminine character and behavior – linguistic skill, imitation, dishonesty, trickery – and comedy. In *Lysistrata*, the use of women as both comic objects and subjects, because of their natural ability to manipulate their language and their appearance, takes center stage. *Thesmophoriazusae*, predictably enough, lays exclusive claim to the manipulation of the female form as a privilege for comedy, not tragedy, and so goes after Euripides and his coterie of tragic and tragicomic women. *Ecclesiazusae* returns to the format of *Lysistrata* and sets feminine comic principles firmly in the unstable and uncertain milieu of early fourth-century politics. *Frogs* includes a few perfunctory and uncomplicated female characters, perhaps because Dionysus himself takes part in the play and provides any and all impetus for gender play, role play, enhanced theatricality, and trickiness. *Ploutos* omits any distinctly significant comic femininity and grants whatever traditional Aristophanic humor that remains to male figures. Thus in this final play, Aristophanes departs from his exploration of the female figure as the ultimate comic instrument.

An analysis of Aristophanic comedy with attention to gender thus offers several salient conclusions about the relationship between humor and femininity in the ancient Greek imagination. First, Aristophanes' portrayal of females, whether abstract concepts in female form, real citizen women, young girls, market women, or foreigners, depends on traditional stereotypes for inspiration. In ancient Greek thought and literature, the feminine is a theatrical phenomenon: women are shifty, transient, insubstantial, deceptive, and imitative. These qualities also belong to comic figures. Whenever any element of femininity is present in an Aristophanic production, an opportunity arises for humor based on theatricality, costume play, or language play. Finally, the convention of male actors playing female roles does appear to intrude into the text, just as it may have intruded into the performance. Femininity is represented by Aristophanes as the site of the ultimate comic figure: completely deceptive because 'she' is not real at all. 'She' must be given shape by a man, and everyone knows that.

TRACES OF THE ARISTOPHANIC FEMALE IN LATER COMIC TRADITIONS

In this section I will briefly survey the appearance and characterization of female figures in a few representative texts from other comic traditions. A complete analysis of these various literary traditions lies beyond the scope of this particular work. Still, it may be useful to point out the occurrence and reappearance of typical Aristophanic trends in other literatures. We can thus note the threads of literary and cultural influence that more modern Western traditions owe to ancient Greece for their configurations of the feminine in comic drama.

We know about New Comedy chiefly from the works of Menander (*c*.342–292 BCE). Menander's distinctly more domestic comedies consistently revolve around a woman, sometimes two, often a wife or a young girl and a courtesan. The plot typically involves a seduction and a subsequent problem with a father or a child, or both. By the play's finale, all disputes are resolved for the better and the action usually culminates in marriage. Female figures indulge in few deceptions, and these deceptions are usually designed to protect other characters rather than to achieve some selfish and fantastic scheme (e.g. the Samia pretends that the disputed child is hers to protect the younger lovers). There is little Aristophanic metatheater.[10] The comedies invoke the passive power of women whom men love, but Menander writes about the humor of desperate domestic situations and that requires the presence of female figures (see Henry 1987). Women do not even indulge in much masquerade: in *Dyskolos*, the youth Sostratos passes himself off as a hard-working farmer in order to impress his lover's misanthropic father, but his lover works no trickery.

The Roman comic poet Plautus (*c*.250–184 BCE), whose work displays a keen awareness and exploitation of the idea of metatheater, plays with the idea of women played by men on stage only slightly.[11] For example, a central joke early on in the *Menaechmi* concerns the theft by Menaechmus of Epidamnus' wife's dress, which he has put on; this is a typical Aristophanic joke about the dress defining the person who wears it (127 ff.).[12] Pseudolus is the metatheatrical trickster of his eponymous play; the central female figure, a young courtesan, functions as the object he must secure for his master. The plays of Terence (195?–159? BCE) also display few of the typical Aristophanic trends in the characterization of female figures.[13] A few women participate in deceptions (notably in *Heauton Timoroumenos* (*Self-Tormentor*) and *Hecyra* (*The Mother-in-Law*)), but their deceptions do not elicit clear-cut metatheatrics.

While female figures cause actions and provide a catalyst for plots and plans in both New and Roman Comedy, their continuation of a tendency toward metatheater diverges from the path established early on and then abandoned by Aristophanes. The clever slave, a role foreshadowed by Xanthias in *Frogs* and later exemplified by Plautus' Pseudolus, takes over as the main metatheatrical leader in the comic play.

It is not until much later that we can pick up a clear Aristophanic thread in Western comic theater, although one might find literary criticism and trickery tinted by femininity in a character like Chaucer's Wife of Bath.[14] Shakespearean comedy provides a more modern example of the comic possibilities of theatrical transvestism and the threat it can pose to the maintenance of any dramatic illusion on stage, especially under the constrictions of the male actor convention. Although there are other Shakespearean plays that concern women disguised as men (*The Merchant of Venice*, *Much Ado*

About Nothing, Twelfth Night, Two Gentlemen of Verona), *As You Like It* provides for my purposes the most provocative examples and appropriate points of comparison.[15] In addition to some transvestism and complicated disguises, *As You Like It* includes jokes about the poet's ability to fool the audience as well as his other characters with the layering of genders upon one figure.

Rosalind and her companion Celia escape into the forest of Arden in search of Rosalind's father, Duke Senior, who has been banished by his brother, Duke Frederick. In order to ensure their safety, Rosalind disguises herself as a young man called Ganymede and Celia becomes the maiden Aliena. Interestingly enough, these disguises appear to suit their individual and feminine bodies also:

> Were it not better,
> Because I am more than common tall,
> That I did suit me all points like a man?
> A gallant curtleaxe upon my thigh,
> A boar-spear in my hand, and – in my heart
> Lie there what a hidden woman's fear there will –
> We'll have a swashing and a martial outside,
> As many other mannish cowards have
> That do outface it with their semblances.
>   (Rosalind; I, iii, 116–24)[16]

Rosalind has selected the features of stereotypical masculinity, perhaps the image of the braggart soldier: height, a sword and spear, and an aggressive, military attitude. She will play this role to protect herself and Celia on their journey. Rosalind also indulges in some parody of such a masculine outlook, suggesting that not all those men who seem to be masculine really are what they seem. The name she takes suggests some homosexuality, and perhaps some feminization.[17] Even so, her gentle dig also affirms the power of a conventional masculine façade, since she needs the costume for her survival. It is clear that Rosalind also separates herself from the image of the brave soldier: her heart remains feminine. Finally, the actor playing Rosalind may also have influenced this speech, especially if he was taller than the actor playing Celia or unusually tall for the role of a young woman like Rosalind.

Later on as Rosalind plays with her disguise, the audience always clearly recalls that Ganymede is Rosalind, especially because she continues to present herself as Rosalind to Celia and only acts as Ganymede in front of others. Ganymede is so effectively played, however, that an unsophisticated country girl named Phebe falls in love with him. To complicate matters, Ganymede offers to act as a surrogate Rosalind for Orlando, whom Rosalind loves. Orlando practices courting Rosalind on a Ganymede who both imitates and is Rosalind. In other words, Rosalind plays the role of a man who imitates Rosalind herself. The audience has x-ray vision, so to speak, at this point in the play (III, ii): they see all three layers of Rosalind's character and hear four different voices in her remarks: those of Rosalind, Ganymede, Ganymede as Rosalind, and, perhaps, the poet.

At times the audience has vivid and direct reminders of Rosalind's real identity when she is dressed as Ganymede. When she cannot hold back her thoughts about Orlando right before she really assumes the masculine role of Ganymede, Rosalind tells Celia: 'Do you not know I am a woman? When I think, I must speak' (III, ii, 263–4).[18] Then, after hearing the story of Orlando's encounter with a lion and seeing Orlando's blood on a handkerchief, Ganymede surprises everyone and, in a symmetrical and stereotypical feminine fashion, faints. Rosalind still controls Ganymede's emotions.[19] In both these instances, Rosalind betrays her feminine nature in a feminine manner: through speech.

Shakespeare also plays with the sexual ambiguity of Rosalind's disguise and its effect upon others. Phebe, for instance, is both perplexed and fascinated by the figure of Ganymede:

> Think not I love him, though I ask for him.
> 'Tis not a peevish boy; yet he talks well.
> But what care I for words? Yet words do well
> When he that speaks them pleases those that hear.
> It is a pretty youth – not very pretty –
> But sure he's proud; and yet his pride becomes him.
> He'll make a proper man. The best thing in him
> Is his complexion; and faster than his tongue
> Did make offense, his eye did heal it up.
> He is not very tall; yet for his years he's tall.
> His leg is but so so; and yet 'tis well.
> There was a pretty redness in his lip,
> A little riper and more lusty red
> Than that mix'd in his cheek; 'twas just the difference
> Between the constant red and mingled damask.
> (III, v, 109–23)

Phebe describes the typically feminine aspects of Ganymede's appearance and personality: his verbal skill, his prettiness, his complexion, his now relatively petite stature, his lips and cheeks. She rationalizes these clues to Ganymede's true gender identity, and takes the feminine or incongruous aspects of his image as authentic rather than suspicious. She does this perhaps out of love, perhaps out of a lack of interpretive sophistication. Or, perhaps, we are to believe that those people in the forest of Arden are more gullible than those in the theater.

At the end of the play, however, Shakespeare lets his Rosalind/ Ganymede have more fun at the expense of the audience. The actor playing Rosalind delivers the epilogue. Rosalind begins the speech by stating that 'it is not the fashion to see the lady the epilogue', and follows through with a remark on how costume determines character: 'I am not furnish'd like a beggar; therefore to beg will not become me'. She refers to the inner workings of the production and reveals that all the parts were played by men:

> If I were a woman, I would kiss as many of you as had beards that pleas'd me, complexions that lik'd me, and breaths that I defied not; and I am sure, as many as have good beards, or good faces, or sweet breaths, will, for my kind offer, when I make curtsy, bid me farewell.
>
> (Epilogue, 17–22)

The actor teases the audience with additional sexual ambiguity. After the play is over, the audience experiences a delayed confusion: which sex does Rosalind parody, male, female, or both?[20] The revelation forces the audience, be it a theatrical or a reading audience, to reflect back upon the play and the 'true' nature of Rosalind's character. That the actor playing her is male could make little difference, but Shakespeare makes a point of telling the audience that Rosalind was played by a man after a presentation of what happens to women who pretend to be men. That is his final touch of humor: 'the boy actor who will play both [Rosalind and Ganymede] will have the best of the joke, and the Elizabethan audience is to share it' (Styan 1975: 165).

The poet had at least three reasons for this. First, this way Rosalind's masculinity becomes grounded in nature, not just in her disguise.[21] Second, he reveals the theatricality of the presentation as part of his comic technique, just as Aristophanes did and in particular with female figures. The play turns itself inside out as part of its comic nature. Finally, he finds a way to confront and diffuse the homosexual undercurrents of the stage performance. Mounting a performance of *As You Like It* with actresses in the appropriate female roles diffuses these undercurrents and much of the humor even further, something

Shakespeare probably did not have in mind, and that is what productions of Aristophanic comedy with actresses playing the female parts do as well.[22]

SUGGESTIONS FOR THE FUTURE

If feminist theater groups want to explore ancient dramatic images of women to empower modern women, they might consider casting and producing *Acharnians* around a female Dikaiopolis.[23] This would require the reformulation of some scenes, perhaps, and the accommodation of some historical inaccuracies (a woman in the assembly participating in the political process, for example). Yet such an adaptation could also foreground both the position of women in society (a woman's voice is often not heard in the public forum, as Dikaiopolis' is not) as well as a woman's often typically individualized solution to a community problem. The finale of the play could, as women's theater groups often desire, offer a positive celebration of female power and ingenuity; with a rejuvenated female Dikaiopolis accompanied, perhaps, by two male peace-treaties, a performance might promise no return to the status quo. Such a production could be truly revolutionary.

A recognition of the significance of gender to *Clouds* could transform productions of that play as well. Playing *Clouds* with a male chorus dressed as women dressed as clouds would highlight the construction of the Clouds' deceptiveness as feminine and enhance the suspicion attached to the figure of Socrates.

Lysistrata could be played by an all-female cast to highlight the construction of male desire and perhaps the complicity of women in the cultural construction of gender roles. Certainly, however, a production of this sort would have to confront the potential for losing the humor in the jokes; it is a reasonable assumption that many audience members might not find this particularly amusing. A cross-gender cast, with male actors playing female roles and female actors playing the male roles, might help expose the paradigmatic nature of the gender characterization. There is plenty of opportunity in this play for the true sexual identity of the actors to be seen through their costumes. If Lysistrata were played by a male actor on the modern stage, her words might be understood quite differently than if she were played by an actress. For one thing, the possibility that she might be best understood as not a real woman, but perhaps a representative of Athena, would become more pronounced and the irony of the representation would be increased. The powers that determine, control, and watch over human communities might be seen not as the Olympic gods but rather as the patriarchal leaders of contemporary society. When Lysistrata is played by a woman, on the other hand, I suspect that problems akin to those that arise from productions of *The Taming of the Shrew* and *As You Like It* may appear: how does a feminist production reconcile the women's return to marriage, silence, and the patriarchal construction of gender roles with the outspokenness of the heroine? Should Lysistrata speak at the end of the play?[24] Should she appear with or without a husband? Who is he? What Athenian man would marry her? What would their life be like after the play is over? Should the play be reset in another time and place altogether? Should she give the play's reconciliation speech, or should she appear silent and assimilated into the group of wives? Should the choruses be played by older women and men? These are the sorts of questions that must be addressed individually by feminist productions of *Lysistrata*. Other, larger questions may also arise. If all roles, both on and off stage, are played by men, can the play truly be called 'feminist'? Can a play that encourages women to solve problems by staging themselves as passive objects of the male gaze be called 'feminist'?

Thesmophoriazusae offers, even on its surface, the simplest option for modern productions, for the cultural and theatrical construction of gender is one of the play's main topics. Playing this comedy with a gender-accurate cast might highlight this issue, especially in the final scenes. An all-male cast here certainly might transform an understanding of the play, turning it into a potential vindication of women's objections to their dramatic portrayals. A director might also choose to underscore the masculine competition over the right to portray women as clever and comic on stage that I have suggested earlier.

Finally, *Ecclesiazusae* offers as many exciting performance possibilities as *Lysistrata* does. While an all-male cast might bring out the false construction and absence of women most effectively, an all-female cast would again reclaim female presence and, in good comic fashion, invert the constructions of gender to emphasize the configuration of masculinity as well as femininity on stage, along with the androgyny of Praxagora. Playing the hag scene with older female actresses would certainly bring home more of its pathos and horror, and provide an opportunity to explore the image of female desire, more than playing it with male actors might.

Playing Aristophanic comedy with female actors would put women in roles that they were not meant to have and that, by definition, can be either completely wrong or completely revolutionary. Still, given that performance conventions in effect during the fifth century have clearly affected Aristophanes' conception of the female as a comic creature, actresses eager to play Lysistrata, for example, should stop to consider the implications of playing such a role. Aristophanic comedy holds great promise for contemporary scholars, students, actors, and audiences; attention should be paid to the dynamics of gender in the text and in the historical conditions of production, both ancient and modern. *Lysistrata, Thesmophoriazusae,* and *Ecclesiazusae* have much more to reveal about men, women, and comedy than they appear to, and it is my hope that other aficionados of Old Comedy will find even more than I have begun to suggest here.

NOTES

PREFACE

1 At the play's opening, she is irritated and frowning (7–8). On Lysistrata's seriousness, Wilhelm Schmid has written, inaccurately, that 'Sie macht keine Witze' (Schmid and Stählin 1946: 330). On the universal hilarity of Aristophanic humor, Cedric Whitman (1964: 22) writes:

> True *joie de vivre* knows no bounds, and whatever sorrows or wistfulnesses are also implicit in the comedies – and they are numerous – there is always the illimitable, libidinous *joie de vivre*, transcending and glorifying the multifarious potpourri of comic experience, redeeming legions of bad puns from their native vapidness, and transforming the most unmentionable coarseness about sex and other bodily functions into an unoffending vision of hilarious nature.

INTRODUCTION

1 See Pickard-Cambridge 1968: 25–42 on the Lenaea, 57–101 on the City Dionysia. Pickard-Cambridge also reproduces the text of relevant inscriptions (*IG* ii^2 2319–23, 2325). Briefer histories of the festivals are given in Dearden 1976 and Simon 1982.
2 On the site of the Lenaea, see Pickard-Cambridge 1968: 37–40 and N. Slater 1986.
3 Our most complete examples of satyr play are found in Euripides' *Cyclops*, in the fragmentary remains of four Aeschylean plays, and in the fragmentary manuscripts of Sophocles' *Ichneutae* and *Inachus*. For more on satyr play, see Guggisberg 1947; Sutton 1974 and 1980. Sutton writes that 'the function of the satyr play in the tetralogy is to allay the anxiety provoked by tragedy' (1980: 165). For illustrations of satyr plays, see Brommer 1959.
4 The most comprehensive survey of evidence about comic costume and past scholarly controversies over the comic phallos is found in Stone 1980.
5 Davis 1978 argues that gender role-reversal can both reaffirm and subvert the social order. I will argue that because Athenian comedy is under the complete control of men, it could never actually undermine Athenian

power structures. Rather, it constructs and reaffirms those power structures.

6 One reason why scholars may disregard the general absence of citizen women characters from the comic stage is the cultural practice of not naming citizen women in public (Thuc. 2. 45. 2; see also Schaps 1977; Sommerstein 1980). In addition, upper-class citizen women, at least, seem to have spent little time in public; comedy may reflect a natural absence of women from the situations that male comic protagonists find themselves in. McLeish, for whom travesty connotes only men dressing as women on stage, discusses travesty acting in *Lysistrata* and *Thesmophoriazusae* but dismisses it in *Ecclesiazusae*, except for the hag scenes (1980: 153–5). Gruber writes that the audience always recognized the difference between an actor and his role and that a transvestite performance caused the constant reassessment of that relationship (1986: 2). After suggesting that the male actor playing Lysistrata influences a spectator's understanding of the play, however, he ventures no further toward explaining that influence. Arnott goes so far as to suggest that male actors in female roles determined the unusual masculinity of female characters, but then does not follow up with further discussion (1989: 87). I follow the lead of Stephens (1990: 292), who writes that

> Like ideology, the functioning of dramatic convention is often hidden, and what appears to the reader/spectator as an engaging story which challenges social convention may also contain a more subtle counterargument which serves to recoup any ground lost in the direction of significant change.

An interesting analysis of female characters in drama which takes the portrayal of women by men on stage as its starting-point is Ferris 1989 (on Greek drama, see ch. 2). In general, this has not been an issue for classicists to address. The standard interpretation of *Ecclesiazusae*, for example, that the women set up a government structured on the principles of the *oikos* which then serves to illustrate the problems of early fourth-century Athens and to celebrate the comic utopia, is usually made without reference to performance practice even by critics who employ contemporary methodologies: e.g. Foley 1981; Saïd 1979. I will address these questions in later chapters.

7 An appropriate parallel to ancient Greek impersonations of women is discussed by Phelan 1988. Her concerns are similar to mine: she tries to understand the theatrical meaning of male actors as women, and she writes of such ancient ritualized dramatic traditions as Balinese dance drama, Indian *kathakali*, Japanese *kabuki*, and Chinese opera, that

> ... classical female roles played by men or women do not, by definition and design, penetrate the 'identity' of any female; they are surface representations whose appeal exists precisely *as* surface. 'Reading' them depends not on plausibility or coherence but rather upon immediate recognition of the comic artifice *and* irreverent idealization of the form which organizes the image the dancer projects.
>
> (Phelan 1988: 109)

NOTES

She goes on to provide an example in the performance of a South Asian boy, Gautam, who dances in the guise of a woman. This dancer is convincingly, yet overdeterminedly, female:

> the excess and 'surplus' encoded within Gautam's surface femininity reminds the spectator of the absence of the female (the lack) rather than of her presence . . . No one forgets that the dancer is male; the invocation of the nonmale is controlled by the security of the performer's male body.
>
> (Phelan 1988: 110)

Jan Kott has discussed the representation of women by men in partially similar terms:

> In fact, femininity only exists in the eyes of men, just as blackness only exists for whites. The Onnagata portrays femininity to a much greater degree than if the actor was a woman. His femininity is the result of study by generations of actors and perhaps even more importantly generations of painters. It is at one and the same time magical and a joke, adoration and humiliation, idealization and desire.
>
> (Bassnett 1987: 236)

In comedy, however, one wonders how much magic, adoration, and idealization takes place. It should also be noted that masculinity exists in the eyes of men as well, masculinity staged for the vision of other men and, perhaps, women.

8 For more on commissioned vases, see Webster 1972: 42–62; 270–300. Only four of the twenty illustrations of comedy in Trendall and Webster 1971 specifically show male actors portraying female characters.

9 Green (1985: 105) writes:

> First, it seems that in vase-painting comic scenes are shown more literally than tragic scenes. This is especially true where representations of actors are concerned: contrast the so-called phylax vases, whether of Attic, other mainland, or South Italian Greek manufacture, with those representing tragedy. The vase painter (and by extension the audience as a whole) remained aware of the conventions of staging, just as playwrights were capable of standing back and making 'objective' comments about their stagecraft or about the costume worn. These conventions could indeed be a source of humour in themselves.

Secondary to Green's identification of the vase as an illustration of Aristophanes' *Birds* is his observation that 'the unique opportunity that the vase provides of comparing text and costume demonstrates how conscious the poet was of performance' (ibid. 118).

10 Another apparent chorus dressed as women appears in Simon 1982: fig. 6. 2. The illustration, by the Sabouroff painter on a red-figure cup dated to *c*.460 BCE, shows actors with silly expressions on their faces dressed in long pleated *chitones* and wearing pointy shoes. They pose with stylized (dancing?) gestures. Although Simon suggests that they are the chorus of a

comedy (p. 14), the men are not masked and no masks are pictured on the vase. The figures are quite clearly men – their beards are rather conspicuous – dressed as women, more in the style of the *symposion* vase, rather than as actors in a comic play. An equally interesting *symposion* vase is reproduced in Halperin 1990: 115. The vase shows male symposiasts celebrating and dressed as women (Attic red-figure cup by the Briseis Painter, signed by Brygos as potter, *c*.480–470 BCE; J. Paul Getty Museum). Halperin chose a provocative illustration. He argues (1990: 146–7) that Socrates dons a female persona to speak as Diotima in Plato's *Symposium* as part of an initiatory process, an idea akin to what I say here about the representation of women in comedy:

> The 'feminine' identity acquired by men in the course of performing rites of initiation must therefore be an incomplete identity, and its status as a fiction – as an impersonation rather than a total appropriation of 'the feminine' – must be exposed by a selective puncturing of the illusion, either by a dropping of the mask or by a thematization of its status as a mask . . . the very act of self-exposure contributes an essential element to the successful operation of the symbolic procedures whereby 'masculine' and 'feminine' identities circulate within a continuous system of male self-representation.

Diotima is not a woman, he writes, but a 'woman'; 'gender is an irreducible fiction' (ibid. 151). The *symposion* vase with illustrations of male revelers dressed as women is peripherally related to the illustration of male actors as women in comedy. The situation is similar: men gathered together representing 'women' for each other, a part of the expression and establishment of masculinity and power. A comprehensive list of such vases, along with a discussion of them as illustrations of the poet Anacreon and his followers and relevant bibliography, is in Kurtz and Boardman 1986. After a survey of the representational evidence, Boardman concludes that the dress these men wear may have been more feminine than the standard dress of Athenian males but that it is not effeminate; he suggests that it is East Greek and Ionian in origin (Kurtz and Boardman 1986: 65).

11 Of vase-painting, Dover writes: 'it was normal practice in archaic black-figure vase-painting to make men and youths black but women white' (1989: 77). Women in *Ecclesiazusae* are identified by the pale skin that an indoor life fosters; men have suntans from being outside. Stone (1980: 24–5) comments on this as being a convenience for the audience as well as an accurate ethnographic observation:

> In dramas where women were not only played by men, but in which transvestism is a favorite theme, a color code would provide a welcome point of reference. For example, a dark or ruddy mask might help the viewer to distinguish a male actor as a male character in female disguise (e.g. Mnesilochus in *Thesm.*) from a male actor as a female character.

12 See also an illustration of young men dressed as maenads with an *aulos* player, dated *c*.550 BCE in Pickard-Cambridge 1962: pl. VI a, no. 20. See also Caruso 1987.

NOTES

13 Bérard and Bron 1989 concerns the representation on vases of men playing satyrs. In a discussion of males 'transformed' into satyrs during a ritual performance, Bérard and Bron mention an illustration of a female satyr. Her female body is pictured from the waist up; she wears a pair of hairy shorts with a tail and phallos attached. Bérard and Bron (1989: 145) write:

> One of the leitmotifs of Dionysiac ceremonies surfaces here again: strange relations are established between the sexes, upsetting all the norms of the city. The intensity of the religious experience is not expressed in the same way for a woman as for a man. She is sometimes disguised as a satyr, but the artifice always remains evident; she never becomes a real satyr.

I am concerned with the representation of real women by male actors, rather than an actor's representation of a mythological, Dionysiac creature. Yet what Bérard and Bron say has relevance here. The vases discussed in this chapter show that, while a male actor might 'become' a satyr (or Dionysus himself) through the Dionysiac magic of ritual performance, an actor is not to be thought of as 'becoming' a woman.

14 The *himation*, a large rectangular piece of wool, often used as a blanket and then wrapped around the body, was draped over the *chiton* differently by men and women. Men usually wore one end draped over the left shoulder, with the rest of the cloth wrapped around the back and the right hip and with the ends brought together in the front. Women wore the cloth over the back of their heads as well (*Ecclesiazusae* 275); see Stone 1980: 155–6. On the semantics of clothing in Athens, see Geddes 1987.

15 The vase illustration here, along with others like it, receives a different interpretation from Brommer 1954 and Beazley 1931: 84. Brommer suggests that the women's heads are attached to hats worn by the men. Beazley interprets them not as masks, but rather as token disguises. He also suggests that the men here represent maenads in a pre-dramatic performance. Webster discusses the evaluations of Brommer and Beazley and writes that 'the extra-mask like the heads on heads . . . provides the audience with further information which the painter could not have given them in a realistic representation' (Webster 1956: 115). What Webster says is thus not much different from what I suggest here: the painter shows the viewer of the vase what the theater audience may have seen or understood in the performance.

16 A female mask floats above the action on several vases, all of which show a comic scene. See Trendall and Webster 1971: IV, 10 and IV, 14. Ibid. IV, 11 (Paestan kalyx-krater, c.360–350 BCE) shows Dionysus and two male characters watching a nude female acrobat; two actors wearing white female masks, which stand out quite clearly from the darker skin on their necks, watch from windows in the background. Although they are fully costumed, their role-playing is made obvious by the contrasting colors of the masks and their skin.

17 Blok 1987 is especially good at pointing out the assumptions that predetermine some scholars' assessment of ancient sources. For more information and bibliography on the social history of women in ancient Greece, see Cantarella 1987; Gould 1980; Just 1989; Pomeroy 1978.

18 The extant literary works by ancient women are collected and translated in Snyder 1989.
19 On Susarion, see Pickard-Cambridge 1962: 183–7 and Chapter 3, n. 9 below. The *Suda* attributes the introduction to drama of women as *prosopa* to Phrynichus. Even Pomeroy devotes only three pages to her discussion of the three relevant Aristophanic plays (1978: 112–14). Lévy 1976b presents an evaluation of women in Aristophanes in light of the iambic tradition of invective against women, but he refers only to the three 'women' plays and makes few general remarks about comedy. On tragedy, there is most recently the idiosyncratic and lengthy Des Bouvrie 1990. There were female figures in satyr play, yet there remains to be published a study of their nature and representation. One of the most common plots for a satyr play was the rescue of a woman from the sexual bondage of satyrs; such a play might end in the marriage of the woman to her rescuer (see Sutton 1980, esp. ch. 10).
20 The relationship between carnival and comedy is developed in Bakhtin 1965. The applicability of Bakhtin's theories to Aristophanic comedy is taken up by Carrière 1979; for a differing opinion, see Rösler 1986. Related information is discussed by Halliwell 1991. For an introduction to the use of humor for social control, specifically the subjugation of women, see Mulkay 1988, esp. ch. 8; also, Apte 1985, esp. ch. 2.
21 The claim is attractive, even if not able to be confirmed (it rests on an argument *ex silentio*: there is no definite evidence of any other such play before *Lysistrata*, so *Lysistrata* appears to be the first).
22 The order of production of these plays is not definitely known. Sommerstein 1977 argues that *Lysistrata* was produced first, at the Lenaea, and that *Thesmophoriazusae* followed at the City Dionysia; he confirms the assertions of Wilamowitz, and many scholars accept these dates (Dover 1972: 169–71; for different reasons, Hubbard 1991: 243–5). Others suggest a different order (Schmid and Stählin 1946: 204 ff.; Gelzer 1970: 1467 ff.), often because *Lysistrata*'s panhellenic wishes seem more appropriate to the City Dionysia and the exclusive literary parody of *Thesmophoriazusae* seems better suited to the Lenaea (McLeish 1980: 28). Others date *Thesmophoriazusae* to 410 BCE, after the oligarchic coup (recently E. Hall 1989b; Vickers 1989; Rhodes 1972).
23 The date of *Ecclesiazusae* is uncertain. 392 and 391 BCE are the popular scholarly suggestions, although some argue for 393 BCE. See, for example, Ussher ed. 1973: xx–xxv; Rothwell 1990: 2.
24 See, for example, Shaw 1975. A convincing counter-argument has been made by Foley 1981, who shows that Shaw's notion of the female intruder encroaching on male territory does not take into account the overlap of female and male domains in the city. For more on this equation, see Ortner 1974.
25 I will treat Zeitlin's analysis of *Thesmophoriazusae* more fully in Chapter 3. Also of interest here is Assaël 1985, which argues that Euripides portrays strong women with good, competent Athenian characters, and that Aristophanes' criticism stems from a desire to suppress such a potentially subversive message. The argument is attractive, yet it is difficult to prove conclusively that Euripides rode any wave of feminist thought in Athens, no matter how small.

NOTES

26 Dover (1989: 73) writes:

> Attic comedy generally assumes that a man who has female bodily characteristics (e.g. sparse facial hair) or behaves in ways categorized by Athenian society as feminine (e.g. wearing pretty clothes) also seeks to play a woman's part sexually in his relation with other men and is sought by them for this purpose.

An excellent recent exploration of gender and sexuality in ancient Greece is Winkler 1990, esp. ch. 2. Central to Winkler's approach (and to other recent work on ancient constructions of sexuality) is Foucault 1985.

27 Mulvey 1988 began this method of investigation. Mulvey's psychoanalytic approach has been taken since then in different directions by other critics. For further reading, see deLauretis 1984; Doane 1986: 176–83; Kaplan 1983: 1–20, 23–35.

28 Dolan, an expert on feminist literary theory, writes an excellent summary of the recent scholarship. I include a brief summary, with bibliography, only to clarify my theoretical viewpoint.

29 'The gaze in performance, although not as carefully controlled as in film, is also based in a narrative paradigm that presents gender and sexuality as a factor in the exchange of meanings between performers and spectators' (Dolan 1988: 14).

30 For details on the audience, see Pickard-Cambridge 1968, ch. 6, and esp. 263–5 for speculation on the attendance of women. Most scholars speculate that women were probably present, although they may have been restricted in some way (Arnott 1989: 5–6; Dover 1972: 16–17; Haigh 1898: 363–8; Walton 1980: 77–8).

31 I offer one example of a seemingly obvious claim about the production of meaning exclusively by men for men that deserves further consideration:

> It is natural that a comic poet should speak of his audience as male, since at Athens it was the taste and judgement of men which carried weight and determined the standing of the poet; positive reactions of approval or disapproval by women in the presence of men would not have been welcomed.
>
> (Dover 1972: 17)

32 Barber 1959 discusses the relationship between festival, role-playing, and ritual transvestism. Five of Shakespeare's comedies feature women dressed as men (*The Merchant of Venice*, *Much Ado About Nothing*, *Twelfth Night*, *Two Gentlemen of Verona*, and *As You Like It*). These plays have recently spawned a great deal of provocative criticism. My research owes a debt to the following works: Belsey 1986; Freedman 1991; Howard 1988 (with further bibliography); Jardine 1989; Rackin 1987. The theme of gender disguise is relatively common in all comedy. Closer to home, some recent American films explore cultural constructions of gender through cross-dressing; see Kuhn 1985. *Ecclesiazusae*, for example, closely follows Kuhn's account of the narrative of sexual disguise in films such as *Tootsie*, *Victor/Victoria*, and *Some Like it Hot*.

33 On the fallacious assumption that theatrical convention is passively accepted by audiences, see M. Carlson 1990: 114–15.

NOTES

1 THE REPRESENTATION OF FEMALE FIGURES IN ARISTOPHANES' PLAYS BEFORE 411 BCE

1 Henry 1988 posits a revised theory for New Comedy. Its emphasis on the importance of the courtesan to the reunification of the family offers a model for the reconsideration of the female figures in Aristophanes' plays.
2 *Acharnians* was awarded first prize at the Lenaea in 425 BCE. It is the earliest of the extant Aristophanic comedies (Aristophanes made his debut in 427 with *Banqueters*, now lost). For a comprehensive treatment of the play, see Edmunds 1980. Edmunds places a slightly different emphasis on theatricality than I do, discounting the dramatic performance of the Rural Dionysia because of Aristotelian inaccuracy. I will show that the procession is carried out as a dramatic performance not necessarily with direct or accurate reference to the festivals that form the origins of comedy.
3 Not much is known about this festival; this scene in *Acharnians* is our most complete source of information. A fertility festival, the Rural Dionysia was held in the month of Poseideon (December–January). The phallos procession, in which Dikaiopolis' slave Xanthias carries the phallos (243, 259–60), was its central feature. The festival had nothing to do with wine; the cause for its association with Dionysus is generally unknown. Each deme held this festival on separately arranged dates. For more details, see Pickard-Cambridge 1968: 42–54; Farnell 1909, vol. 5: 204; Parke 1977: 100–3. The phallic procession of the Rural Dionysia in *Acharnians* may or may not be related to the development of the festivals of Dionysus at Athens where playwrights presented their work. In *Acharnians*, the procession is presented as a kind of play-within-the-play; if the Rural Dionysia were believed, in 425 BCE, to have been the festival from which these later celebrations were derived, then the metatheatrical flavor of the scene would have been even stronger.
4 Of this festival Pickard-Cambridge (1968: 51) writes:

> It is clear from the inscriptions that the festivals also afforded the demes an opportunity to mimic the city, and to assert their identities as states within the state, by proclamations of crowns for benefactors and a reflection in little of the institutions of the city.

Now the meaning of Dikaiopolis' name bears relevance: he is 'just city'.
5 I am following Coulon 1923, vol. 1; the translations are mine. Although modern editors no longer ascribe any lines to Dikaiopolis' wife, the *editio princeps* (printed in 1498) does attribute lines 244 and 253–8 to her.
6 On this phenomenon, see Schaps 1977 and Sommerstein 1980.
7 Aristotle (*Poetics* 1449 a 12) claims that tragedy and comedy originated in improvisation, tragedy with the improvisation of poets of the dithyrambic chorus, comedy with the leaders of the phallic song and dance, two types of poetry still performed in Aristotle's day in many cities. For modern scholarship on the origins of comedy, a complex subject with a lengthy history itself, see Pickard-Cambridge 1962: 132–94; Giangrande 1963.
8 Dikaiopolis' description of the family reveals a not unusual definition of his wife, who will appear later on. He says to Amphitheus: 'You, taking the eight drachmas, make a peace treaty with the Lacedaimonians for me

alone and my children, and my consort' (ἐμοὶ σὺ ταυτασὶ λαβὼν ὀκτὼ δραχμὰς / σπονδὰς πόησαι πρὸς Λακεδαιμονίους μόνῳ / καὶ τοῖσι παιδίοισι καὶ τῇ πλάτιδ·, 130–2). Dikaiopolis divides the parties interested in peace into three parts: himself, his children, and 'the one nearest to me' (ἡ πλᾶτις, wife, from πέλας, 'nearby', also related to ὁ πελάτης, 'one who approaches', such as a client or a dependent (LSJ)). Van Daele translates ἡ πλᾶτις as 'ma chère compagne'. Sommerstein 1984b translates it as 'consort'. Although Sommerstein notes the rarity of the word and its incongruity next to παιδίοισι (1984b: 164 *ad* 132), its sense is quite clear: she is defined in relation to him. Dikaiopolis' definition is traditional: 'Elle se détermine et se différencie par rapport à l'homme et non celui-ci par rapport à elle' (de Beauvoir 1949: 15). Later on Dikaiopolis calls her his wife (γυνή, 262), but it is worthwhile to notice that his word choice neglects their legal and emotional relationship. Dikaiopolis is the center of things, surrounded by his family. Even the syntax of his statement emphasizes him alone: ἐμοί and μόνῳ frame the request; subsequent mention of his children and wife seems like an appendix. Despite its strangeness, ἡ πλᾶτις calls more attention to Dikaiopolis than to his wife, for it points to him through her. At the risk of positing an overly construed point, the position of his wife at the edges of his universe (even further removed than the children) nevertheless grants her a good position for observation.

9 When these meanings are revealed, the girl says, 'Mother, hand up the phallos (soup-ladle) so that I might pour the semen (soup) over this vagina (little cake) here'. The ladle represents the phallos, source and container of the liquid. Henderson argues that ἔτνος refers to *secreta muliebra* (1975: 144–5). But the girl only pours the sauce from the ladle; she does not supply it. Together with the lines of Trygaeus' daughter in *Peace* (discussed below), the lines spoken here constitute an apparent anomaly: unmarried women of marriageable age, commonly referred to as 'maidens', never speak in fifth-century comedy. Dikaiopolis' and Trygaeus' daughters must be quite young, perhaps somewhere between 5 and 12 years old.

10 Potential sexuality is important; she is in preparation for the role of wife and mother. Parker even prefaces his translation of these lines with stage directions that suggest Dikaiopolis' distress at the girl's 'gawky adolescence' (1961: 25). That adolescence suggests imminent sexual maturity.

11 βλέπουσα θυμβροφάγον, 'looking as though you have eaten savory', is an obscure phrase, but it seems to suggest that she pucker her lips in an exaggerated fashion, to look prim and proper instead of attractive. Sommerstein suggests 'an acid, unfriendly look' (1984b: 168 *ad* 254), since it would be inappropriate for girls like her to smile in public; Starkie wants her to look prim and, like any decent woman, not call too much attention to herself (1909: 61 *ad* 254).

12 See also Sommerstein: 'Throughout the passage, Dicaiopolis pretends that the procession is to be watched by a large crowd' (1984b: 168 *ad* 254).

13 Another young girl is the subject of the phallic hymn that Dikaiopolis sings during the procession. Dikaiopolis fantasizes about meeting a young woodland girl stealing wood and 'seizing her about the middle, throwing her down, joining together, and deflowering her' (271–5). Here is a vision

of what will come to be a typical comic female: crafty (as a thief), mute, the center of a dramatic presentation, and the focus of overbearing male sexuality. Dikaiopolis does not present her with what might be thought of as a particularly pleasant sexual encounter; he expresses his sexual desires bluntly and aggressively. Still, they are only desires: we never see them actually carried out. Dikaiopolis is in fact quite self-centered; he makes the peace for himself and does not always think of its repercussions for others. This fantasy girl confirms a status quo in the relations between men and women in Dikaiopolis' plan. For Dikaiopolis, a utopian vision of peace (and sex) does not necessarily include only the females in his family. See Dover 1972: 63–5, for a thorough analysis of the Megarian scene. I differ from him on a few points.

14 The Megarian tells his daughters: "Ἀκούετε δή, ποτέχετ' ἐμὶν τὰν γαστέραν'. The usual idiom is 'προσέχω τὸν νοῦν' (LSJ; cf. *Knights* 1014; *Clouds* 575; *Birds* 688). The girls speak and understand regular language and they are small; my guess is that they are very young, between 4 and 6 years old, perhaps.

15 MacMathúna writes that μηχανή is the broadest term Aristophanes uses for a trick, 'a "way out" or means of rescue for the person employing it, regardless of the nature of the device' (1971: 1); he applies it to the stratagem which does not involve deceit. The Megarian's plan is clearly a μηχανή that involves deceit, a trick that is the basis for the performance that the Megarian puts on with his costumed daughters. MacMathúna offers a stimulating analysis of the scene and a discussion of μηχανή but does not mention the theatrical overtones of the Megarian's μηχανή. Yet he concludes that three charades, with the Megarian, the Boeotian, and the Informer, 'illustrate three main strands of Aristophanic comedy, the vulgar, the intellectual parody, and the political' (1971: 40). Females are an integral feature of all three: they are the necessary sexual ingredient of vulgar comedy, the personifications of intellectual parody, and the medium of political comedy.

16 The idea of a silly, vulgar Megarian trick was proverbial. Aristotle (*Poetics* 1448 a 29) explains and rejects the claim that the Megarians are responsible for the development of comedy. The Megarians in Greece claim that it developed when they formed a democracy. The Megarians in Sicily point out that the comic poet Epicharmus came from their island. Pickard-Cambridge generalizes that although the details and the possibility of the Megarians' invention of comedy or of their inventing the claim itself are sketchy, there must be some vestige of truth in them; at least there was a tradition of this belief in Aristotle's day (1962: 178–87). What matters here is that we recognize the allusion to their claims and acknowledge the dramatic context of the scene.

17 Stone argues that the girls here put on real costumes, pigskins with hooves still attached and half-masks fashioned as snouts, since the verbs the Megarian uses to order them to put on the costumes are περίθεσθε and ἀμφίθεσθε, words suited to the 'putting around' of garments (Stone 1980: 415; after Starkie 1909: 434 *ad* 35). Her comment is important and, if correct, confirms Aristophanes' conception of this scene as a play-within-the-play complete with new costumes for the female characters.

NOTES

18 There is also a pun here on the word for little girl, κόρη. Κόρη sounds like χοῖρος, which has a suspicious etymology (from χῆρ, cf. Lat. *horreo*) that makes the joke even more aggressive towards women (Chantraine 1980, vol. 4. 2: 1266–7; Frisk 1970, vol. 2: 1108). The pun does not exist in English. Radermacher 1940 disputes a possible pun on χοῖρος/κόρη at *Frogs* 337–8, but with the play on words here, it would seem that the pun is a usual one, especially in reference to sacrifices to Demeter and Persephone.

19 The obscenity of this scene is not in contention, but a clear interpretation of lines 786–7 makes the crudeness of the Megarian's metaphor more apparent. Dikaiopolis complains that a piggy like this is not able to be sacrificed because it lacks a tail; the Megarian replies: 'Well, it is young still, but when it grows up to pig-hood, it will have a big, fat, red one'. Dover believes that he refers to the phallos that the girl will attract as an adult (1972: 67). There is no indication, however, that this tail (κέρκον, 785) belongs to anyone but the piggy; it just as likely refers to the girl's mature genitalia. Cf. *Clouds* 538; *Peace* 927, 1531 for the adjectives of size and color (Henderson 1975: 128). Sommerstein also comments on the immature size of this χοῖρος (1984b: 196 *ad* 785). There is no solid proof to back up the speculation that a joke is being made here about the *kerkos* belonging to the boy actor who will grow up to play adult roles (and wear the comic *phallos*), but I call attention to that possibility anyway. It is reasonable to assume that boys would have played children's roles, since a violation of the male actor convention seems unlikely (so Stone 1980: 348). Acting appears to have been a profession that ran in families; perhaps young boys learned to act by playing such minor roles as children (on acting families, see Sutton 1987). While this speculation cannot be verified, a parallel exists in the theatrical conventions of Renaissance England, where boys played the parts of women early in their careers in preparation for later adult male roles: see, for example, Rackin 1987.

20 ἐρεβίνθους, phallos; ἰσχάδας, σῦκα: genitals in general (Henderson 1975: 118; cf. *Peace* 1350, *Ecclesiazusae* 708).

21 Pigs were sacrificed to Demeter at Eleusis and at the Thesmophoria. Despite what Dikaiopolis thinks about sacrificing pigs to Aphrodite, they were associated with her at the Adonia, although the three festivals are not at all related (Burkert 1985: 242–6). Pigs were sacrificed to Aphrodite in a few places: Argos (Athen. 3. 96 a), Cyprus (Antiphanes, fr. 126) and others (Strabo 9. 5. 17). The scholion for 793, however, claims that many Greeks did not sacrifice pigs to Aphrodite because of their sinister associations with Adonis' death (Sommerstein 1984b: 196 *ad* 793).

22 'She represents the sexual nature of Dikaiopolis' (and the poet's) conception of peacetime' (Henderson 1975: 61). The symbolic link between women and peace made in Western culture is an obvious and traditional one here. In the Iliad, Hektor expresses the equation 'war is of men as peace is of women' in his well-known request of Andromache:

> ἀλλ' εἰς οἶκον ἰοῦσα τὰ σ' αὐτῆς ἔργα κόμιζε,
> ἱστόν τ' ἠλακάτην τε, καὶ ἀμφιπόλοισι κέλευε
> ἔργον ἐποίχεσθαι· πόλεμος δ' ἄνδρεσσι μελήσει

NOTES

πᾶσι, μάλιστα δ' ἐμοί, τοὶ Ἰλίῳ ἐγγεγάασσιν.
(6.490–3)

Go therefore back to our house, and take up your own work,
the loom and the distaff, and see to it that your handmaidens
ply their work also, but the men must see to the fighting,
all men who are the people of Ilion, but I beyond all others.
(Lattimore 1951: 166)

Here in *Acharnians*, Dikaiopolis clearly links war with men and peace with women when he agrees to give the bride's attendant part of his 'peace' wine since, as a woman, she had no part in the war (161–2). *Lysistrata*, of course, revolves completely around this symbolic link, eventually reversing and dissolving the Homeric formula (538). There is a great deal of modern scholarship on the equating of women with peace and men with war, an equation which certainly continues to be a strong component of Western thought today. See, for instance, Macdonald 1987; for a discussion of the equation, and of contemporary images from the nuclear disarmament movement that link women and peace, see the first half of Carroll 1987.

23 *Knights* won the first prize at the Lenaea. For a fuller analysis of the play with emphasis on metatheatricality, see Engle 1983; also Bennett and Tyrrell 1990 on the *pharmakos*.

24 Sommerstein (1981: 213 *ad* 1306) notes:

these ships think and talk like women, and sometimes they are described in language similar to that which would be used of women. So here this virgin ship, which has yet to make her 'maiden' voyage, is spoken of in terms appropriate to a human virgin 'who had never come near a man'.

25 The text does not indicate how the Spondai are clothed, but most often the silent female figures present at the end of an Aristophanic comedy appear to inspire the sexual rejuvenation of the hero with their nude bodies. They would have been played by male actors in costumes representative of women's bodies (Stone 1980: 147–50).

26 *Clouds* was performed at the City Dionysia in 423 BCE. The text of *Clouds* that exists today is apparently the second version of the play. After the original production, placed third in the competition, Aristophanes revised it and sent it out as a written text (Dover 1972: 103–5). See also Hubbard 1986.

27 I have followed Dover 1968.

28 Leo Strauss concludes that the Clouds function as the equivalent of the Muses: 'the clouds are the goddesses of imitation and therefore the natural teachers of all imitative or likeness-making arts, and hence in particular of the art of speaking' (1966: 18).

29 Bergren 1983 establishes this in Hesiod, Homer, and Stesichorus, especially in reference to the figure of Helen, but her argument is limited to archaic writers. Woman's ability to deceive through language relates directly to her knowledge of the truth and to her relationship with the Muses, the female divinities who know the truth and how to say things that seem like the truth, an ability that men adopt later. Her words may be applied to the Cloud-chorus in *Clouds* as well: 'In these figures we see a degree of

NOTES

knowledge attributed to the female that results in a capacity for double speech, for both truth and the imitation of truth, a paradoxical speech hopelessly ambiguous to anyone whose knowledge is less than the speaker's' (Bergren 1983: 70). I have used West 1966 and 1978.

30 I have translated some of the rhetorical terms in line with Dover's notes (1968: 142–3 *ad* 317–18) and LSJ. Κρούειν: to strike 'an audience with a telling point or an opponent with an argument which discomfits him'; καταλαμβάνειν: to 'check' 'an unfavorable reaction from the audience or an argument in which an opponent trusts'.

31 This concept of femininity as changeable or unstable seems basic to Greek thought. Semonides (7), for example, discusses the mind of woman in a similar vein. He compares woman's mind to several animals: a pig, a dog, a horse, etc. At one point he says that woman is as changeable as the sea. Semonides also does not conceive of women as simply 'being women'. For him, woman, and her mind, is always 'like' something; he cannot say 'Woman is' or 'Woman is X'.

32 *Wasps* won second prize at the Lenaea. For a fuller discussion of the play, see the introduction to MacDowell 1971. The politics of the play are discussed in Konstan 1985.

33 Sommerstein says that this means that he looks 'like a woman in acute distress' (1983: 241 *ad* 1413). In Greek mythology, Ino was the sister of Semele, the mother of Dionysus. When Semele died before giving birth to Dionysus, Zeus sewed the baby up in his thigh. When he was born, he was given to Ino to care for. Driven mad by a jealous Hera, Ino leapt into the sea.

34 *Peace* was performed at the City Dionysia and won the second prize. For a more comprehensive analysis of the play, see Newiger 1980.

35 I have followed Coulon 1923, vol. 2. The scholiast quotes two lines from Euripides' *Aeolus* (Euripides fr. 17). The girl also puns on the proverbial insult, 'to go to the crows', and displays an Homeric vocabulary with μεταμώνιος (*Iliad* 4. 363; *Odyssey* 2. 98; 18. 332, 392; 19. 143). See Merry 1900: 12–13; Platnauer 1964: 76 *ad* 114; Rau 1967: 92–3; Rogers 1913a: 16–18; and Sommerstein 1984c: 140.

36 In explaining the problem with identifying the nature of these figures, Whitman (1964: 111) writes:

> Opora (Harvest) and her companion Theoria (Embassy) are figures which, like Demos in the *Knights*, waver tantalizingly between the abstractions which they represent and the attractions of the way they are represented. Peace is herself transcendent, and was probably represented by a statue; her two attendants, however, prefigure respectively the immanent aspects of private and public peace, or more accurately, peace in the country and peace in the city. Such female figures form a regular part of the Aristophanean exodus, though not always with such explicitly allegorical significance.

Although they are attractive women, the two aspects cannot really be separated. Whitman's translation of *theoria* slightly misrepresents her name: θεωρία means being a spectator, or viewing, although it can also be used to identify a delegation of ambassadors. Her mask is, in fact,

NOTES

apparently quite a vision (534). Since she smells of the theater and the accompaniments of dramatic festivals (530–2), it seems appropriate to understand her as unambiguously allied with the spectacle of theater.

37 This must have made quite an impression: Eupolis, in Autolykos (fr. 62 *PCG*), and Plato Comicus, in *Nikai* (fr. 86 *PCG*), both made fun of the statue that represented Eirene here.

38 Newiger even admits that this is only possible because of their sex: 'And the manner in which the Council could "concern itself" with the young female character, Theoria, embodiment of the festival, is reflected once more in sexual imagery made possible by Theoria's sex' (1980: 226).

39 The scene in which Trygaeus and his friends pull Eirene out of the cave also appears to recall a satyr-play by Sophocles, 'Pandora, or the Hammerswingers', illustrated on a vase dated to *c*.460 BCE (Brommer 1959: 51–2, fig. 49). In this painting, Pandora rises up from the earth and Prometheus stands behind her, holding a torch in either hand, while hammer-wielding satyrs dance around them. Thus some genre parody cannot be ruled out. Donald Kagan writes that Aristophanes' *Peace* shows Athenians ready for peace and with worries 'far from their minds' (1974: 348). On the contrary, the figure of Eirene here is beautiful and desirous on the surface, but perhaps just a mute statue whose voice, Hermes, may trick her people. Peace is unsettling simply because it may not last and Athens may be disappointed.

40 *Birds* was performed at the City Dionysia, where it placed second. *Birds* has proven to be one of Aristophanes' most popular and intriguing plays. For fuller treatment of its play with language, fantasy, and the polis, see Konstan 1990; on the play of language and theater, see Dobrov 1990.

41 Tereus, married to Procne, daughter of Pandion king of Athens, raped her sister Philomela and cut out her tongue so that she would not tell Procne. Philomela wove her story into the illustrations on a tapestry, however, and in revenge Procne murdered her son and served him to Tereus. Philomela was turned into a swallow, Procne into a nightingale, and Tereus into a hoopoe. On the popularity of the Tereus and Procne story and cult, see Burkert 1983: 179–85. Pausanias records a sculpture of Procne and Itys placed on the Acropolis and dedicated by Alcamenes (1. 24. 3). The origin of this statue is unknown, but some scholars have speculated that it was dedicated in honor of the success and popularity of Sophocles' play *Tereus*. The date of *Tereus* is also unknown, but it can be placed between 430 and 414 (the date of *Birds*). The few fragments of Sophocles' play indicate that Procne delivered speeches lamenting the traditional treatment and roles of women in marriage, reminiscent of the sentiments of Euripides' Medea. As part of a parody, perhaps, Aristophanes has made the otherwise murderous and opinionated Procne conspicuously silent. On the possibility of Sophoclean parody, see Hofmann 1976: 106. Sutton 1984: 127–32 collects the fragments of *Tereus*.

42 Although Pozzi's desire to retain the manuscript spelling 'Peisthetairos' is reasonable, I follow the generally accepted 'Peisetairos' as the spelling of the hero's name (see Pozzi 1986: 119).

43 The text is cited from Coulon ed. 1928.

44 Although sometimes κυνῆ means phallos, it is also an hetaira name (Henderson 1975: 133; cf. *Wasps* 1032; *Peace* 755; *Knights* 765). Dearden

believes that this is just a joke about the elaborate head-dress that the actor must be wearing; perhaps it looks like a ship or has wings of some sort (1976: 119). If so, then the joke insults Iris with the obscene pun and also calls attention to her costume.

45 I tend to agree with Henderson (1975: 85):

> The arrival of Iris, messenger girl of Zeus (1202 ff.), provides Peisthetairus with an opportunity to demonstrate both his sexual superiority over the gods and his heroic rejuvenation. Where the gods had been free in the past to have their way with mortal women, Peisthetairus now turns the tables on them by capturing and hubristically mistreating their pretty envoy. From the first, Peisthetairus whittles away Iris' air of superiority by means of sexual *double entendres* (1204, 1206, 1214 ff.).

46 The suggestion that Prometheus' presence in *Birds* parodies a previous treatment of the Prometheus story has been posited, most often in reference to an Aeschylean version of the myth. The passage in question probably contains allusions to Aeschylus' *Prometheus Bound*. Herington 1963 reopens the case for a conscious parody of Aeschylus' *Prometheia* in this part of *Birds*, and summarizes the history of the debate. Rau 1967 reviews Herington's article and stresses the cunning of the Hesiodic Prometheus over the stubborn Aeschylean Prometheus: 'von der für den tragischen Prometheus wesentlichen *trotzigen* Auflehnung ist nichts zu bemerken, wohl aber zeichnet sich der Aristophanische Prometheus durch die *List* des Hesiodischen aus' (1967: 176). Hofmann 1976 points out the connections this Prometheus shares with both his Aeschylean and Hesiodic counterparts. Recently Auger 1979 has suggested that the scene recalls the Hesiodic Prometheus and the Hesiodic pattern of marriage and sacrifice that leads to the iron age. It is from her article concerning the role of women in the Aristophanic utopia that I form my ideas here.

47 Dover (1972: 142) writes that:

> since he [Prometheus] was worshipped at Athens in Aristophanes' time, it was emotionally necessary for the Athenians either to refrain from asking themselves whether Zeus and Prometheus were still enemies or to believe that Prometheus had been released from his bondage and reconciled to Zeus.

This ambiguity concerning the status of the feud between Prometheus and Zeus is just what fuels the doubts about Prometheus' advice. That an Athenian audience would have to think about the issue at all is significant because Peisetairos himself does not think about it, even though he recognizes Prometheus' signature craftiness (προμηθικῶς, 1511).

48 Βασίλεια appears usually in reference to goddesses, princesses, or queens (e.g. *Peace* 794; Aeschylus, *Persians* 623, *Agamemnon* 84; Euripides, *Electra* 988; Homer, *Odyssey* 4. 770; Pindar, *Nemean* 1. 59 (LSJ)). Consequently, some scholars choose to see her simply as a princess. Reckford sees her as the princess who marries the hero in a fairy tale (1987: 529 n. 73). Other scholars have linked her with several divinities. Sheppard 1909 argues that she is the Basilissa to whom a mountain is dedicated, along with Dionysus, and so that we are to think of her as an imaginary goddess, 'the consort of

comedy'. Cook suggests that the marriage between Peisetairos and Basileia parodies the hieros gamos of Zeus and Hera, which makes sense because Peisetairos will be taking Zeus' place and so by analogy Basileia assumes Hera's place (Cook 1913). Newiger believes she is a goddess of some sort allied with Zeus (1957: 91–9; on the literal representation of a metaphor on stage, see also Newiger 1980). Since she distributes Zeus' thunderbolts, Whitman writes about her as though she were Athena and appeared on stage complete with helmet and aegis (1964: 196–7). Hofmann cites three possible models for the marriage of Peisetairos and Basileia: the ritual wedding of Dionysos and the wife of the Archon Basileus at the Anthesteria, the apotheosis of Heracles and his union with Hebe, and the *hieros gamos* of Zeus and Hera (1976: 145–7). Βασίλεια has also been considered a personification of royalty through her link with the word βασιλεία, 'hereditary kingship, dominion' (LSJ); as such, she represents Peisetairos' assumption of Zeus' throne. Apropos of the difference between Βασίλεια and βασιλεία, Pozzi's suggestion (1986: 127 n. 25) is sensible:

> Yet *Basíleia* must evoke *basileíâ* and the ambiguity serves as a clue to her role. Peisthetairos receives the scepter, symbol of the supreme rule, and marries the goddess who once sat by Zeus and will hence be his own *paredros* (1752), thus becoming a god himself.

Nothing prevents her figure from combining the attributes of both the goddess and the abstract noun.

49 As Auger points out, she is not given as a gift, she is gained through extortion (1979: 84). Auger's final point is that Aristophanes borrows the Hesiodic myth to subvert it: the gift of a woman in *Birds* (and in *Peace*) does not so much define the human condition as it allows Peisetairos to join the gods (ibid.). But I argue that the play also borrows Hesiodic ambivalence towards woman and Prometheus, through the acquisition of Basileia, which makes Peisetairos' rule not necessarily any better than Zeus'. Konstan 1990 also senses some uncertainty at the end of the play, but for different reasons.

50 Stone even suggests 'that a transparent *chiton* or *nebris* may have been added over the grotesque padding to produce a ridiculous, mock-sexy image' (Stone 1980: 303).

2 WOMEN AS WOMEN, MEN AS MEN: *LYSISTRATA*

1 A recent example comes from the back jacket of Sommerstein's edition of *Lysistrata* (1990):

> It is astonishing to think that this play was first performed exactly 2,400 years ago, because of all of Aristophanes' great comedies, *Lysistrata* seems to speak most clearly to our own age. It could perhaps be described as the world's first and indeed still the world's greatest feminist drama.

2 'In the *Lysistrata* we find a *play* instead of a collection of single scenes; a play informed by a single idea, and a plot in which each link in the chain is forged upon the preceding' (Grene 1937: 122). See also Gelzer 1975; for a

brief summary of scholarly admiration for the play's structure, see Henderson 1987b: xxvi.

3 Although Rosellini 1979 argues for a staging of femininity, I will show that the play is equally a staging of masculinity. After all, the phallos is the most salient feature of the play; Henderson (1975: 98) writes:

> The men in the play are characterized by their phalluses, from Lysistrata's first revelation of the plan by πέους (cock) in 124, to its glorious realization in the later spectacle of the men trying vainly to conceal their monstrous erections and psychic desperation.

See also Whitman 1964: 209.

4 There is, for example, no mention of the apparent originality of the plot in Dover 1972, a book which is widely regarded as the best introduction to Aristophanes. Henderson, the strongest proponent of the possibility that *Lysistrata* is the first ancient Greek comic play to feature women in central roles, never makes anything of this assertion interpretively and writes that 'the appearance of a heroine was unusual and perhaps a novelty: although female choreutai were not uncommon in comedy there are no earlier examples of a female protagonist like Lysistrata' (1987b: xxviii); see also Henderson 1980: 170; 1987a: 107. Recently, Dillon 1987 has proposed a reason for the innovation: the Spartan investment of Dekeleia in 413 BCE and the subsequent need for attention to Athenian defenses.

5 The fragments of Aristophanes' *Women Pitching Tents* (dated to sometime after 420 BCE) indicate that the play concerns women who set up tents to watch and perhaps judge a performance of some sort. Unfortunately, exact details of the plot and the date of this play are both unknown. A brief discussion of the fragments appears in N. Slater 1990b; see also Henderson 1987b; Richter 1934. Aristophanes wrote a *Danaids* around 420 BCE; he also wrote a *Lemnian Women* (*c*.413 or 412) and a *Phoenician Women* (*c*.409), so it appears that he was at least working with the idea of women as central to comedy prior to the time of *Lysistrata*. For a discussion of the relationship between Aristophanes' *Lemnian Women* and *Lysistrata*, see Martin 1987: 101–5. For information on the fragments of Old Comedy, see Kock 1888); Kassel and Austin (eds) 1983–91, *et al.*). Among the known titles of comedies dated before 411 BCE that indicate the presence of women on stage in some capacity are Cratinus' *Thracian Women* (442) and *Delian Maidens* (424). Pherecrates wrote two plays with women at the center, much in the tradition of *Lysistrata*. While the plot of *Old Women* (date unknown) remains unclear, fragment 34 seems to indicate that at some point in the play, a peace treaty was established, perhaps between the women and the men. In 413 Pherecrates wrote *The Kitchen, or The All-night Festival*, which probably parodied such a midnight celebration and may have featured some female characters. Fragment 64 reveals a debate about the proper jobs for men and women. The most well-known of the fragmentary comedies which appear to have used females is *Cities* (422 BCE) by Eupolis. In this play there is an allegorized marriage of the allied cities to Athens. The play seems to have had a chorus of women who represented these cities (frs 206, 231–3). The plot also apparently included parodies of certain marriage customs (frs 213, 229, 240). After the productions in 411

BCE of *Lysistrata* and *Thesmophoriazusae* (which does not have female protagonists proper, but rather features characters who disguise themselves as women throughout the play), Pherecrates wrote *Sovereignty* (410 BCE, although the dating of this play is uncertain; see Edmonds 1957: 259). This play shows signs of Aristophanic influence: the women are described as saviors of the city (fr. 187 Kock; cf. *Lysistrata* 29–30). Sometime between 410 and 404, Theopompus wrote *Women in the Army*, the details of which are unknown. Philyllius wrote a *Cities* also, perhaps in 411. The details of this play are unclear. Strattis wrote a *Phoenician Women* (409). In 404, Cephisodorus wrote *Amazons*. At about the same time as Aristophanes' *Ecclesiazusae* (392 or 391), Nicochares wrote a *Lemnian Women* (393). Both Philyllius and Theopompus wrote their own versions of *The Festival of Aphrodite* (388 or 387), around the time of Aristophanes' *Ploutus* (388).

6 Many of the extant tragedies prior to *Lysistrata* feature female protagonists: Aeschylus' *Agamemnon*, and even *Eumenides* (458 BCE); Sophocles' *Antigone* (441), *Electra* and *Trachiniae* (dates unknown, but thought to be early); Euripides' *Alcestis* (438), *Medea* (431), *Hippolytus* (428), *Trojan Women* (415), *Helen* (412). The dearth of specific material from satyr plays prevents any comprehensive statement about the portrayal of women in that genre and its relationship to the portrayal of women in comedy. We do know that one common satyr-plot was the rescue of a woman (Sutton 1980: 147; e.g. perhaps Euripides' *Helen* and *Andromeda*), and so women must have been represented in these plays, but how is just beyond our present reach. Sophocles also presented satyr plays with the titles *Pandora* and *Nausicaä*. If Euripides' *Alcestis* can be used as an example along with other dramas like *Iphigeneia among the Taurians* and *Helen*, it shows that Euripides, as we might expect, featured women in different sorts of tricky and deceptive roles in his pro-satyric works also.

7 Unfortunately, no source for ancient acting techniques exists. We can only surmise that ancient actors, like their modern counterparts, studied for their roles in part by observing each others' work, and that they used the performances and styles of others as a guide for their own performances. See Aristotle, *Poetics* 1461 b 33–5, where the actor Mynniscus criticizes the performance of another actor; such criticism implies observation and study. In support of this supposition, I offer the words of N. Slater, from a paper on the growth of the concept of 'actor' in ancient Greece (1990c: 389–90):

> The narrowing in the choice of tragic subjects which seems to begin in the course of the fifth century may be related to the developing skills of the actors. Aristotle says that some myths are better suited to tragedy than others. One can only speculate that acting plays a part here. One representation of Orestes can build on another, both histrionically as well as poetically. The urn supposedly containing Orestes' ashes is as much a creation of performance as of poetry, if not more. How an actor realizes a scene on stage creates just as much anxiety of influence for future performers as do the words of the text. . . . Thus as the storehouse of myths for tragedy begins to contract ever so slightly, the actors begin to portray characters whom other actors have portrayed

NOTES

before. As this process accelerates, it creates the standards by which quality of acting can be judged and actors typed in their abilities to represent certain kinds of characters.

Slater hypothesizes about the continued performance of tragic characters in a way that relates inversely to my hypothesis about *Lysistrata*: just as there were many previous portrayals of Orestes (or Heracles, for example), so there were no previous Lysistratas to exert influence on the comic actor. Again, acting styles in satyr play may have influenced comic actors also, but we cannot know to what extent and in what fashion. Certainly, if women were usually mute and/or waiting to be rescued in satyr plays, then they influenced the composition and performance of a woman like Lysistrata very little.

8 Apropos of tragedy, Bassi (1989: 22–3) has written that

> the representation of women was perhaps the greatest task of illusion with which the playwright was confronted. . . . We know, . . . in general, how a mortal woman looks and sounds. The costume, mask, speech patterns, and gestures of the male actor playing a female must therefore perform a more arduous task of mimetic deception . . . the more the female character is meant to be like a mortal woman, the more difficult it is for the male actor to be able to play her role convincingly.

The same rule holds true for comedy. The relationship between the female and imitation in tragedy is clearly and forcefully discussed by Zeitlin 1981. Zeitlin argues elsewhere that mimesis is 'the art of imitation through which characters are rendered lifelike, and plot and action offer an adequate representation of reality. Yet mimesis also focuses attention on the status of theater as illusion, disguise, double-dealing, and pretense' (1985: 84). Sometimes scholars have used the difficulty of the representation of women by men to justify the other conventions of dramatic costume, namely the mask and the body-hiding clothing: men needed the mask, for example, in order to represent women in the first place (see, for instance, Haigh 1898: 274; Webster 1970: 35–6).

9 While female characters in the play may express, at times, the sentiments of real Athenian women (for example, about giving birth to sons who must go to war: *Lysistrata* 588–90; 651), that the representation of them was realistic in any accurate historical sense seems unlikely. Actors in Old Comedy wore padded and wrinkled sleeves and leggings underneath their costumes, as well as pads on their bellies and rear ends. They also wore masks (a mimetic necessity as well as a dramatic convention). Henderson points out that over this padding the women's clothing would have been representative of what such women wore in real life (1987b: xliv). On costumes for female characters, see Stone 1980: 297–308.

10 Critics are hardly in agreement upon this matter, however. Whitman writes that 'the role [of Lysistrata] can be played properly only by an actress of singular grace and charm' (1964: 202). Arnott, on the other hand, suggests (1989: 87) that

> casting would have worked against such realism: the female parts were played by men. This prevailing masculinity seems to have affected the

NOTES

writing. We notice that the principal female characters are, at least by Greek standards and probably by ours also, highly masculine.

On the basic premise that dramatic 'illusion as a psychological phenomenon was entirely alien to Greek theatrical audiences (and that the use of the term with reference to Greek drama is an anachronism)', see Sifakis 1971: 7. Sifakis goes on to outline a theory of realistic drama and argues that Greek drama, particularly comedy, was not realistic to begin with.

11 Aristophanes' interest in metatheatricality has become an increasingly popular topic for scholars. Among those whose work intersects the boundaries of gender impersonation, and which has influenced my own, are Kowzan 1983; Muecke 1977; N. Slater 1985 and 1990b; Taplin 1986; and Zeitlin 1981 and 1985. For my purposes, questions of both breaking the dramatic illusion and direct audience address are somewhat peripheral (see Bain 1977). My definition of metatheatricality encompasses more a calling attention to the trappings of theater as theater and the implicit or explicit likening of life to dramatic performance. For instance, see the now classic Abel 1963. Muecke (1977: 55) writes quite aptly:

> drama requires a twofold reaction from the spectator, who must on the one hand be imaginatively involved in the fiction which is being presented, and on the other detached enough to allow him to 'read' or 'decode' the play according to the rules of theatrical discourse.

12 A story about Polus of Aegina, a popular actor in the fourth century, offers an example:

> Soon after the death of a favorite son, he happened to be acting the part of Electra in the play of Sophocles. In the scene in which Electra takes in her hands the urn supposed to contain the ashes of Orestes, and pours forth a lamentation over his death, Polus came on stage with the urn containing the ashes of his own son, and holding it in his hands proceeded to act the scene with such profound depth of feeling as to produce the greatest impression of grief upon the audience.
>
> (Gell. *NA* 7. 5, cited in Haigh 1898: 316–17)

See also Figures 1–4.

13 The question of whether the male actor significantly affects the representation of Lysistrata raises, for me, an unanswerable historical question: who played Lysistrata? We know that the *didaskalos* was Kallistratos (*hypothesis* 1; MacDowell 1982), who had produced Aristophanes' *Banqueters* (427 BCE), *Babylonians* (426), *Acharnians*, and *Birds*. Otherwise, we know nothing definite about the production, festival, or prize received (Henderson 1987b: xv–xvi). There is no evidence to point to Aristophanes as the main comic actor here as there is in *Acharnians*, for example; on that play and Aristophanes as Dikaiopolis, see Foley 1988. While comic poets once played the protagonists in their own plays, by 411 this practice had largely stopped. Acting eventually became a profession separate from playwriting:

> Thus in the early fifth century, actors existed primarily in relation to the piece they enacted. Their performance was not separable from the

overall performance of the drama. Gradually, this began to change. We can describe a parallel evolution in which their part of the drama increased in both size and complexity without yet determining causality between the two. It is only logical to assume that, insofar as the victorious poets tended to employ the same actors, at first in subordinate roles, then later as protagonists, the actors' skills improved apace. At some point the poets ceased to act, in recognition of the fact that mimetic skill was now a significant factor in the success or failure of the piece as a whole.

(N. Slater 1990c: 389)

Ghiron-Bistagne summarizes the historical information (1976: 136–54).

14 Foley comes to a similar conclusion from a different perspective: 'the women have not, like their dangerous sisters in tragedy, truly crossed from their enclosed domestic world into an unconfined public one but have conducted their intrusion still metaphorically contained by the boundaries and values proper to respectable women' (1977: 7). Although the women in *Lysistrata* assume the traditionally male role of establishing public policy, they do not cross over completely into the realm of male identity; rather, they carry out their plan by enacting a concentrated femininity.

15 The absurdity of holding a sex strike at home when the men are away at war in the first place has been well noted. Henderson (1987b: 75) argues that Lysistrata proceeds with the plan under 'comic logic':

having secured the wives' agreement about the complaint (the war has made sexual partners scarce), Lysistrata proceeds to offer a plan based on the opposite assumption (husbands are at home)... Henceforth we are to imagine the husbands to be at home ...

While a certain amount of absurd impossibility is always central to Aristophanes' comic sense, my theory alleviates the need for such logic. Lysistrata's plan proceeds under the logic that posits 'women will be women' and 'men will be men', or 'if women are women (A), then men will be men (B)'. She provides for (A) and (B) follows, even if a slightly ironic rearrangement of roles is required. Martin discusses the problem of 'comic logic' and suggests a way of looking at *Lysistrata* in relation to the myth and cult of the Lemnian women that also removes the need for such logic (1987: 83).

16 Hdt. 4. 110–17 recounts ancient beliefs about the Amazons (see esp. 110 and 117). Apropos of the depiction of women in ancient Greek literature in general, Herodotus' account of the Sauromantian women (who, he claims, have descended from the Amazons) includes several of the elements common to the characterization of women in comedy. He claims that the Amazons arrived at the cliffs of Lake Maeotis after the battle of Thermodon, where they were taken prisoner by the Greeks; they killed their captors and, not knowing how to sail, were at the mercy of the sea and the wind. Drifting to land, they seized the first band of wild horses and proceeded to raid the Scythian territory. The Scythian men did not recognize them, not by language, clothing, or ethnic identity, and only learned that the intruders were women by examining the dead bodies left after a battle. They send some young men to camp near the Amazon camp,

NOTES

to become familiar with the Amazons, and to infiltrate and intermarry within the new group. The two groups intermingle and eventually pair off. Like comic women, the Amazons show more facility with language than the men: in ch. 114 they are able to learn Scythian, while the men are not able to learn whatever the Amazons speak (later we learn that the women learn Scythian imperfectly and so the Sauromantians now speak a kind of Scythian dialect, ch. 117). A belief in the natural but imperfect relationship between women and language, so well employed in *Ecclesiazusae*, is not limited to Herodotus; How and Wells' commentary subscribes to it also: 'The greater aptness of the Amazons is a delightful touch of nature; but they were inaccurate (cf. σολοικίζοντες *c*. 117), as lady linguists often are' (1912: 341). Like the women in *Lysistrata*, the Amazons are also eventually 'tamed' by marriage.

17 A few examples of stories about women in groups show that this pattern pervades ancient Greek thought about women: consider the stories of the Bacchae, the Lemnian women, the Amazons, and more specifically, the women in *Thesmophoriazusae* and *Ecclesiazusae*, who meet in a group to plot destruction of things male. Of course, women who act alone also cause trouble: e.g. Clytemnestra, Medea, Helen.

18 I have followed Henderson 1987b. Unless otherwise noted, the translations are taken from Henderson 1988. πανοῦργος is the standard Aristophanic term for a trickster and appears only once in *Lysistrata*. It endows the women with trickery and deceitfulness.

19 For a review of the linking between the feminine, women, and mimesis, see Zeitlin 1981. Bassi also discusses woman as a mimetic construct, never allowed to represent herself and conceived as a substitute (1989: 23). Here, the women act as substitutes for the men, since the men have abdicated their interests in the *oikos*.

20 Loraux does describe this concept of woman as an ungraspable entity imperfectly disguised by clothing apropos of Pandora rather than of the women in *Lysistrata*: 'la créature de la *Théogonie* n'est pas un déguisement trompeur; son voile ne dissimule pas qu'elle est autre chose qu'une femme – un dieu, un démon, un homme –, il ne cache rien parce que la femme n'a pas d'intérieur à masquer' (1981: 86).

21 The crafty seductress is a traditional literary image of woman: e.g. Hera (*Iliad* 14), Helen, Circe, Calypso, and even Penelope to a certain extent. Here, the image of woman is a heavy-handed stereotype. Zeitlin has written of the inherently feminine affinity for theater: 'Woman is the mimetic creature par excellence, ever since Hesiod's Zeus created her as an imitation with the aid of the other artisan gods and adorned her with a deceptive allure' (1985: 85).

22 Cartledge particularly notes the overwhelming masculinity of Spartan society, and that at times 'Spartan women were trained to act, and obliged to look, like men' (1981: 105), even though this was done with an 'overriding emphasis placed on their child-bearing potential and maternal roles' (ibid.). The masculinity of Spartan women in comparison to Athenian ideology about the femininity of Athenian women could have been an easy joke, especially during the war. Ταῦρος, bull, can refer to the phallos (Henderson 1975: 127). While it may thus identify Lampito as a woman (suggested by ἀταυρώτη, unmarried/unmanned, at 217; cf. Aesch.

NOTES

Ag. 245), it may also contribute to her gender ambiguity, for ταῦρος can also refer to the vagina and to the rear end, usually in reference to the preferences of aggressive homosexuals (Henderson 1975: 133, 202–3).

23 Kalonike turns the Corinthian woman into a physical representative of her city's most famous geographic feature, the Gulf of Corinth. Other male poets have imagined woman's body as a map, sometimes for seduction (e.g. Donne, Elegy 15, esp. lines 25–30), sometimes for a comic routine (e.g. Shakespeare, *The Comedy of Errors*, III. ii. 114–48).

24 I use my own translation here. Henderson's is more contemporary but less literal: 'No wonder men write tragedies about us. We're nothing but a diaper and a bed' (1988: 23). He cites the allusion to Sophocles' (second?) *Tyro*, produced after 420 BCE, in which Tyro was seduced by Poseidon and gave birth to Polias and Neleus, whom she sent off in a little boat (Henderson 1987b: 84). The children were reared by shepherds and reunited with their mother later in the play. Henderson also repeats the scholiast's explanation: Poseidon and a boat = συνουσιάζειν καὶ τίκτειν. Both Henderson and the scholiast read the allusion accurately, the way a male audience would and should, for Aristophanes. However, a modern audience of women (with full information about the myth) might recognize the woman here as a victim of rape and might see the boat as a sign of the difficult necessities of unexpected and unwanted motherhood.

25 Henderson's translation catches the joke well: he has Lysistrata call Lampito the 'manliest of women' (1988: 24).

26 In this case, the women will eventually 'sacrifice' wine, but it is worth noting that τόμια were usually the testicles of the sacrificial victim (Henderson 1987b: 90). The immediate reaction of the audience upon hearing this word might have been great amusement, given what the women have agreed to give up for the sake of peace.

27 The details about Helen's breast are unique to Euripides' version of the story as recounted in *Andromache* (Henderson 1987b: 86), although the trope of Menelaus' inability to act in front of Helen is found in both the *Little Iliad* and Ibycus. The date for *Andromache* is not definitely known, but it can be narrowed down to sometime around 425, give or take a few years (Stevens 1971: 19). Appropriately, the theme of *Andromache* is domestic disharmony; for more on this, see Storey 1989. Recall also that Clytemnestra bares her breast to Orestes in *Choephoroi* in an attempt to disarm him (896–8). The allusion reverberates with the image of dangerous women.

28 The stereotype is discussed by Halperin 1990: 129–30. Some heroes exhibit such characteristics: cf. e.g. Odysseus' ability to resist the Sirens' song (*Odyssey* 12) and his resistance to Circe (albeit with some help from Hermes in *Odyssey* 10).

29 Henderson writes: 'it is important for Lysistrate's characterization that she finds it easy to divorce herself from the home and its concerns, whereas the other wives experience constant homesickness not exclusively connected with their longing for sex' (1980: 171). See also Martin 1987: 85.

30 'Notice that Lysistrate does not here or subsequently deny that the wives are frivolous and inferior. She emphatically says that these inherent weaknesses can be used as strengths when properly employed (or rather,

not employed). She herself does not share in the weaknesses' (Henderson 1980: 172).
31 Again I rely on Henderson's anticipation of my point: 'Here the warlike Lysistrate must be guided by her more feminine colleagues' (1980: 181).
32 'Lysistrate knows how to reach the hearts of her bibulous co-conspirators, and even the male audience would agree that she has struck the right note' (Henderson 1980: 182).
33 The names 'Lysistrata' and 'Lysimache' carry just about the same meanings: 'Lysistrata' = 'disbander of armies' and 'Lysimache' = 'disbander of battle'. Also, in 411 BCE the name of the priestess of Athena Nike was Myrrhine.
34 The Adonia was a festival in honor of Adonis celebrated by women but not officially sanctioned or recognized by the state. Celebrations apparently took place on rooftops, and involved the growing of 'Adonis gardens' and the performance of lamentations for the dead god (Henderson 1987b: 119; Burkert 1985: 176–7). Keuls (1985: 30) suggests that allusions to the Adonia in *Lysistrata* indicate that Aristophanes believed that its celebration provided the women of Athens with a certain amount of freedom of expression, sexual and otherwise:

> Through the Adonia women voiced a claim to an active role in sex relations. Aristophanes, whose play *Lysistrata* was heavily inspired by the Adonia, was well aware of this. In fact, he had one of his characters phrase for the first time the feminist slogan 'up from under'. Lysistrata, in order to bolster the courage of her female co-conspirators, dreams up a fake oracle, foretelling the victory of the lowly over the proud; 'Does that mean that we women shall lie on top?' asks an unnamed woman (773).

35 Aristophanes will eventually suggest that any grotesque exaggeration of gender behavior can be funny; the humor just depends on your method of interpretation. To the wives, the macho soldiers bullying their way through the market, eating everything in sight, are hilarious. The magistrate thinks they are manly (τοὺς ἀνδρείους, 558) and perhaps sees an epic image. Lysistrata thinks they are ridiculous (τό τε πρᾶγμα γέλοιον, 558) and sees a comic image, perhaps an image of the comic theater (Lamachus of *Acharnians*, for example). On Lamachus as a representative of tragedy who is vanquished in a contest with the comic hero, see Foley 1988.
36 Henderson writes of this and notes the 'virtual oxymoron' of the concept of a female mind (1987b: 163).
37 Henderson also makes a very fine distinction between the use of the intransitive and transitive senses of this verb, claiming that the intransitive form can also mean 'to fornicate' (1975: 152). If he is correct, then my suggestion about Lysistrata's βινητιῶμεν is strengthened. The wives are clearly trying to get home for legitimate sex with their husbands; Lysistrata uses the word that indicates a desire for sex with anyone, spouse or not. She therefore speaks very much like a man, especially like the men at the end of the play. It is interesting to note that Henderson skirts the issue in his

NOTES

translation, rendering Lysistrata's line as 'I'll make it short: they're dying to get laid' (1988: 53). I thank James R. Baron for first pointing out to me the problems of Lysistrata's word choice here (in correspondence).

38 Rothwell is correct in arguing that 'Lysistrata's rhetorical abilities differ from Praxagora's' (1990: 91). His explication points out how Praxagora is characterized as a *rhêtôr*. For my purposes, Lysistrata is simply a good speaker; she has no need of the formalized skills of a *rhêtôr*. Rosellini argues that the women, including Lysistrata, have no idea of the real significance of the language they use and so their plan will end in chaos (1979: 21).

39 Kinesias' name is constructed from the vulgar meaning of κινεῖν; Henderson translates Kinesias' line as 'Rodney Balling, from Bangtown' (1988: 60). Myrrhine's name echoes a common vulgar description for female genitalia: μυρρίνη, 'myrtle' (Henderson 1975: 134–5).

40 Although the idea of seduction usually connotes the erotic persuasion of a woman by a man, there is a tradition of the seduction of men by women in Greek literature. The rhetoric of persuasion rather than the structure of seduction scenes is examined in Gross 1985. Gross's analysis works under the assumption that all seduction is undertaken by men upon women (see ch. 2, 'The Rhetoric of Seduction'). Women, according to Gross's analysis, use rhetoric to persuade their lovers to remain with them (ch. 3, 'The Rhetoric of Abandonment'). Epic provides us with several examples of what has been called 'the allurement scene', in which a female persuades, or tries to persuade, a male into a sexual or otherwise erotic liaison (Forsyth 1979). For example, Aphrodite seduces Anchises in the *Homeric Hymn to Aphrodite* (53–201) and Hera seduces Zeus in *Iliad* 14. 159–328 (although he returns the advances). Whether the participants in allurement scenes are divine or mortal, the pattern of action remains basically the same. The pattern is also present in *Iliad* 3 between Helen and Paris, and in the *Odyssey* between Circe, Calypso, Nausicaä, Penelope, and Odysseus. Forsyth presents a subtle analysis of Homer's manipulation of the elements of seduction in his portrayal of Penelope (1979: 114–17).

41 Some critics do not question the femininity of Myrrhine here. Rosellini, for example, comments on Myrrhine's ability to impede the seduction by following all the rules for seduction assiduously (1979: 23). McLeish writes that 'the Myrrhine/Kinesias scene in *Lysistrata* would not work unless Myrrhine is thought to be not only feminine but attractive as well' (1980: 154). On the other hand, Walton (1987: 206) has written that

> *Lysistrata* is at heart a 'drag' play. The jokes are those of men dressed up as women, not of women being women.... Lysistrata is a part written to be performed by a man. So are the other women of Athens, Myrrhine among them, whose encounter with her husband gets comically close to the sexual act without quite consummating it. A major part of the comedy as written relies on the fact that this husband and wife, both male, both masked, could not behave exactly like husband and wife.

42 Naked women were probably played by male actors in bodysuits made up to represent the female body (see Henderson 1987b: 195; also Willems

NOTES

1919: 381–95. Stone summarizes much of the evidence and the scholarly debate (1980: 147–50).

43 Lysistrata directs Diallage to hold the ambassadors 'gently' (οἰκείως) and 'like a woman' (ἀλλ' ὡς γυναῖκας εἰκός, 1118). If the men will not extend their hands, she instructs Diallage to take hold of their phalloi (τῆς σάθης ἄγε, 1119; see Henderson 1987b: 197).

44 The comment also seems to be a joke about the alleged homosexuality (and preference for being the passive partner) of Lysistratos of Amphitrope (Henderson 1987b: 195).

45 Not only does Aristophanes quote Euripides here, but he also significantly alters the context of the line. In fr. 484, Melanippe cites her mother Hippe as the source of her wisdom. That Lysistrata claims wisdom from her father and other old men sets her off as unique: a female with an appropriately ambivalent gender identity. The reference also seems redolent of Athena, the daughter of a father without a mother.

46 In his commentary, Henderson has Lysistrata exit at 1189 and points out that it is unclear whether she leads in the wives at 1273 (1987b: 206–7, 213–14); her purpose is served and she is no longer needed. In his translation, he points out that *Ecclesiazusae* follows a similar pattern. In that play, 'Aristophanes similarly abandons a heroine when the plot no longer needs her' (Henderson 1988: 78). Since the translation is designed for modern production, he also suggests that a modern director may want to adapt the end of the play to a modern audience's sensibility and let Lysistrata perform the Athenian ambassador's speech at 1273–90 (ibid. 82). Sommerstein, on the other hand, on the authority of other scholars, assigns the speech to Lysistrata (1990: 221).

47 If the play was produced at the Lenaea, then it was produced shortly before the oligarchic coup and the reorganization of government in Athens. Political strife is indicated in *Lysistrata*, but impending solutions are not. My concern here is with a vision of the effects of war upon those at home, which is ostensibly the concern of *Lysistrata*.

48 On a related note, Keuls writes that Aristophanes wrote *Lysistrata* in response to the mutilation of the herm statues which occurred in Athens shortly before the launching of the Sicilian expedition and cast a pall of superstition over the city (Thuc. 7. 75; 7. 87). She suggests (1985: 345) that Aristophanes knew who was responsible for the vandalism:

> I can see no other explanation for Aristophanes' sudden preoccupation with female protest than that he, and at least a part of the audience, knew or even suspected that the castration of the herms had been perpetrated by women, a suspicion which by now could not possibly find overt expression.

> I would suggest, however, that *who* vandalized the herms is almost immaterial here. The phallos is quite conspicuous in *Lysistrata* (as Keuls notes), and rather than a veiled revelation of the guilty party, the play instead celebrates the possibility of normal life, the return of the phallos, in an otherwise emasculated city.

NOTES

3 MEN AS WOMEN: *THESMOPHORIAZUSAE*

1 The date of *Thesmophoriazusae* is not absolutely verifiable, and some scholars support placing it in 410 (see Sommerstein 1977). At the end of this chapter I will offer some suggestions that support the dating of *Thesmophoriazusae* as at least following *Lysistrata*, if not specifically at the City Dionysia of 411.
2 No specific name for this relative, referred to alternatively as the Old Man, the Kinsman, and the Relation, survives. In the text, he is called ὁ κηδεστής, the 'relation by marriage' (LSJ suggests 'father-in-law'). The sigla and scholia give him the name Mnesilochus, which is used by many scholars (e.g. Reckford 1987; Whitman 1964; Zeitlin 1981), but there is no proof that this was the name Aristophanes meant him to have (Dover 1972: 165). I follow Hansen's generalized translation and will refer to him as the Relative (see H. Hansen 1976).
3 Aristophanes' model for this plot is not exactly the idea of 'women on top' as much as it is the idea of men intruding into groups of women alone together. There are two tragic stories which provide a paradigm for this plot. One, cited by Aelian (fr. 44 Hercher) and Suidas, concerns Battus, the king of Cyrene, who desired to learn the secrets of the Thesmophoria. The priestess refused to allow him to participate fully, but did allow him to watch the first part of the ritual. He sees the women bloody from their sacrifices, and, as he watches, in a group they turn upon and castrate him (as a secret and illegal spectator, he becomes part of their ritual sacrifice). The second story, from Pausanias (4. 17. 1), tells of Aristomenes' imprisonment of women who have sequestered themselves in the temple of Demeter for a festival celebrated by women only. The women defend themselves with the knives and skewers used for the ritual sacrifices. Aristomenes escapes death, however, with the help of one of the priestesses. For more detail and specific reference to the violence of the women in the Thesmophoria, see Detienne 1979: 184–6. Here Aristophanes puts Euripides at the center of a potentially tragic plot and then provides him with a comic way out. It has also been noted that the shape of *Thesmophoriazusae* recalls Euripidean escape plots (see E. Hall 1989b: 41–3; Zeitlin 1981: 181–2).
4 On the Thesmophoria in general, see Burkert 1979, 1983 and 1985; Detienne 1979; Farnell 1909, vol. 3: 75–112; Zeitlin 1982. Farnell is particularly detailed on the epithet θεσμοφόρος given to Demeter and how it expresses 'the pre-eminent interest of Demeter in political order and the law-abiding life' (Farnell 1909, vol. 3: 75). Just what laws (θεσμοί) Demeter is thought to have brought is unclear; Farnell concludes that her interests lie primarily in the order and structure she grants to marriage.
5 Detienne also focuses upon the inherent paradox of Demeter *thesmophoros* as a limiter of women (1979: 183–4).
6 Here I disagree with Reckford (1987: 309), who writes:

> It is the women of Athens and Greece, and Lysistrata (or Lysimache) behind them, and the goddesses behind her – Athena, Artemis, Aphrodite – who have that final power to save, to which even Dionysus seems to defer in the present play [*Lysistrata*]. In the

NOTES

Thesmophoriazusae, it will be the great goddesses, Demeter and Persephone, together with Athena.

The representation of these goddesses and their powers would not even be possible without Dionysus and without men.

7 Several scholars have recently published lists of examples for this lack of interest in *Thesmophoriazusae* (see, for instance, Moulton 1981: 108 n. 1; Zeitlin 1981: 170 n. 4). On parody of the format of the *ecclesia*, see Haldane 1965. Haldane's analysis of the close parody of prayer and response formulae in this scene reveals a double vision close to what I shall argue here:

> While the two prayers of the Kerukaina work out in their different fashions the analogy between the religious and political sides of the women's gathering, those of the chorus, by highlighting first the one and then the other, form both complement and contrast to the spoken prayers and to each other. In the same way, individual words and phrases become facets reflecting the basic incongruity of the comic situation.
>
> (Haldane 1965: 45–6)

Vickers 1989 finds an almost infinite number of political allusions in these plays and his findings have been met with great scholarly skepticism; while the credibility of them all is questionable, we must still admit that there may be more to the political aspect of this play than previously thought.

8 The term *parabasis* means 'a stepping aside', and refers to a feature present in most, but not all, of Aristophanes' extant comedies: *Acharnians, Knights, Wasps, Birds,* and *Clouds* all have a parabasis; it appears in an alternate or partial form in *Peace, Lysistrata, Frogs,* and *Thesmophoriazusae*; neither *Ecclesiazusae* or *Wealth* has one. In the parabasis, the chorus usually 'step aside' from their character and from the main action of the play to address the audience directly about poetic ideas, the value of the poet, and to present a defense of the play (or previous plays). They may also remind the judges of the importance of voting for this particular play as the first prizewinner. Technically speaking, 'the parabasis was originally a semi-dramatic, or even a non-dramatic, sequel to the dramatic action of the *agôn* by the *komastai*' (Pickard-Cambridge 1962: 199). On the origins of the parabasis, see Sifakis 1971. On the parabasis and its relation to spectators, and for some interesting comments on how the parabasis reverses the relationship between actors and spectators, see Hubbard 1991: 13–15.

9 Hubbard also argues compellingly that the parabasis of *Thesmophoriazusae* returns and refers to themes found in *Lysistrata* (1991: 182–99). His argument also highlights Aristophanes' interest in the image of women in comedy. A clear exposition of the parabasis can be found in Moulton 1981: 127–34. Moulton remarks that 'the insistent ironic emphasis on τὸ κακόν adverts, perhaps, to the maxim of the Sixth century comic poet Susarion: κακὸν γυναῖκες' (1981: 128). Susarion's work can be dated to *c*.581–560 BCE (Pickard-Cambridge 1962: 183). The fragment of Susarion that he refers to reads: ˙κακὸν γυναῖκες· ἀλλ' ὅμως, ὦ δημόται, / οὐκ ἔστιν οἰκεῖν οἰκίαν ἄνευ κακοῦ. / καὶ γὰρ τὸ γῆμαι καὶ τὸ μὴ γῆμαι κακόν' ('Women are bad, but still, o countrymen, even though they are bad, it is

NOTES

not possible to keep a household without one. For marrying is bad but not marrying is also bad'; I have followed Kock 1888; the translation is mine.) (Pickard-Cambridge 1962: 183–7 is extremely skeptical about the relationship between Susarion and Old Comedy, and even about the existence of Susarion.) If Moulton's suggestion is correct, then the self-consciousness of Aristophanes' writing here is stronger than previously suspected. Aristophanes alludes to the earliest comic poet, whose surviving work indicates that the degrading of women is a very old comic subject, even for Aristophanes. While setting himself squarely within the old traditions of Greek comedy, Aristophanes also goes one better than Susarion. While the 'women' of *Thesmophoriazusae* attempt irony, they actually display their inability to construct a completely convincing argument, especially because they have displayed and confirmed their rascal behavior already. The play confirms that women are τὸ κακόν; while Aristophanes gets away with portraying them as such easily, Euripides does not.

10 For text I am following Rogers 1920; unless otherwise noted, all translations cited in this chapter are also Rogers 1920.

11 There is general critical agreement on this point. For instance: 'The image of the women, with its conflation of the male and female spheres, constitutes a quintessential comic emblem, wherein the harmonies of gender and of sex roles, and of the very language used to symbolize them, are challenged' (Moulton 1981: 133). Also:

> The parabasis should have been the place for the women to show their positive and beneficial side, and they attempt to do so; but Aristophanes seems to have found the task difficult. The comparison of the bad performances of specific men with the virtues implied in ordinary women's names is feeble, either as argument or humor, and the poet, perhaps realizing the fact, cut the parabasis short.
>
> (Whitman 1964: 224)

12 I will show what Henderson asserts: 'a flesh-and-blood man like the Relation cannot be turned into a tragic heroine simply by depilation and a change of clothes' (1975: 89). He can, however, become comic.

13 Keen observers in the theater might also notice the self-referentiality and self-parody in the structure of this scene. In *Acharnians*, Dikaiopolis seeks Euripides' help in designing a costume to elicit pity from his audience (the chorus of angry Acharnians, who need softening in their opinion of Dikaiopolis' private peace). When he approaches Euripides' house, Dikaiopolis learns from the servant that Euripides is inside composing (399). Eventually, Euripides is rolled out of the house (409; he too reclines while composing) and provides Dikaiopolis with a costume of rags left from his previous production of *Telephus*. In *Thesmophoriazusae*, Euripides must borrow costumes from an even more decadent composer and be reduced to the strategies of an Aristophanic hero. There is also much *Telephus* parody still to come. See Miller 1948; Rau 1967: 42–50, esp. 46; also Pickard-Cambridge 1946: 101–2.

14 Both Rogers 1920 and Hall and Geldart 1907 give the Relation the name Mnesilochus in their Greek versions of the play. I will follow the custom of

NOTES

these editors in citations of the Greek and the custom of critics in discussion of the passages in English translation.

15 μέλας, dark, and καρτερός, big and strong ('brawny'), are fairly common masculine traits. For example, καρτερός is used of Heracles at *Frogs* 464; of Zeus at Aeschylus, *Septem* 517; of Ajax at Sophocles, *Ajax* 669. Μέλας is used of men at Plato, *Republic* 474e; Demosthenes 21. 71 (LSJ). The masculinity of dark skin is the logical correspondent to the femininity of light skin (*Ecclesiazusae* 62–4); see also Dover 1989: 76–8. Δασυπώγων, shaggy-bearded, a reasonable expectation for the appearance of any masculine Athenian, appears only here (LSJ). The ironic incongruity of Agathon's costume is noted by Stone 1980: 346–7. Dover discusses what little evidence there is about the real Agathon; the relationship between his representation here and his real interests and habits is unknown (1989: 144).

16 The main Greek verb of sight, ὁράω, dominates the passage, appearing in different forms at lines 26, 32, 33, and 34. There is no controversy over the meaning of this verb: to see, to look at, to behold. While it is too common a word to hold primary and specific theatrical connotations, the visual nature of the theater is nevertheless quite obvious (cf. Aristotle, *Poetics* 1449 b 33, 1450 b 20 on ὄψις, spectacle). Here it may be worth recalling the overwhelming emphasis on sight in Sophocles' *Oedipus Tyrannus*, for example. Sight is metaphorical for Oedipus not only in terms of his particular condition; it is theatrical, for Oedipus acts out stories and roles that become visible to the audience, to the people in Thebes, and, upon further contemplation, to himself.

17 λάθρᾳ indicates secrecy. στολή indicates equipment in clothing; cf. *Thesm.* 851. It often appears to be used in a military sense (*Ecclesiazusae* 846; Aeschylus, *Supplices* 764, *Persae* 1018) and also of ethnic garb (Hdt. 4. 78; Euripides, *Rh.* 313; Xenophon, *Cyr.* 8. 1. 40; LSJ). This suggests that the word connotes not just simple clothing but rather clothing as gear, equipment, costume, and spectacle. Ἀμφιέννυμι quite clearly refers to the wearing of clothing, and Aristophanes often uses it to refer to the wearing of costume (*Wasps* 1172; *Ecclesiazusae* 879).

18 The text indicates that Agathon is wheeled both out (οὐκκυκλούμενος, 96) and back into (εἰσκυκλησάτω, 265) his house. According to Pickard-Cambridge, these verbs (also at *Acharnians* 408–9) signal the only textual evidence for the possible use of the *ekkyklema* in the fifth century (Pickard-Cambridge 1968: 100). Supporting evidence comes from lexicographers and scholiasts. Scholarly opinion on the actual use of the *ekkyklema* as stage equipment here is divided, however. H. Hansen 1976: 170–3 summarizes the evidence succinctly. Webster 1970: 9 and Pickard-Cambridge 1968: 102–3 argue that Agathon is brought out as he reclines on a wheeled couch, not on the *ekkyklema*, for there is no documented use of the *ekkyklema* in this way for the fifth century, nor would there have been space for it to move through the doorway of the scenery for Agathon's house, nor would there be any need for any other stage equipment besides the wheeled couch. Arnott 1962: 78–90, esp. 84, and H. Hansen argue convincingly, on the basis of other evidence, that the *ekkyklema* could have been used at least to move Agathon here. In addition, the bold use of the *ekkyklema*, which was a scenic device common to tragedy, to facilitate the arrival and departure of

NOTES

the highly theatrical Agathon would only support and strengthen the metatheatricality of Agathon's appearance.

19 I follow van Leeuwen (after Dindorf) here and read δόκιμον rather than Rogers' δοκίμῳ or Meineke's δοκίμων (van Leeuwen 1904: 24). The syntax of line 125 balances more evenly with δόκιμον modifying κίθαρίν in line 124. Rau discusses the hymn as a parody of dithyrambic poetry (1967: 104–8). H. Hansen (1976: 169) makes some dramaturgical suggestions that are helpful in imagining the effect of this gender confusion on stage:

> Ostensibly the major portion of this prayer is not womanish, but one suspects that Agathon intoned the phrase 'manly shout' so as to get as loud a laugh as possible, and when he spoke the chorus' lines, he probably minced about in some fashion. The phrase 'mother of hymns', while hardly unusual, is significant in a play where the theme of sexual rôle-reversals will loom so large, and in such close conjunction with the phrase 'manly shout'.

20 Saïd discusses this passage as a parody of a scene between Lycurgus and Dionysus in Aeschylus' *Edonians* (1987: 230). The Relative addresses Agathon with Lycurgus' words in that play (see frs. 57–67 Radt). The resemblance of Agathon to Dionysus here strengthens the theatrically aggressive tone of the play. Not only will the Relative receive instruction and a costume for his female impersonation from a real effeminate poet, but also from a representative of Dionysus himself. The precursors to Euripides' *Bacchae* are clear here. The scene also continues parody of a tragic plot and suggests that the Relative is in a dangerous position, for Lycurgus was punished for his mockery and rejection of Dionysus with homicidal madness. For a technical discussion of the parody of Aeschylus, see Rau 1967: 108-11; on Dionysus, effeminacy, and the image of the female on stage, see Zeitlin 1985. Fr. 332 of *Thesmophoriazusae* B (407/6?) also consists of a detailed list of feminine costume requirements (Kassel and Austin 1983–91, vol. 3. 2: 183–7). Snyder 1974 suggests that Agathon perhaps resembles Anacreon here, linking his appearance here to painted representations of Anacreontic singers, particularly one in the Boston Museum of Fine Arts.

21 Henderson's translation (1975: 158). Gruber remarks about the 'lewd desires' that Agathon arouses in the Relative, but considers them part of the Relative's mockery of Agathon rather than expressions of real desire aroused by the sight of an effeminate male (1986: 25).

22 Dover points out that the use of both κατάπυγον and εὐρύπρωκτος in reference to a specific person does not always or necessarily suggest an accusation of taking the passive role in a homosexual relationship; the words may also simply imply 'worthlessness, inferiority or shamelessness in general' (1989: 143). It seems quite clear in Agathon's case, however, that homosexuality and effeminacy are quite to the point. I agree with Henderson, who argues that their appearance here is 'distinctly homosexual' (1975: 210). The roles are also discussed by Winkler along the lines of hoplite and *kinaidos*: the hoplite is characterized as courageous, manly, and active, the *kinaidos* as cowardly, effeminate, and passive (1990: 46–54).

NOTES

23 Cf. the discussion above (Introduction, pp. 6–7) of two vase-paintings depicting actors in female roles (Trendall and Webster 1971: III. 1, 2; III. 1, 25); with the inscription *KALO[S]* (ΚΑΛΟ[Σ]), the vase appears to be erotically dedicated to the male actor who played a woman's part. The theme of male spectators becoming sexually attracted to male actors in female roles is found in Japanese stories about Kabuki drama also.

24 Rogers' note *ad* 205 hits the mark here: 'Euripides will be detected as being a *man*; Agathon will be suspected as coming to play a *woman's* part, and to steal away, by attracting to himself, the love which the women would otherwise enjoy' (1920: 24).

25 This singeing and shaving episode is lengthy, yet critical opinion on its function and meaning forms no clear consensus. On the one hand, some scholars dismiss it: Whitman 1964 makes no comment, Dover discusses the singeing only to point out its illogicality and its role as an opportunity for slapstick (1972: 163). On the other hand, Gruber notes a link between the Relative's transvestism and Pentheus' in Euripides' *Bacchae*, before he goes on to discuss the public humiliation that the episode inflicts upon the Relative for his 'transsexual impulses' (1986: 27). Gruber's likening of the Relative's transvestite disguise to Pentheus' is not wholly convincing, however. Euripides in *Thesmophoriazusae* has no ulterior motive in using his relative as a go-between; Dionysus in *Bacchae* does, and his intention to punish Pentheus for his impiety is quite clear. The Relative resists his role as a woman; Pentheus, under the spell of the god, does not. The only significant force that ties these two scenes together (aside from their generic similarities) is the eventual triumph of the spirit of Dionysus (over Demeter here, over skeptics in *Bacchae*) at the end of the play. More illuminating is Zeitlin's discussion of the dressing scene in *Bacchae* (1985: 74–5). As Pentheus is made to submit to physical changes as a sign of femininity, so the Relative here submits his masculine body to the artificial changes that create 'woman'. The scene in which the Relative and Euripides play dress-up in a parody of feminine vanity is as much a sign of femininity as is the actual appearance of the Relative in women's clothes. Zeitlin also makes my point of *Bacchae*: 'the fact that Pentheus dons a feminine costume and rehearses in it before our eyes exposes perhaps one of the most marked features of Greek theatrical mimesis: that men are the only actors in this civic theater' (1985: 65).

26 Razors remove facial and body hair; flames from a singeing instrument (here, a torch; in *Ecclesiazusae*, a lamp (λύχνος), 12–13) remove pubic hair. In *Ecclesiazusae*, the women throw away their razors in order to cultivate masculine hairiness (65–7). The razor is thus closely linked to femininity: it appears on a list of feminine equipment (Aristophanes fr. 320). Dover speculates that Agathon did not actually shave his facial hair (as he apparently did his body hair), but rather that his beard has been trimmed as closely as possible (1989: 144). The slight presence of beard stubble on his face might thus enhance his gender ambiguity. On depilation, see Bain 1982 and Kilmer 1982.

27 Adult Athenian men sported full, trimmed beards, which are thus associated with robust male sexuality. Their absence is conversely associated with effeminacy and femininity. Compare, for instance, the

women of *Ecclesiazusae* who must wear false beards to disguise themselves as men (24–7).

28 καταγέλαστος, 'ridiculous', often describes a self-consciously comic character or situation: *Lysistrata* 751, 907, 1020, 1024; *Ecclesiazusae* 126.

29 Euripides most likely hands the Relative a mirror (probably the mirror that Agathon held at line 140) at line 234. Rogers suggests understanding the word κάτοπτρον after φέρε there, but that is not even necessary. It is clear from the context that the Relative acquires a looking-glass in which to view his reflection.

30 Gruber is accurate in identifying the Relative here as 'a theatrical phenomenon' (1986: 27).

31 As Saïd notes, 'Le passage du masculin au féminin, qui est toujours imposé au personnage de l'extérieur est une dégradation' (1987: 236).

32 The singeing episode generates two obscene *double entendres*, the significance of which remains less than subtle. The relative fears that, once singed, he will resemble a δελφάκιον, literally a suckling pig. The word often also describes a mature woman's vagina (*Acharnians* 786; *Lysistrata* 1061; see also Henderson 1975: 132). The fear proves to be groundless: once he is exposed, the last thing the Relative's genitals resemble is a δελφάκιον. Κέρκος is a slang term for penis (cf. *Acharnians* 785, 787; Henderson 1975: 128). Perhaps the singeing actually achieves the opposite effect from the one intended: rather than making the Relative's crotch appear more feminine, it makes his κέρκος all the more conspicuous. This exposure of what disguise is meant to hide is, of course, characteristic of Aristophanic comedy.

33 The στρόφιον appears also at *Lysistrata* 931; fr. 647 (incert.); Pherecrates fr. 100. See also Stone 1980: 184–5.

34 See *Clouds* 51; *Lysistrata* 44–51, 645. Compare Blepyrus' κροκωτίδιον at *Ecclesiazusae* 332: he has put on his wife's dress because she has taken his cloak. Dionysus at *Frogs* 46 also wears the κροκωτός farcically, underneath his Heraclean lion-skin. The association of this garment with Dionysus may be strong. The only men who wear it (with the exception of Blepyrus) are effeminate in the manner of Dionysus. See also Stone 1980: 174–6.

35 On the ἱμάτιον, see Introduction, n. 14. The Relative probably wraps his cloak in the feminine style, with the right side of the cloth draped as a hood over the back of his head. Cf. *Ecclesiazusae* 73–5, 275 (where the women wear their cloaks in the masculine style). This style of draping is illustrated in Figure 4.

36 λαλεῖν is often used of women's speech; recall its appearance at the entrance of the gender-bending Agathon, line 138. It implies gossip, babble, and nonsense. Cf. *Thesm.* 393, 578, 717, 1108, 1109, 1082, 1087; *Lysistrata* 442, 627; *Ecclesiazusae* 16, 119, 120, 129, 1058.

37 The daughter's name is a diminutive form of the slang χοῖρος, 'cunt', often used to describe women; cf. *Acharnians* 729–835 (see above, Chapter 1, pp. 28–9).

38 The balance of gender-role reversal seems to be a festive requirement: if women act like men, then men must act like women (see Zeitlin 1981: 178; 1985: 66–7).

39 Aristophanes dramatizes an assembly meeting twice, once in *Acharnians* and again here in *Thesm.*; an account of an assembly meeting appears in

NOTES

Knights, and the assembly is both rehearsed and described in *Ecclesiazusae*, although in that play we do not actually witness the meeting at which the women carry out their plan. Rogers 1920: 34 *ad* 295 details the elements parodied in this play; my concern is not so much the imitation of male behavior on the part of the women here, although certainly the idea of male actors as women imitating men is present, but rather to note that at this *ecclesia* the women adapt the practices of assembly meetings to their own needs and purposes (see also Haldane 1965). The juxtaposition of the Relative/imitation woman with these 'real' women is enough to jeopardize the pretense of costume and role. Harriott (1986: 151) writes:

> they [the audience] will be curious to see how long it is before the kinsman's female impersonation is detected and whether he gives himself away by some slip. Secondly, they will expect to hear the women's case against Euripides and its refutation by his agent. Thirdly, they will surely be intrigued by the idea of women taking part in an Assembly and in particular by the opportunity of witnessing part of a secret, exclusively female rite, as recreated by the dramatist. In these conditions the male Assembly will function as standard for comparison, not as target.

Harriott is correct in saying that 'there is no reason to suppose that a negative attitude to Assemblies as such underlies this scene' (ibid. 154). Unlike the male attenders at the assembly in *Ecclesiazusae*, the women of this assembly know how to recognize an imposter. Rather, perhaps the ritual secrecy of the Thesmophoria is exposed here just as the ritual secrecy of the actor's disguise has been exposed.

40 Procne reveals the secret to the imitation of women on stage in the extant fragment of her speech. She says, 'Now, outside [my father's house] I am nothing. Very often, in fact, I have looked at the nature of women in this way, that we are nothing' (νῦν δ' οὐδέν εἰμι χωρίς. ἀλλὰ πολλάκις / ἔβλεψα ταύτῃ τὴν γυναικείαν φύσιν, / ὡς οὐδέν ἐσμεν). Recall that Procne is present in *Birds* also, although there she appears after her murder of Itys and her metamorphosis into a nightingale.

41. σκοπέω means to behold or contemplate, more in specific terms than in general (as ὁράω). In this case, the word is accurate: as spectators, these men have had their gaze fixed upon the specific behavior of specific women, their wives, because of the stage vision of a specific woman.

42 Artemis is often invoked by women: see *Thesm.* 742; *Lysistrata* 435, 922, 949; *Ecclesiazusae* 90, 136.

43 The original reads: 'there is nothing worse than a bad woman' (τῆς μὲν κακῆς κάκιον οὐδὲν γίγνεται Γυναικός, fr. 494 Nauck; see also Webster 1967: 150–7). Aristophanes adds the tag 'except women in general' (πλὴν ἄρ' εἰ γυναῖκες). The joke is on the theater as well, for all these bad women are brought to life by men.

44 Agraulus, Rogers explains *ad* 533, otherwise known as Ἄγλαυρος, was a daughter of Cecrops, one of the mythological founding heroes of Attica. She seems, along with her sisters, an appropriate deity for an Athenian woman to invoke.

45 Stone imagines Kleisthenes in a long *chiton* and an effeminate hairstyle (342), and reproduces a vase illustration of an effeminate man thought to

represent him (Stone 1980: fig. 6). Kleisthenes is one of Aristophanes' favorite targets. He appears as a character only in this play, but he is mocked in every other play except *Peace*, *Ecclesiazusae*, and *Wealth*. The most well-known, and for this instance most appropriate, passage for comparison occurs at *Clouds* 355, where Strepsiades learns that the protean and female clouds have taken the shape of women because they have seen Kleisthenes in the audience (see above Chapter 1, p. 33). Dearden hypothesizes that the same actor played both Agathon and Kleisthenes (1976: 99). It is nice to imagine the ironic and comic effects of an actor who specialized in such effeminate roles appearing later as the overly masculine Scythian archer (also as per Dearden's suggestion).

46 Kleonymus is a man noted for his corpulence and eating habits (*Acharnians* 88, 844; *Knights* 958, 1293) and, accused of having thrown away his shield in the midst of battle, ridiculed as an effeminate coward (*Knights* 1372; *Clouds* 353–4; *Wasps* 15–23; *Peace* 446, 670–8, 1295–301; *Birds* 289–90, 1470–81); see Dover 1989: 144. He is also feminized in *Clouds* when his name, being used as an example of a noun, is declined in the feminine (670–80). Rogers writes: 'Fritzsche thinks it an intentional stroke of humour that the wife of Κλεωνύμη (*Clouds* 680) should be the first suspected of being a man' (1920: 65–6 *ad* 605). Halliwell suggests that she would have been padded in emulation of her husband's body (1982: 154).

47 Ferris (1989: 27) writes of this as a scene of phallos worship:

just as Mnesilochus conspires with his phallus to prevent the women from discovering his true identity, so do the Athenian (male) citizens of Aristophanes' audience conspire with themselves and the actors: what joy, what gaiety our phallus brings, how it binds us, male performers and male audience, in the gleeful power of possessing one.

48 Muecke makes a smart distinction between the representation of a Euripidean play for strategic purposes and the parody of a Euripidean play (1977: 65). In this case, the parody of *Telephus* appears only as a side-effect of the Relative's desperate escape strategy. The *Telephus* is also parodied in *Acharnians* (430–556; see Rau 1967: 19–42).

49 Muecke convincingly suggests 'represent the characteristic features of', rather than 'parody', as an interpretation of μιμήσομαι (1977: 65–6). On the parodical adaptation of *Helen*, see Rau 1967: 53–63.

50 Rogers notes *ad* 858 that an oath to Hekate φωσφόρος connotes quaintness, and that here the line alludes to Euripides' *Helen* 569: ὦ φωσφόρ' Ἑκάτη, πέμπε φάσματ' εὐμενῆ. The oath to Hekate was an oath used by women (cf. *Ecclesiazusae* 70), as was the oath to 'the two goddesses', Demeter and Persephone (cf. *Ecclesiazusae* 155–9).

51 The metaphor of spinning in this description of Euripides as ἱστιορράφος is telling. The verb ῥάπτειν, to spin, often refers to the design of comic plots (e.g. *Ecclesiazusae* 24, where it refers to the false beards worn by the women). Euripides is, in fact, a spinner of plots, and in this case he is forced to become a comic plotter, just like a woman (see Rogers 1920: 100 *ad* 935).

52 Other men in women's clothes experience a symbolic death. In *Lysistrata*, the Proboulos first becomes a woman and then a corpse (the better for Lysistrata to silence and disregard him, 531–613); in *Ecclesiazusae*, Blepyrus is rendered sterile and constipated in his wife's dress (311–71).

NOTES

53 The play is lost except for some fragments. Rau discusses the literary details of the parody (1967: 65–89); see also Zeitlin 1981: 190–4.
54 He is in many ways a standard comic figure: the all-brawn, no brains foreigner. Compare, for instance, Pseudabartas in *Acharnians*, the Triballian god in *Birds*, and even the Spartan Lampito in *Lysistrata*. For a comprehensive discussion with bibliography of the treatment of the Scythian archer, see E. Hall 1989b; a much shorter discussion may also be found in Long 1986: 106–7.
55 Problems with the staging here are discussed by H. Hansen 1976: 181–3. His suggestion that Euripides plays the part of Echo while visible to the audience is clever and playful. The effect of Euripides as the embodiment of the disembodied Echo would be all the stronger in this way.
56 *Pace* E. Hall, who writes: 'by his "rational" dispersion of the tragic illusion, the archer shows that he is going to be harder to deceive than his counterparts in satyr play or tragedy' (1989b: 50).
57 I agree with Rogers, who writes: 'such a hymn is more especially appropriate to the divine patron of the drama at the Dionysian festivals' (1920: 107 *ad* 999).
58 As E. Hall points out, 'Euripides must find another strategy which makes no intellectual demands on the Scythian, because he can only be defeated on a physical level' (1989b: 50). She finally assesses the role of the Scythian as a representative of that other 'other', the non-Greek, who cannot participate in paratragedy and so must finally be defeated by Greeks in common and with Greek ingenuity; 'the play's last laugh is not on Agathon nor Cleisthenes nor Euripides and his kinsman, nor even on the women of Athens, but on the dense and uncouth barbarian' (ibid. 52). Bobrick 1991 suggests that this scene parodies, in particular, Euripides' *Iphigeneia in Tauris*, which was produced a year or two before *Helen*, probably around 413. Thus Aristophanes presents another travesty of Euripidean escape motifs. Bobrick's suggestions are intriguing and do not contradict mine. Perhaps Aristophanes here makes Euripides direct and act in a comic version of a specific play.
59 In this, I agree with Hubbard, who has advanced an argument for dating *Lysistrata* to the Lenaea and *Thesmophoriazusae* to the City Dionysia of 411 BCE on the basis of intertextuality (1991: 187–99 and appendix 4).
60 Reckford (1987: 299–300) writes:

> It [*Thesmophoriazusae*] suggests that Athenians can play many parts, can survive humiliation and defeat, can find a way out of seemingly hopeless difficulties . . . No role is final, and no situation, if you are irrepressible like Euripides' relative. There is always another role to play. And the next role, the next disguise – or its stripping off – may show you, and show the polis, the real way out.

4 WOMEN AS MEN: *ECCLESIAZUSAE*

1 This event is not entirely without historical precedent. Xenophon provides an example of a dramatic manipulation in the real *ecclesia*. After the battle of Arginousae (406 BCE), at the celebration of the Apatouria, Theramenes

organized a large group of supporters who attended the assembly in costume, dressed as though they were the mourning relatives of those who had perished in the battle. They arranged for Callixenus to accuse the generals, and by means of their number and presence in the *ecclesia*, they managed to sway the vote to guilty against the generals (Xenophon, *Hell.* 1. 7. 8ff.; see also B. Strauss 1987: 29–30). The anecdote shows how theatrical a meeting of the real *ecclesia* might have been. For a group to infiltrate an open-air meeting with varied attendance and to force through a proposal by the strength of their number is not far-fetched. In fact, however, the events of *Ecclesiazusae* could never have happened: women in Athens most likely never cross-dressed.

2 While all costume ideas remain speculative, we can deduce some information like this from the text. Laconian shoes were men's shoes with full uppers, fastened with straps, and usually red or white in color (see Stone 1980: 226). They signify social status and gender (*Wasps* 1157–8; *Thesmophoriazusae* 142).

3 Saïd also notes that the mask calls attention to the artificial whiteness of a woman's skin (1987: 227).

4 Apropos of the realistic representation of women on stage is Saïd's provocative suggestion that 'on peut penser qu'un théâtre qui donne de la virilité une représentation caricaturale (le phallus de cuir) devait avoir recours à des procédés du même ordre pour représenter la fémininité' (1987: 228). She goes on to speculate that the representation of naked women at the end of comedies must, then, have been by male actors in costume.

5 Ussher is the only commentator on this play even to mention falsetto: 'male actors hardly employed falsetto (whatever they might do on occasion, *Th.* 267)' (1973: 70; see also ibid. 89 *ad* 101). The situation in *Thesmophoriazusae* that Ussher cites (where the Relative, about to portray women farcically, mocks feminine voices) differs fundamentally from the situation of an actor who portrays a woman for a basic stage illusion. Higher-pitched female voices may, however, be an issue later on (line 149); see also West 1987: 38, 191.

6 I am following the text of Ussher 1973. The translations are mine.

7 Euripides' *Phoenician Women* begins with a similar address to Helios. His *Cyclops* speaks of Hephaistos and his lamp (Ussher 1973: 70 *ad* 1).

8 Ἀπόρρητα are secret, hidden places; the word often refers to the components of mystery offerings and sacred rites. It seems to be a common Greek way to refer to the female body (LSJ), although Henderson 1975 does not list this as a common word for women. Ussher mentions its overtones of 'not quite polite to speak of' (1973: 73 *ad* 12–13). An extremely provocative work on the understanding of the female body in ancient Greece can be found in Sissa 1990. Sissa's thesis, that virginity was understood by the Greeks as a moral rather than a physical condition, and that the site of virginity was understood to be a mouth kept open or closed, depending on moral choices, has some implications for the study of women in Aristophanic comedy. Surely the loquacity of comic women is related to their allegedly voracious sexual appetites, while the virtuous speech of a woman like Lysistrata matches her ambiguous, yet arguably chaste, sexuality, especially if she is to be linked with the priestess of Athena Polias.

NOTES

9 The first speaker in the assembly of *Thesmophoriazusae* laments that men have locked up the stores; not only was the distribution of grain stores a woman's job but snitching a bit of food was their prerogative (418–21). The Relative accounts for much of woman's stereotypical behavior himself, however, which colors his claim: that claim certainly has origins in a male point of view. Saïd also points out how Praxagora's account of feminine behavior and taste adheres to traditional literary treatments of women (Saïd 1979: 40–1).

10 The text is corrupt here. I read τᾶς ἑταίρας in line 23, with the codices and Ussher 1973: 75. Although described in the scholia as a politician who decrees separate seats for women, men, and *hetairai*, Phyromachos was most likely a tragic actor infamous for his mispronunciations. *Hetairas* is a mispronunciation of *hedras*, which has two meanings: a seat to sit on and the seat with which one sits, one's rear end.

11 LSJ lists both these meanings for ῥάπτειν. As a metaphor, κακὰ ῥάπτειν appears at *Odyssey* 3. 118, *Iliad* 18. 367; φόνον, θάνατόν, μόρον τε ῥάπτειν at *Odyssey* 16. 379, 422. The word appears in Aristophanes at *Knights* 784, *Clouds* 538, and *Wealth* 513, but does not have the same significance in those places.

12 Sources on the Skira are confusing and scholarly accounts are equally muddled. See Brumfield 1981: 156–81; Deubner 1932: 40 ff.; Farnell 1909, vol. 1: 292; Parke 1977: 160; Simon 1983: 19–24. Burkert explains that the Skira was one of the few days on which women were allowed to leave the confines of their quarters, to participate in the procession from Athens to Skiron. He reasons that since the women formed their own organization at this festival and the balance of the home was upset, the day also served to unsettle the male population (1985: 230). He also emphasizes that the Skira was a festival of inversion, with a procession away from Athens and women leaving their homes: 'a day when all is reversed: the domestic and family orders are abolished, marriage suspended' (1983: 45). As such, it provides an appropriate place to formulate this plan. The Skira and the Thesmophoria are related by both being festivals of Demeter and celebrated by women alone. The Skira is a new year festival; the Thesmophoria is a seed-time festival. The Skira contrasts with the Adonia, however, the festival linked to *Lysistrata* (387–96), by its embrace of the erotic rather than the maternal. On the disunion of these festivals, especially due to ritual and physical smells, see Detienne 1977: 80. Detienne's analysis is given sensitive and trenchant criticism in Winkler 1990. Winkler (1990: 189) uncovers what he calls Detienne's 'phallocratic bias' and, inspired by the laughter often associated with the several festivals for women only, argues that these were occasions for women to celebrate their power over the giving and creation of life, and that by virtue of her public duty of silence and decency, an ancient Greek woman was thus privy to a 'double consciousness' about how she was supposed to be and how she really was. Lysistrata displays such a double consciousness, perhaps, although her friends and associates may not. That all three of these plays mention festivals for women only as places for plotting is not surprising, given the Greek male imagination and its tendency to fantasize about the trouble women might get into when they are together without men.

NOTES

13 Women could hardly imitate adult Athenian men without them. Aristophanes commonly associates beards with robust sexuality and, conversely, their absence with effeminacy: *Acharnians* 120–1; *Wasps* 476; *Lysistrata* 1072; *Thesmophoriazusae* 33, 190, 191–2, 214–35, 575, 583; *Ecclesiazusae* 24–5, 68–71, 118, 121, 126–7, 145, 273, 493–4, 501–2. In each case, beards are associated with manliness while clean-shaven men are allied with women and effeminacy. See also Saïd's review of costume details (1987: 226–31). On the practice of feminine depilation, see Bain 1982; Kilmer 1982.

14 The walking-stick, βακτηρία, was carried by men in the assembly, old men, men who lived in the country, beggars, and apparently Spartan sympathizers (Stone 1980: 225; 246–7). Each of the six references to the βακτηρία in *Ecclesiazusae* calls attention to the stick as a prop for the imitation of men. In general, Aristophanes mentions it either as an element of low humor (*Acharnians* 682; *Wasps* 1296; *Clouds* 541; *Wealth* 272) or as part of a costume ensemble (*Acharnians* 448; *Wasps* 33). In *Ecclesiazusae*, Woman A uses a theatrical term to describe carrying it: ἐξηνεγκάμην (Ussher 1973: 85 *ad* 76–7). Rothwell provocatively suggests that it may have phallic significance here (1990: 84). Laconian slippers can also carry a theatrical connotation. They signify a certain social status and gender. At *Wasps* 1157–8, Philocleon wears them after his metamorphosis into a well-dressed gentleman. At *Thesmophoriazusae* 142, the effeminate Agathon does *not* wear them. It is not chance that Praxagora emphasizes these two parts of the women's costumes: they are two stereotypical features of male comic costume. It should be clear that the women produce a theatrical performance as well as a deception.

15 See Ussher 1973: 89 *ad* 95–7; the scholiast on *Frogs* 965 writes μέγαν ἔχων πώγωνα ('having a large beard').

16 The scholiast explains that Agyrrhios was once in a homosexual relationship, as εὐρύπρωκτος (literally, 'wide-assed'; see Henderson 1975: 210): Ussher 1973: 89 *ad* 102–4.

17 Σύμβολον, token, has here both a literal and a figurative meaning. On the one hand, the women need their tokens for entry into the assembly meeting. On the other hand, σύμβολον can also be used to indicate the phallos, another item that the women need for entry into the assembly. Cf. *Birds* 1214, where the sense depends on ἐπιβάλλειν to connote sexual violence (Henderson 1975: 124). Here the sense depends as much upon production and staging as upon suggestive vocabulary.

18 Ussher concurs with such speculation: 'His costume is almost certainly phallic (1973: 121 *ad* 317–19). Blepyrus uses different words for the same garment, but this dress is referred to with words (ἡμιδιπλοίδιον, κροκωτίδιον) that identify it as specifically for women; it is probably a woman's *chiton* dyed orange-yellow. The use of the diminutive presumably enhances its cuteness and femininity. Similarly, Persian slippers are exclusively for women (Stone 1980: 227).

19 My conclusions here were drawn quite separately from Saïd's, but hers (1987: 235–6) are worth noting:

> Enfin, et l'*Assemblée des femmes* ne manque pas de le souligner, le costume ne modifie jamais que l'apparence et se révèle impuissant à

transformer le caractère. . . . Il démontre aussi l'inégalité des sexes. Le passage du masculin au féminin, qui est toujours imposé au personnage de l'extérieur est une dégradation. Au contraire le passage exceptionnel, du féminin au masculin (même s'il est, comme le précédent condamné à être imparfait par la permanence d'un «visage» et d'un «corps» auxquels la comédie ne touche pas) est toujours le résultat d'un libre choix et apparaît comme une promotion.

20 Ussher has emended ἄκουσαι and ἔχουσιν in 503, I think correctly. He argues that not only does the line read more clearly with the emendations, but that if ἄκουσ' is correct at *Peace* 612, it parallels the personification of the beards here (1973: 145 *ad* 503). The emendation also gives τὸ σχῆμα the force I emphasize here. If we look back at τὸ σχῆμα at 482, we see that the women were concerned that someone might discover the trick by watching their bodies (τὸ σχῆμα) as they walked. τὸ σχῆμα has another use in reference to deceptive appearance (Euripides, fr. 25. 2).

21 I accept Ussher's reading according to the codices here. The feminine participle (ἡμῶν προσιουσῶν, also Hall and Geldart 1907, vol. 2), which Faber thinks more conspiratorial, loses the play on masculine speech and identity that turns up at other points, especially in the rehearsal scenes. Ussher's defence of the masculine participle is sound – 'Woman A and her friends are dressed as *men*. She wants not so much to act her part out fully (she is more absent minded, 189) as to give the audience a chuckle' (1973: 77) – but does not take into account that to give the audience a chuckle will be, precisely, to act out the part.

22 Cf. Praxagora's praise of the lamp at line 16. In *Thesmophoriazusae*, after the Relative has put on women's clothes, he has to learn to speak like a woman. Euripides tells him to babble, so that he can be a woman convincingly with his voice (267–8). Cf. also Pherecrates fr. 64, where a man apparently performs a woman's task and spends the day babbling.

23 Ussher (1973: 97 *ad* 155) shows that the oath characterizes Athenian women in particular (*Ecclesiazusae* 532; *Acharnians* 538; *Lysistrata* 148). On this, and the differentiation between male and female speech in general and the need for more attention to these differences in Greek and Latin, see Gilleland 1980.

24 A parallel oath to Artemis occurs at *Thesmophoriazusae* 517. For women who invoke Artemis in order to be more feminine (and more chaste), see *Lysistrata* 435, 922, 949. Oaths are powerful comic weapons. Compare Blepyrus' invocation of Hermes, the tricky god of lies, when he agrees that the women do not falsify his character (445).

25 At 242, Woman A turns it around and uses it to praise Praxagora for her speaking ability. The usage is ironic, since Praxagora has successfully imitated a man and Woman A insists on praising her as a woman. Woman A is always mindful of the actor underneath the costume.

26 Rogers writes: 'She is addressing the audience in the theatre as though they were the people assembled in the Pnyx. There would be no women in either place' (1913b: 28 *ad* 165).

27 We know little about Epigonos; he is not named elsewhere in Aristophanes (Ussher 1973: 99 *ad* 167–8).

28 Ussher points out the similarity between her statement and Creon's in Sophocles' *Oedipus Tyrannus* 630 (1973: 100 *ad* 173–4). Creon is right in

NOTES

claiming his share of the land. To the audience of *Ecclesiazusae*, however, who know that she is really a woman, Praxagora claims an untenable share. Ussher 1973: 99 is right in saying that paratragedy is not intended here, but Praxagora still borrows tragic words, valid male speech, with which to costume her comic female character. This is not paratragedy but a linguistic disguise. Rothwell analyzes the relationship between Praxagora and rhetoric in detail (1990: 82–92). He establishes that Praxagora's character is modelled after the traditional figure of the *rhêtôr*, and argues for a positive assessment of Praxagora's persuasive skills. Rothwell is concerned strictly with the fictional world of the play, however. Certainly *peithô*, as he assesses it in *Ecclesiazusae*, has as much to do with theater as it does with seduction and political argumentation. Still, the argument that Praxagora is successful as a *rhêtôr* in the assembly because she appears to be an attractive young man and so of erotic interest to a male audience (98) supports my suggestions about the staging of her character for the male gaze and also the staging of her character as of ambiguous gender.

29 There seem to be no satisfactory answers as to why Praxagora and her husband were living on the Pnyx. Ussher lists the possibilities: because of the proscriptions of the Thirty; because of the flight of farmers to Athens at the beginning of the Peloponnesian War; because of the flight before Lysander (1973: 108 *ad* 243–4). None of these provides a logical and acceptable solution, however.

30 The prototype for this attitude toward women can be found in Hesiod, *Theogony* 590–602 (about the race of women after Pandora), and also in Semonides 7. In Aristophanes, for example, see *Clouds* 43–55 (Strepsiades' comments about marriage and his wife); also *Thesmophoriazusae* 389–94 (the women accuse Euripides of portraying women in this way, although they appear to fit the model) and 418–28 (because of their behavior, the women's husbands have locked up all the stores of grain and wine and the women can no longer filch them).

31 This passage shows that what Henderson has written (1975: 101) about the prologue holds true for the rest of the play:

> Just as Praxagora's euphemisms impose a linguistic artifice upon what is most accurately expressed by means of blunt language, so her fantastic ideas constitute an attempt to impose a noble and selfless social order upon what proves to be an ignoble and selfish society. Both impositions are manifest failures.

32 The usual feminine version of ὁ στρατηγός is ἡ στρατηγίς. Ὁ στρατηγός does not always connote military power (LSJ). It seems appropriate to use the masculine form of the noun, since Praxagora has dressed herself up as a man and is performing what is essentially a male task. The word appears at 491, 500, 727, 835, and 870; also Pherecrates, fr. 235. LSJ seems to disapprove of the word as a feminine noun, saying that the feminine usage at lines 491 and 500 is 'merely comic' (1652); so also Peppler 1918: 179. It is a comic but no less significant way of describing Praxagora and her acceptance by the group in a male role as a male figure, despite her sex.

33 The equation, for men, of female clothes and death seems somewhat pervasive: cf. *Lysistrata* 387–475 (the Proboulos scene). Just as Blepyrus

NOTES

resembles a corpse with only a bit of feminine attire, so Praxagora and her friends need the vitality and power of masculine clothing to carry out their plan.

34 Διδάσκω is the common term for producing a play (*Frogs* 1206; cf. *Ecclesiazusae* 215, 514, 662). Praxagora also uses technical terms to refer to the spectators (θεῶνται, θεαταῖς). That Praxagora's words refer to her plan and to a plan for drama has been noticed before (Foley 1977: 15 n. 32).

35 In matter of cultural fact, the idea of *gynaikokratia* is not new to men at all, although all the exempla of women in charge tend to confirm the need to keep men in charge: cf. Clytemnestra, Omphale, the Amazons, and the Lemnian Women; see above, Chapter 2. See also, Pembroke 1967; Vidal-Naquet 1981.

36 Ussher explains that she simply uses a generalized masculine form, presumably as a universal neutral as in the English universalized 'he', 'his' (1973: 157; see also Rogers 1913: 88 *ad* 589). He is not necessarily wrong. Still, the masculine form stands out when used by and in reference to a woman, and its application to Praxagora as she goes over her plan, in charge of the government, like a man and not like a woman, seems rather appropriate. Rothwell concurs that Praxagora, a woman, is the leader of the conspiracy because of '(a) the blurring of lines between women and the attractive youth trained in rhetoric, a stock figure in comedy; (b) the long-standing tradition that women have verbal skills' (1990: 103).

37 Cf. 160, where a woman trying to act like a man swears by Apollo. Blepyrus swears by Apollo when Praxagora abolishes the judicial system (659) and turns the courts into dining-halls (676–80). Ussher remarks that Blepyrus swears indiscriminately, an opinion difficult to justify in a play where oaths have such pointed significance, but somewhat accurate for the buffoon that Blepyrus is. See, for instance, his oath to Hermes at 445. Blepyrus also swears by Dionysus before he mentions his shoes (344–5), an oath that befits a man dressed in woman's clothes (he is the only character in *Ecclesiazusae* to swear by Dionysus). Dionysus has a mythic history of wearing feminine attire and encouraging others to do the same, often to ill effect. In addition, he is the god of the theater and the correct god to invoke when describing costumes and disguises.

38 See above, Chapter 2, pp. 58–62.

39 The young woman mentions a lover named Epigenes at 931. Ussher does not give the youth this name; Henderson 1987a and Sommerstein 1984a do.

40 For an excellent overview of the representation of older women in Attic comedy, see Henderson 1987a, although it will be shown later that we disagree on the interpretation of this scene. Henderson seems more amenable to an ironic interpretation of this episode in 1975: 100–4. The general features of the elderly woman in Aristophanes, based mainly on this episode and on a character in *Wealth*, are described in Oeri 1948: 7–32. White skin is mentioned as usual for women (*Ecclesiazusae* 63–4, 385–7). It was commonly enhanced with white lead; Theophrastus describes its preparation (*Lap.* 56), and Xenophon warns his wife about it (Oec. 10. 2, 7): Ussher 1973: 195 *ad* 878–9. On the parallel that exists between the

NOTES

relationship of women to cosmetics and that of orators to rhetoric, see Rothwell 1990: 67.

41 The garment suggests seductiveness: it is worn by prostitutes (*Ecclesiazusae* 721), the color is attractive to women (ibid. 332), Lysistrata advises her friends to wear theirs in their actions to stop the war (*Lysistrata* 46, 51, 219), and it is worn at festivals (ibid. 645). In *Lysistrata* young women employ the κροκωτός for teasing their husbands, while here the dress and its implied circumstances are wholly inappropriate for an old woman. The Relative also wears one borrowed from Agathon (*Thesmophoriazusae* 253). Cf. Blepyrus' mocking appearance in the κροκωτίδιον earlier (332).

42 Saïd writes: 'La communauté des femmes a abouti au triomphe de la mort' (1979: 60). For non-ironic evaluations of *Ecclesiazusae*, see Konstan and Dillon 1981; Henderson 1987a; Sommerstein 1984a.

43 Bowra 1958 presents a close consideration of the duet in terms of its origins and possible inspirations. He comes to the conclusion that the song has similarities with several other love poems and other bawdy drinking-songs. Bowra says little about the place of the duet in the scheme of *Ecclesiazusae*, and his remarks are colored by a predetermined idea of social structure and a preconception of 'low-class society' among people who might know these lyrics. He accuses Aristophanes of debasing lyric poetry with this parody. Debase it he may, but not maliciously: this is what comedy is all about. Olson 1988 argues plausibly that the lyric presents a parody of the *paraclausithyron*, with gender-role reversals in line with Praxagora's social reforms.

44 Gross writes that the duet parodies sophisticated literary diction, and that this parody is brought on by the exuberance of the lovers' adolescent eroticism (1985: 32, 51). The lovers are terribly eager for one another, but the desperate mockery of Sapphic love lyric also draws attention to the strangeness and barrenness of a law that will not allow young lovers to be together. If Gross is correct, then Aristophanes mocks two literary traditions here.

45 Cf. Sappho, fr. 130 L-P (Bowra 1958: 385). The difference between Sappho's poem and Aristophanes' is that Aristophanes has stressed the physical nature of the young woman's desire, especially with διακναίσας; Sappho's Eros λυσιμελής is a divinity and the personification of desire, with lovely images following him.

46 McLeish sees naïveté in the old woman's remarks (1980: 99), but that is hardly supported by the aggressive nature of the scene. This woman knows very well that she speaks in obscene *double entendres*. McLeish also points out that the actor himself may enjoy this travesty of coy femininity, adding to the powerful homoeroticism of the scene.

47 A *lekythos* is a small or medium-sized pitcher for oil or other liquids. White-ground *lekythoi* have figures painted on a backwash of white lead paint, and were used as offerings to the dead and as memorials. The old woman's face must look as pale as the background of a *lekythos* painting.

48 Ussher suggests not only Death (who causes the vases to be painted) as the lover but also the vase-painter, who paints only women with one foot in the grave (1973: 214 *ad* 995–7). Some see a reference to Aristophanes the vase-painter or to an undertaker as the lover (Rogers 1913: 151). Quincey has suggested that *lekythos* here is part of a colloquial metaphor; the young man

NOTES

really just compares the old woman's painted and inflated cheeks to the sides of a pot: 'That *lekythos* and *lekythoi* were in common colloquial use at Athens for the inflated cheeks is strongly suggested by certain passages in Aristophanes' *Ecclesiazusae*' (1949: 40). Quincey's three points of evidence are that the *lekythos* remark is in response to a request for a kiss (and the woman's lips are puckered and her cheeks puffed out), that there are many allusions to make-up and paint, and that the colors of the make-up recall the red and white colors of a white-ground *lekythos*. His paper is not unconvincing, but I prefer to think of the woman as literally resembling a memorial vase-painting for her deceased self through her failed attempts at rejuvenation through paint.

49 Ἔμπουσα was a monster who could assume many forms (Taillardat 1962: 64). Cf. *Frogs* 290–2 and also Bdelycleon's description of Philocleon as 'a boil dressed up in garlic' (*Wasps* 1172). There are several other entrances of grotesquely costumed characters in Aristophanes (*Acharnians* 63–4, 156–8, 575–86). Chapman clearly explains that such scenes 'tend to remind the audience that they are looking at actors in comic costume and thus rupture the dramatic illusion, but there are several scenes in which Aristophanes seems to go even further and parody the grotesqueness and extravagance of comic costume' (1983: 15). This costumed hag appears in one of these scenes. Aristophanes appears to use ἠμφιεσμένη when describing someone dressed in an outrageous costume, as this hag's surely must be (cf. Old Woman A, 879; also *Wasps* 1172; *Thesmophoriazusae* 92, where Euripides describes how the Relative will infiltrate the Thesmophoria; and ibid. 840, in description of Hyperbolus' mother). Here its use calls attention to the old woman's dress as costume.

50 πίθηκος, monkey, also describes a person's character, but cf. *AP* 11, 196. 1: Bito's nose is three times worse than a monkey's. It also describes sycophants: *Peace* 1065, *Birds* 440, fr. 394 (Taillardat 1962: 228). πιθηκισμός also refers to a trick (*Knights* 887); the animal vaguely recalls the theme of deception.

51 Phryne was a common name for an old whore (Ussher 1973: 225–6), as well as for a toad. Taillardat (1962: 64–5) makes an applicable point in showing that the same expression, 'having something on the jaws', describes the way that the women wear their beards (σάκον πρὸς τοῖν γναθοῖν ἔχουσα, 502). If this woman has a slight beard that adds to her unattractiveness, then she adds to the confusion that disguise causes in the play. The women who wore beards previously gained some power by doing so and did not lose their femininity; this woman has developed a natural bit of masculinity.

52 τῷ βουλομένῳ (987), ἔδοξε ταῖς γυναιξίν (1015), and ἔστω (1019) are all formulaic expressions found in decrees; cf. 455, 615, 987, 1019, and *Thesmophoriazusae* 373. Ussher gives some inscriptional examples to confirm the style (1973: 216 *ad* 1011–20).

53 Again, my conclusions parallel Rothwell's: 'Nevertheless, although they follow and enforce Praxagora's laws, they represent failures of persuasion or seduction and thus are anti-types to Praxagora: their make-up notwithstanding, they lack Praxagora's erotic appeal' (1990: 72).

54 The identity of this man is disputed, with scholars arguing both for Blepyrus and for an unnamed citizen; see Olson 1987. The symbolic role

reversal between husband and wife seems the important point, however; whether the man is Blepyrus or not matters little to my interpretation.

55 'Linguistic feminism' may be defined as the acknowledgement through language of women as individuals and as a group. Nussbaum 1985 offers a simple explanation and example, using Plato, of the misunderstandings this can cause for translators. For example, the maid made the appropriate adjustment for her owner at 1126. This passage where the man seems only to invite men has caused trouble for commentators of *Ecclesiazusae*. He may simply mean, as Ussher suggests, 'everyone from six to sixty' in a colloquial sense. Ussher also suggests that women may not have been mentioned either because of convention or because they were not present in the audience (1973: 231 *ad* 144–8). If women were not mentioned as a matter of polite convention, then the man still refuses to acknowledge the new social structure. The problem with this society is that there has been little linguistic change, except by the slave-girl, even though the women are trying to institute social reform.

56 Saïd smartly remarks that the mish-mash of this dish causes all its elements to lose their identities and form a 'mot-merde', which is appropriate for Blepyrus and his preoccupations with defecation and food (1979: 55).

57 I disagree with MacMathúna, who writes that, in Aristophanes, physical trickery is comic and harmless and rhetorical trickery is serious and dangerous (1971: 236). In *Ecclesiazusae*, both types of trickery are equally comic and dangerous. Aristophanes makes us examine which is which. MacMathúna also writes (ibid.) that the most substantial trick that the women pull off is their vote in the assembly:

> Their trick, then, has to be viewed as mainly physical: their dressing up as men and flooding the assembly is what wins for them. Rhetoric indeed plays a part in the trick – the proposal has to be made and made well, if the fervid enthusiasm of its women supporters is not to arouse fatal suspicion; but it is of importance chiefly in the measure of its effect on the physical disguise.

I would argue that their rhetorical trickery is in the service of the physical disguise but is of no less importance, especially in its implications for the *gynaikokratia* itself. After all, the physical deception neither secures the plan's success nor works after the new government has begun.

58 David 1984 recounts the clear antagonism between rich and poor in fourth-century Athens.

59 For a complete analysis of the population of Athens in the fourth century, see M. H. Hansen 1986, which calculates the citizen population of Athens on the basis of army and navy figures. It seems beside the point to go into his calculations here. Pomeroy also notes that there was an unusually large proportion of women to men in the city (1978: 69).

60 Dillon 1987 argues that the Spartan investment of Dekeleia in 413 BCE inspired Aristophanes' new approach to the traditional comic themes of peace, fertility, and sexuality in *Lysistrata*. If we accept that this event, which occurred outside of Athens, could cause Aristophanes to reappraise his presentation of peace, then we may accept that social conditions within Athens could do so as well. Such a pattern has also been recognized in other

5 THE LEGACY OF ARISTOPHANES' WOMEN

1 The festival at which *Ploutos* was produced and the prize it was awarded are unknown. Aristophanes had produced a play with the same name in 408 BCE; however, scholars have indicated through studies of the play's political references that the *Ploutos* we possess was written in 388, shortly before Aristophanes' death (Dover 1972: 202).
2 I have followed the text of Stanford 1963.
3 Euripides' *Alcestis* (438 BCE) was, interestingly enough, performed in the position of a satyr play, fourth after three tragedies. Its treatment of the figure of Alcestis as a woman played by a male actor for performance purposes is taken up by Bassi 1989. It seems likely that tragic and/or satyric portrayals of Heracles that are now unknown to us are being parodied here (e.g. perhaps a play of the story about how Heracles wore women's clothes when in service to Omphale).
4 Henderson notes that the promise of these dancing girls occasions the change of costume (1975: 93), a point which may or may not have to do with their femininity.
5 In an attempt to avoid other difficulties of the text, Dover suggests that the chorus be split into two groups, one male, one female, from lines 440–6 (1972: 179); I follow his interpretation. Stanford leaves the lines to the chorus as a group, as do Hall and Geldart 1907; Rogers 1919 gives 440–6 to the Coryphaeus (1919: 66–8).
6 In Middle Comedy, of which only a few examples exist (*Ecclesiazusae* is often cited as more of Middle than Old Comedy), the plot rests on schemes of less outrageous fantasy, domestic situations begin to command attention, the chorus tends to take a smaller, more subordinate role, and the stock characters of master and slave, old men in argument, courtesans, cooks, parasites, and professional soldiers normally appear. For a good introduction, see Webster 1953. These trends can be seen already in *Frogs* as well as in *Ecclesiazusae*.
7 I have followed Hall and Geldart 1907. Two missing choral songs interrupt the dialogue after 770 and 801; they are not counted in the line count. For two interpretations of *Ploutos* in relation to social conditions in fourth-century Athens, see Konstan and Dillon 1981 and Sommerstein 1984a.
8 The personification of abstract principles bears some inconsistency. For example, the gender assignments in *Ploutos* generally reverse those of *Peace*. In *Peace*, the principles of peace, plenty, and festival are female; the principle of poverty and destruction is male. On the tendency in Western thought to personify abstract principles as female, see Warner 1985.
9 ὁ πλοῦτος, wealth (m.), becomes the proper noun Πλοῦτος, Ploutos, the god of wealth. Ἡ πενία, poverty (f.), becomes the proper noun Πενία, Poverty (cf. Alc. 92, Pl. *Symp.* 203b).

NOTES

10 Men still serve exclusively as actors, however. On the system of signs and meanings in performances of Menander's comedy, see Wiles 1991. Wiles does not focus upon the gender confusion caused by the interplay between actor and character in performance, yet he does acknowledge it (1991: 17):

> In any given performance some sign systems are dominant, and serve as points of articulation for others. Thus a drag act is articulated upon costume ... Mask and costume plainly were discrete sign systems – Aristophanes mocked Euripides for dressing a king in rags, using mask and costume to send contradictory messages.

11 On Plautus and metatheater, see N. Slater 1985, which elucidates the clever slave as the most common orchestrator of trickery through metatheater in Plautus.

12 I have followed Moseley and Hammond 1933.

13 For a good treatment of Terence's work, see Goldberg 1986. Terence might be called metatheatrical, for he often has characters call attention to themselves as performers of a play for the audience's enjoyment and his plays generally rework the plots of previous plays. Still, the female figures display little of the theatrical trickery of Aristophanic females. For a general introduction to Roman comedy, see Norwood 1952; for interpretations of specific plays, see Konstan 1983.

14 In brief, she offers a clever interpretation of scriptural texts (9–162), praises feminine talent for prevarication (224–34), discusses the problems caused by women's talent for costume (337–56), and deception (357–61; 400–2), and her own plot was hatched during the religious festival of Lent (543–7). She boasts of her own trickery: 'And thus of o thing I avaunte me, / Atte ende I hadde the bettre in ech degree, / by sleighte, or force, or by som maner thing, / As by continuel murmur or grucching' (403–6).

15 The original casts of these plays were no doubt entirely male. *As You Like It* is dated to 1599 or 1600, and the first woman did not appear on the English stage until 1660. The theme of gender disguise was common in Elizabethan drama and not limited only to Shakespearean comedy. See, for instances of women dressed as men and men playing women's roles, Bradbrook 1952; Curry 1955; Freeburg 1915; and Rackin 1987.

16 All quotations are from *As You Like It* Kittredge 1936 and will be cited parenthetically by act, scene, and line number.

17 Ganymede was a handsome prince of Troy whom Zeus abducted to serve as his cupbearer and, probably, lover (*Il.* 20. 231–35; *Hymn to Aphrodite* 5. 202–17; Apollodorus 2. 5. 9, 3. 12. 2).

18 Dawson cites other examples and writes: 'She reveals her most "feminine" aspects here, just before she begins playing her role in earnest' (1978: 31). Recall that this happens to the women in *Ecclesiazusae* also, primarily in regard to their speaking as men. Dawson's treatment of Shakespearean comedy echoes my approach to Aristophanes: 'This book examines a number of Shakespeare's plays from the point of view of their reflexivity, that is, their use of self-conscious techniques which radically affect the relation of the audience to the play' (ibid. xii).

19 Of the handkerchief scene, Styan concurs: 'Her grief unmasks the true Rosalind, and the audience is required at the last to make its greatest shift in perception' (1975: 166). The interchange of Rosalind's voice and

NOTES

Ganymede's voice is literally line by line. When Rosalind speaks from Ganymede's mouth, we know that the statement makes sense from Rosalind, but to those on stage who hear only Ganymede, the comment is a riddle. The double-voiced Ganymede has been appreciated by all critics of *As You Like It* and so I will not comment on it at any length; see Chapter 4 above for an application of its precepts to *Ecclesiazusae*. The most elegant consideration of Rosalind and Ganymede has been written by Brown. He describes the effect in this manner: 'Within the predominantly wide focus of the comedy, a double vision gives a kind of flickering intensity, and during a few moments of avowal, for some of the audience, the dramatic focus may be still, deep, and intimate' (J. R. Brown 1979: 81).

20 As a matter of fact, the actor playing Rosalind only appears costumed as a woman three times in the play: twice at the beginning (I, ii; I, iii) and once again at the end (V, 102 ff.). That we see Rosalind as Rosalind so seldom may blur the parody even further.

21 Richmond points this out: '[Rosalind] is costumed as a boy and "her" maleness is even finally acknowledged openly in the play's epilogue' (1971: 141).

22 On *As You Like It* as misunderstood as long as it is played by a male and female cast as if the female roles were written for actresses, see the remarks of McKellen 1992. There are other English plays deserving of attention in this fashion, but there is not enough room to discuss them all here. For instance, see Jonson's *Epicoene, or The Silent Woman*; also Ferris 1989: 53. S. Carlson 1991 presents a provocative and interesting study of women and their relation to English comic drama. Female tricksterism through costume and imitation has not entirely disappeared from popular comedy. The recent American film *Working Girl*, for instance, features a comic heroine with a selfish fantasy (to move from her lower social status and job as a secretary to a higher-paying and higher-profile executive position) and an Aristophanic scheme (she masquerades as her boss by cutting her hair, wearing her boss's clothes, and imitating the speech patterns of an upper-class American from the East Coast). The heroine's masquerade is presented as a seamless feat, for the film sees wearing cosmetics and different kinds of clothing as feminine traits; the men all dress the same.

23 πόλις is actually a feminine noun, but 'Dikaiopola' would be more obviously feminine to a modern audience.

24 Lysistrata says at 1182 that her job is done when the peace is ratified, and so it is not clear that she speaks again. Against the manuscripts, Henderson 1987b assigns 1273–8 to the Athenian Ambassador rather than Lysistrata herself. To remedy the problem of dramatic incompleteness that arises with her absence from the play's final moments, he suggests that a mute Lysistrata escorts the wives on stage for the finale. I agree rather with Neuberg, who argues in his recent translation for Lysistrata as speaker of 1273–8 for dramatic reasons (1992: 86–7).

BIBLIOGRAPHY

Abel, L. (1963) *Metatheatre*, New York: Hill & Wang.
Ackroyd, P. (1979) *Dressing Up, Transvestism and Drag*, New York: Simon & Schuster.
Amussen, S. (1988) *An Ordered Society: Gender and Class in Early Modern England*, Oxford: Blackwell.
Apte, M. L. (1985) *Humor and Laughter: An Anthropological Approach*, Ithaca, NY, and London: Cornell University Press.
Arnott, P. (1962) *Greek Scenic Conventions in the Fifth Century BC*, Oxford: Oxford University Press.
—— (1989) *Public and Performance in the Greek Theatre*, New York and London: Routledge.
Assaël, J. (1985) 'Misogynie et féminisme chez Aristophane et chez Euripide', *Pallas* 32: 91–103.
Auger, D. (1979) 'Le théâtre d'Aristophane: le mythe, l'utopie et les femmes', *Les Cahiers de Fontenay* 17: 71–102.
Austin, C. (1974) 'Adnotatiunculae in Thesmophoriazusas', *Proceedings of the Cambridge Philological Society* 20: 1–2.
Austin, G. (1990) *Feminist Theories for Dramatic Criticism*, Ann Arbor, Mich.: University of Michigan Press.
Bain, D. (1975) 'Audience Address in Greek Tragedy', *CQ* 25: 13–25.
—— (1977) *Actors and Audience: A Study of Asides and Related Conventions in Greek Drama*, Oxford: Oxford University Press.
—— (1982) 'Κατωνάκην τὸν χοῖρον ἀποτετιλμένας (Aristophanes, *Ekklesiazousai* 724)', *LCM* 7: 7–10.
Baker, R. (1976) *Drag: A History of Female Impersonation on the Stage*, London: Triton Books.
Bakhtin, M. (1965) *Rabelais and His World* (trans. H. Iswolsky, 1984), Bloomington, Ind.: Indiana University Press.
Barber, C. L. (1959) *Shakespeare's Festive Comedy*, Princeton, NJ: Princeton University Press.
Baron, J. R. (1990) 'Drag Humor in Aristophanes' Comedies', unpublished paper.
Barrett, D. (trans.) (1964) *The Frogs and Other Plays*, Harmondsworth: Penguin.

BIBLIOGRAPHY

Bassi, K. (1989) 'The Actor as Actress in Euripides' *Alcestis*', in J. Redmond (ed.) *Women in Theatre*, Cambridge: Cambridge University Press, 19–30.

Bassnett, S. (1987) 'Perceptions of the Female Role: the ISTA Congress', *New Theatre Quarterly* 11: 234–6.

Beacham, R. (1992) *The Roman Theatre and its Audience*, Cambridge, Mass.: Harvard University Press.

Beazley, J. (1931) *Attic Vase Paintings in the Museum of Fine Arts, Boston*, vol. 2, Cambridge: Cambridge University Press.

Bell-Metereau, R. (1985) *Hollywood Androgyny*, New York: Columbia University Press.

Belsey, C. (1986) 'Disrupting Sexual Difference: Meaning and Gender in the Comedies', in J. Drakakis (ed.) *Alternative Shakespeares*, London and New York: Methuen, 166–90.

Bennett, L. J. and Tyrrell, W. B. (1990) 'Making Sense of Aristophanes' *Knights*', *Arethusa* 23: 235–54.

Bérard, C., Bron, C., Durand, J.-L., Frontisi-Ducroux, F., Lissarrague, F., Schnapp, A., and Vernant, J.-P. (1989) *A City of Images: Iconography and Society in Ancient Greece* (trans. D. Lyons), Princeton, NJ: Princeton University Press.

—— and Bron, C. (1989) 'Satyric Revels', in C. Bérard, *et al. A City of Images: Iconography and Society in Ancient Greece* (trans. D. Lyons), Princeton, NJ: Princeton University Press, 131–50.

Bergren, A. (1983) 'Language and the Female in Early Greek Thought', *Arethusa* 16: 69–95.

Blau, H. (1990) *The Audience*, Baltimore, Md: Johns Hopkins University Press.

Blok, J. (1987) 'Sexual Asymmetry: A Historiographical Essay', in J. Blok and P. Mason (eds) *Sexual Asymmetry*, Amsterdam: Gieben, 1–57.

Bobrick, E. (1991) 'Iphigeneia Revisited: *Thesmophoriazusae* 1160–1225', *Arethusa* 24: 67–76.

Bowie, A. M. (1982) 'The Parabasis in Aristophanes: Prolegomena, *Acharnians*', *CQ* 32: 27–40.

Bowra, C. M. (1958) 'A Love-Duet', *AJP* 79: 376–91.

Bradbrook, M. C. (1952) 'Shakespeare and the Use of Disguise in Elizabethan Drama', *Essays in Criticism* 2: 167.

Brommer, F. (1954) 'Kopf über Kopf', *Antike und Abendland* 4: 42–4.

—— (1959) *Satyrspiele: Bilder Griechischen Vasen*, Berlin: De Gruyter.

Brown, C. (1983) 'Noses at Aristophanes, *Clouds* 344?', *Quaderni urbinati di cultura classica* n.s. 14: 87–90.

Brown, J. R. (ed.) (1979) *Much Ado About Nothing and As You Like It: A Casebook*, London: Macmillan.

Brumfield, A. C. (1981) *The Festivals of Demeter and Their Relation to the Agricultural Year*, New York: Arno.

Burkert, W. (1979) *Structure and History in Greek Mythology and Ritual*, Berkeley and Los Angeles: University of California Press.

—— (1983) *Homo Necans: The Anthropology of Ancient Greek Sacrificial Ritual and Myth* (trans. P. Bing), Berkeley and Los Angeles: University of California Press.

—— (1985) *Greek Religion* (trans. J. Raffan), Cambridge, Mass.: Harvard University Press.

BIBLIOGRAPHY

Burns, Edward (1990) *Character: Acting and Being on the Pre-modern Stage*, New York: St Martin's.
Burns, Elizabeth (1973) *Theatricality: A Study of Convention in the Theatre and in Social Life*, New York: Harper & Row.
Byl, S. (1982) 'La métis des femmes dans *L'Assemblée des Femmes* d'Aristophane', *Revue belge de philologie et d'histoire* 60: 33–40.
Cantarella, E. (1987) *Pandora's Daughters* (trans. M. Fant), Baltimore and London: Johns Hopkins University Press.
Carlson, M. (1990) *Theatre Semiotics*, Bloomington, Ind.: Indiana University Press.
Carlson, S. (1991) *Women and Comedy*, Ann Arbor, Mich.: University of Michigan Press.
Carrière, J.-C. (1979) *Le Carnaval et la politique: une introduction à la comédie grecque*, Paris: Société d'Éditions Les Belles Lettres.
Carroll, B. (1987) 'Feminism and Pacifism: Historical and Theoretical Connections', in R. R. Pierson (ed.) *Women and Peace: Theoretical, Historical and Practical Perspectives*, London: Croom Helm, 2–28.
Cartledge, P. (1981) 'Spartan Wives: Liberation or Licence?', *CQ* 31: 84–105.
—— (1990) *Aristophanes and His Theatre of the Absurd*, Bristol: Bristol Classical Press.
Caruso, C. (1987) 'Travestissements dionysiaques', in *Images et société en Grèce ancienne*, Lausanne: Institut d'Archéologie et d'Histoire Ancienne, 103–10.
Case, S.-E. (1985) 'Classic Drag: The Greek Creation of Female Parts', *Theatre Journal* 37: 317–28.
—— (1988) *Feminism and Theatre*, London: Macmillan.
Chancellor, G. (1979) 'Implicit Stage Directions in Ancient Greek Drama: Critical Assumptions and the Reading Public', *Arethusa* 12: 133–52.
Chantraine, P. (1980) *Dictionnaire étymologique de la langue Grecque*, Paris: Klincksieck.
Chapman, G. A. H. (1983) 'Some Notes on Dramatic Illusion in Aristophanes', *AJP* 104: 1–23.
Cohen, D. (1989) 'Seclusion, Separation, and the Status of Women in Classical Athens', *G&R* 36: 3–15.
Cook, A. B. (1913) 'Nephelokokkygia', in E. C. Quiggin (ed.) *Essays and Studies Presented to William Ridgeway*, Cambridge: Cambridge University Press, 213–21.
Coulon, V. (ed.) (1923) *Aristophane*, vols. 1–5, Paris: Budé.
—— (ed.) (1928) *Aristophane: Les Oiseaux*, Paris: Budé.
—— (1957) 'Aristophanes, Thesmophoriazusen 1015–1055', *Rheinisches Museum* 100: 186–98.
Croiset, M. (1909) *Aristophanes and the Political Parties at Athens* (trans. J. Loeb), London: Macmillan.
Curry, J. V. (1955) *Deception in Elizabethan Drama*, Chicago: Loyola University Press.
Dane, J. A. (1988) *Parody: Critical Concepts versus Literary Practices, Aristophanes to Sterne*, Norman, Okla.: University of Oklahoma Press.
David, E. (1984) *Aristophanes and Athenian Society of the Early Fourth Century BC*, Leiden: Brill.
Davis, N. Z. (1978) 'Women on Top: Symbolic Sexual Inversion and Political Disorder in Early Modern Europe', in B. Babcock (ed.) *The Reversible World:*

Symbolic Inversion in Art and Society, Ithaca, NY, and London: Cornell University Press, 147–90.
Dawson, A. B. (1978) *Indirections: Shakespeare and the Art of Illusion*, Toronto: University of Toronto Press.
Dearden, C. W. (1976) *The Stage of Aristophanes*, London: Athlone.
de Beauvoir, S. (1949) *Le Deuxième Sexe*, Paris: Gallimard.
deLauretis, T. (1984) *Alice Doesn't: Feminism, Semiotics, Cinema*, Bloomington, Ind.: Indiana University Press.
des Bouvrie, S. (1990) *Women in Greek Tragedy* (Symbolae Osloenses, supp. 27), Oslo: Norwegian University Press.
Detienne, M. (1977) *The Gardens of Adonis: Spices in Greek Mythology* (trans. J. Lloyd; originally published 1972), Atlantic Highlands, NJ: Humanities Press.
—— (1979) 'Violentes «eugénies». En pleines Thesmophories: des femmes couvertes de sang', in M. Detienne and J.-P. Vernant (eds) *La Cuisine du sacrifice en pays grec*, Paris: Gallimard, 183–214. [Published in English as 'The Violence of Wellborn Ladies: Women in the Thesmophoria', in M. Detienne and J.-P. Vernant (eds) (1989) *The Cuisine of Sacrifice among the Greeks* (trans. P. Wissing), Chicago: University of Chicago Press, 129–47.
Deubner, L. (1932) *Attische Feste*, Berlin: Keller.
Dickinson, P. (trans.) (1970) *Aristophanes: Plays II*, Oxford: Oxford University Press.
Dillon, M. (1987) 'The *Lysistrata* as a Post-Dekeleian Peace Play', *TAPA* 117: 97–104.
Doane, M. A. (1986) *The Desire to Desire: The Woman's Film of the 1940s*, Bloomington, Ind.: Indiana University Press.
Dobrov, G. (1990) 'Aristophanes' *Birds* and the Metaphor of Deferral', *Arethusa* 23: 209–33.
Dolan, J. (1985) 'Gender Impersonation Onstage: Destroying or Maintaining the Mirror of Gender Roles?', *Women and Performance* 2: 5–12.
—— (1988) *The Feminist Spectator as Critic*, Ann Arbor, Mich.: UMI Research Press.
Dover, K. J. (ed.) (1968) *Aristophanes: Clouds*, Oxford: Clarendon Press.
—— (1972) *Aristophanic Comedy*, Berkeley and Los Angeles: University of California Press.
—— (1989) *Greek Homosexuality: Updated and with a new Postscript*, Cambridge, Mass.: Harvard University Press.
DuBois, P. (1982) *Centaurs and Amazons*, Ann Arbor, Mich.: University of Michigan Press.
Edmonds, J. M. (ed.) (1957) *The Fragments of Attic Comedy*, vol. 1, Leiden: Brill.
Edmunds, L. (1980) 'Aristophanes' *Acharnians*', *YCS* 26: 1–41.
Ehrenberg, V. (1951) *The People of Aristophanes: A Sociology of Old Comedy*, Oxford: Oxford University Press.
Eitrem, S. (1944) 'Les Thesmophoria, les Skirophoria et les Arrhétophoria', *Symbolae Osloenses* 23: 32–45.
—— (1947) 'A Purificatory Rite and some Allied "Rites of Passage"', *Symbolae Osloenses* 25: 36–53.
Engle, J. M. (1983) 'Playing about the Stage: Poetics, Ritual, and Demagogy in the *Knights*', diss., Princeton University.

Epstein, P. D. (1981) 'The Marriage of Peisthetairos to *Basileia* in the *Birds* of Aristophanes', *Dionysius* 5: 6–28.
Farnell, L. M. (1909) *Cults of the Greek City-states*, New Rochelle, NY: Caratzas (1977).
Ferris, L. (1989) *Acting Women: Images of Women in Theatre*, New York: New York University Press.
Fetterley, J. (1978) *The Resisting Reader*, Bloomington, Ind., and London: Indiana University Press.
Fitts, D. (trans.) (1957) *Aristophanes: Four Comedies*, New York: Harcourt, Brace & World.
Foley, H. P. (1975) 'Sex and State in Ancient Greece', *Diacritics* 4–5: 31–6.
—— (1977) 'The "Female Intruder" Reconsidered: Women in Aristophanes' *Lysistrata* and *Ecclesiazusae*', *CP* 77: 1–21.
—— (1981) 'The Conception of Women in Athenian Drama', in H. P. Foley (ed.) *Reflections of Women in Antiquity*, New York: Gordon & Breach, 127–68.
—— (1988) 'Tragedy and Politics in Aristophanes' *Acharnians*', *JHS* 108: 33–47.
Forsyth, N. (1979) 'The Allurement Scene: A Typical Pattern in Greek Oral Epic', *CA* 12: 107–20.
Foucault, M. (1985) *The Use of Pleasure* (trans. R. Hurley), New York: Vintage.
Freeburg, V. O. (1915) *Disguise Plots in Elizabethan Drama*, New York: Columbia University Press.
Freedman, B. O. (1991) *Staging the Gaze: Postmodernism, Psychoanalysis, and Shakespearean Drama*, Ithaca, NY: Cornell University Press.
Frisk, H. (1970) *Grieschisches etymologisches Wörterbuch*, Heidelberg: Winter.
Frontisi-Ducroux, F. and Lissarrague, F. (1990) 'From Ambiguity to Ambivalence: A Dionysiac Excursion through the "Anakreontic" Vases', in D. M. Halperin, J. J. Winkler, and F. I. Zeitlin (eds), *Before Sexuality: The Construction of Erotic Experience in the Ancient Greek World*, Princeton, NJ: Princeton University Press, 211–56.
Gardner, J. F. (1989) 'Aristophanes and Male Anxiety: The Defence of the *Oikos*', *G&R* 36: 51–62.
Geddes, A. G. (1987) 'Rags and Riches: The Costume of Athenian Men in the Fifth Century', *CQ* 37: 307–31.
Gelzer, T. (1970) 'Aristophanes der Komiker', in A. Pauly, G. Wissowa, *et al.* (eds) *Realencyclopädie der classischen Altertumswissenschaft*, suppl. 12, Stuttgart: Druckenmüller, cols 1392–569.
—— (1975) 'Tradition und Neuschöpfung in der Dramaturgie des Aristophanes', in H. J. Newiger (ed.) *Aristophanes und die alte Komödie*, Darmstadt: Wissenschaftliche Buchgesellschaft, 283–316.
Gentili, B. (1979) *Theatrical Performances in the Ancient World*, Amsterdam: Gieben.
Ghiron-Bistagne, P. (1976) *Recherches sur les acteurs dans la Grèce antique*, Paris: Société d'Éditions les Belles Lettres.
Giangrande, G. (1963) 'The Origins of Attic Comedy', *Eranos* 61: 1–24.
Gilleland, M. (1980) 'Female Speech in Greek and Latin', *AJP* 101: 180–3.
Goldberg, S. (1986) *Understanding Terence*, Princeton, NJ: Princeton University Press.

BIBLIOGRAPHY

Goldhill, S. (1990) 'The Great Dionysia and Civic Ideology', in J. J. Winkler and F. I. Zeitlin (eds) *Nothing to Do with Dionysus?*, Princeton, NJ: Princeton University Press, 97–129.

Gould, J. (1980) 'Law, Custom and Myth: Aspects of the Social Position of Women in Classical Athens', *JHS* 100: 38–59.

Green, J. R. (1985) 'A Representation of the *Birds* of Aristophanes', in *Greek Vases in the J. Paul Getty Museum*, vol. 2, Malibu, Calif.: J. Paul Getty Museum, 95–118.

Grene, D. (1937) 'The Comic Technique of Aristophanes', *Hermathena* 50: 87–125.

Gross, N. P. (1985) *Amatory Persuasion in Antiquity*, Newark, Del.: University of Delaware Press.

Gruber, W. E. (1983) 'Systematized Delirium: The Craft, Form, and Meaning of Aristophanic Comedy', *Helios* 10: 97–111.

—— (1986) *Comic Theaters: Studies in Performance and Audience Response*, Athens, Ga.: University of Georgia Press.

Guggisberg, P. (1947) *Die Satyrspiele*, Zurich: Lehmann.

Haigh, A. E. (1898) *The Greek Theatre*, 2nd edn, Oxford: Clarendon Press.

Haldane, J. A. (1965) 'A Scene in the *Thesmophoriazusae* (295–371)', *Philologus* 109: 39–46.

Hall, E. M. (1989a) *Inventing the Barbarian: Greek Self-definition through Tragedy*, Oxford: Clarendon Press.

—— (1989b) 'The Archer Scene in Aristophanes' *Thesmophoriazusae*', *Philologus* 133: 38–54.

Hall, F. W. and Geldart, W. M. (eds) (1907), *Aristophanis Comoediae*, vols. 1–2 (reprinted 1982), Oxford: Clarendon Press.

Halliwell, S. (1982) 'Notes on Some Aristophanic Jokes (*Ach.* 854–9; *Kn.* 608–10; *Peace* 695–9; *Thesm.* 605; *Frogs* 1039)', *LCM* 7: 153–4.

—— (1991) 'The Uses of Laughter in Greek Culture', *CQ* 41: 279–96.

Halperin, D. M. (1990) 'Why is Diotima a Woman?', in D. M. Halperin, *One Hundred Years of Homosexuality*, New York: Routledge, 113–51.

Hansen, H. (1976) 'Aristophanes' *Thesmophoriazusae*: Theme, Structure, and Production', *Philologus* 120: 165–85.

Hansen, M. H. (1986) *Demography and Democracy: The Number of Athenian Citizens in the Fourth Century BC*, Herning, Denmark: Systime.

—— (1987) *The Athenian Assembly in the Age of Demosthenes*, New York and Oxford: Blackwell.

Harriott, R. (1962) 'Aristophanes' Audience and the Plays of Euripides', *Bulletin of the Institute of Classical Studies* 9: 1–8.

—— (1986) *Aristophanes: Poet and Dramatist*, Baltimore: Johns Hopkins University Press.

Hartog, F. (1988) *The Mirror of Herodotus: The Representation of the Other in the Writing of History* (trans. J. Lloyd), Berkeley and Los Angeles: University of California Press.

Henderson, J. (1975) *The Maculate Muse*, New Haven: Yale University Press.

—— (1980) '*Lysistrate*: The Play and its Themes', *YCS* 26: 153–218.

—— (1987a) 'Older Women in Attic Comedy', *TAPA* 117: 105–29.

—— (ed.) (1987b) *Aristophanes: Lysistrata*, Oxford: Clarendon Press.

—— (trans.) (1988) *Aristóphanēs' Lysístrata*, Cambridge, Mass.: Focus Classical Library.

—— (1990) 'The *Demos* and the Comic Competition', in J. J. Winkler and F. I. Zeitlin (eds) *Nothing to Do with Dionysus?*, Princeton, NJ: Princeton University Press, 271–313.
Henry, M. (1988) *Menander's Courtesans and the Greek Comic Tradition*, Frankfurt and New York: Lang.
Herington, C. J. (1963) 'A Study in the *Prometheia*, Part II: *Birds* and *Prometheia*', *Phoenix* 17: 236–43.
Hofmann, H. (1976) *Mythos und Komödie: Untersuchungen zu den Vögeln des Aristophanes*, Hildesheim: Olms.
How, W. W. and Wells, J. (1912) *A Commentary on Herodotus*, vol. 1, Oxford: Clarendon Press.
Howard, J. E. (1988) 'Crossdressing, the Theatre, and Gender Struggle in Early Modern England', *Shakespeare Quarterly* 39: 418–40.
Hubbard, T. K. (1986) 'Parabatic Self-criticism and the Two Versions of Aristophanes' *Clouds*', *CA* 17: 182–97.
—— (1991) *The Mask of Comedy: Aristophanes and the Intertextual Parabasis*, Ithaca, NY: Cornell University Press.
Hude, C. (1908) *Herodoti Historiae*, vols 1–2, Oxford: Clarendon Press.
Isager, S. and Hansen, M. H. (1975) *Aspects of Athenian Society in the Fourth Century BC* (trans. J. H. Rosenmeier), Odense: Odense Universitetsforlag.
Jardine, L. (1989) *Still Harping on Daughters: Women and Drama in the Age of Shakespeare* (2nd edn), New York: Columbia University Press.
Just, R. (1989) *Women in Athenian Law and Society*, London and New York: Routledge.
Kagan, D. (1974) *The Archidamian War*, Ithaca, NY: Cornell University Press.
—— (1987) *The Fall of the Athenian Empire*, Ithaca, NY: Cornell University Press.
Kaplan, E. A. (1983) *Women and Film: Both Sides of the Camera*, New York: Methuen.
Kassel, A. and Austin, C. (eds) (1983–91) *Poetae Comici Graecae*, vols. 2, 3. 2, 4, 5, 7, Berlin: De Gruyter.
Keuls, E. (1985) *The Reign of the Phallus*, New York: Harper & Row.
Kilmer, M. L. (1982) 'Genital Phobia and Depilation', *JHS* 102: 104–12.
Kirk, I. (1987) 'Images of Amazons: Marriage and Matriarchy', in S. MacDonald, P. Holden and S. Ardener (eds) *Images of Women in Peace and War*, London: Macmillan, 27–39.
Kittredge, G. L. (ed.) (1936) *The Complete Works of William Shakespeare*, New York: Grolier.
Knox, B. M. W. (1964) *The Heroic Temper*, Berkeley and Los Angeles: University of California Press.
Kock, T. (ed.) (1888) *Comicorum Atticorum Fragmenta*, Leiden: Teubner.
Konstan, D. (1983) *Roman Comedy*, Ithaca, NY: Cornell University Press.
—— (1985) 'The Politics of Aristophanes' *Wasps*', *TAPA* 115: 27–46.
—— (1990) 'Aristophanes' *Birds* and the City in the Air', *Arethusa* 23: 183–207.
—— and Dillon, M. (1981) 'The Ideology of Aristophanes' *Wealth*', *AJP* 102: 371–94.
Kowzan, T. (1975) *Littérature et spectacle*, Paris: Mouton.
—— (1983) 'Les comédies d'Aristophane, véhicule de la critique dramaturgique', *Dioniso* 54: 83–100.

Kuhn, A. (1985) *The Power of the Image: Essays on Representation and Sexuality*, London: Routledge & Kegan Paul.

Kurtz, D. C. and Boardman, J. (1986) 'Booners', in *Greek Vases in the J. Paul Getty Museum*, vol. 3, Malibu, Calif.: J. Paul Getty Museum, 35–70.

Lattimore, R. (trans.) (1951) *The Iliad of Homer*, Chicago: University of Chicago Press.

Lefkowitz, M. K. (1984) 'Aristophanes and Other Historians of the Fifth-century Theater', *Hermes* 112: 143–53.

Levine, D. (1987) '*Lysistrata* and *Bacchae*: Structure, Genre, and "Women on Top"', *Helios* 14: 29–38.

Lévy, E. (1976a) *Athènes devant la défaite de 404: histoire d'une crise idéologique*, Paris: de Boccard.

—— (1976b) 'Les femmes chez Aristophane', *Ktèma* 1: 99–112.

Lewis, D. M. (1955) 'Notes on Attic Inscriptions II: Who Was Lysistrata?', *Annual of the British School at Athens* 50: 1–12.

Lewis, P. (1989) *Comic Effects: Interdisciplinary Approaches to Humor in Literature*, Albany: State University of New York Press.

Littlefield, D. J. (1968) *Twentieth Century Interpretations of The Frogs*, Englewood Cliffs, NJ: Prentice-Hall.

Long, T. (1986) *Barbarians in Greek Comedy*, Carbondale and Edwardsville, Ill.: Southern Illinois University Press.

Longo, O. (1990) 'The Theater of the *Polis*', in J. J. Winkler and F. I. Zeitlin (eds) *Nothing to Do with Dionysus?*, Princeton NJ: Princeton University Press, 12–19.

Loraux, N. (1981) *Les Enfants d'Athéna: idées athéniennes sur la citoyenneté et la division des sexes*, Paris: Maspéro.

Lucas, D. W. (1980) *Aristotle: Poetics*, Oxford: Clarendon Press.

Macdonald, S. (1987) 'Drawing the Lines: Gender, Peace and War: An Introduction', in S. MacDonald, P. Holden and S. Ardener. (eds) *Images of Women in Peace and War*, London: Macmillan, 1–26.

MacDowell, D. M. (ed.) (1971) *Aristophanes: Wasps*, Oxford: Oxford University Press.

—— (1982) 'Aristophanes and Kallistratos', *CQ* n. s. 32: 21–6.

McKellen, I. (1992) Address to the National Press Club, Washington, DC, June 1992.

McLeish, K. (1980) *The Theatre of Aristophanes*, New York: Taplinger.

McLuskie, K. (1987) 'The Act, the Role, and the Actor: Boy Actresses on the Elizabethan Stage', *New Theatre Quarterly* 3: 120–30.

MacMathúna, S. F. (1971) 'Trickery in Aristophanes', diss., Cornell University.

Martin, R. P. (1987) 'Fire on the Mountain: *Lysistrata* and *The Lemnian Women*', *CA* 6: 78–105.

Merry, W. E. (ed.) (1900) *Aristophanes: Peace*, Oxford: Clarendon Press.

Mikalson, J. D. (1975) *The Sacred and Civil Calendar of the Athenian Year*, Princeton, NJ: Princeton University Press.

Miller, H. W. (1946) 'Some Tragic Influences in the *Thesmophoriazusae* of Aristophanes', *TAPA* 77: 171–82.

—— (1947) 'On the Parabasis of the *Thesmophoriazusae* of Aristophanes', *CP* 42: 180–1.

BIBLIOGRAPHY

—— (1948) 'Euripides' *Telephus* and the *Thesmophoriazusae* of Aristophanes', *CP* 43: 174–83.
Moreau, J. (1938) 'Note sur le vers 1174 des *Thesmophories* d'Aristophane', *Antiquité classique* 7: 227–31.
Moseley, N. and Hammond, M. (eds) (1933) *T. Macci Plauti Menaechmi*. Cambridge, Mass.: Harvard University Press.
Mossé, C. (1973) *Athens in Decline: 404–86 BC* (trans. J. Stewart), London and Boston: Routledge & Kegan Paul.
Moulton, C. (1981) *Aristophanic Poetry* (Hypomnemata 68), Göttingen: Vandenhoeck & Ruprecht.
Muecke, F. (1977) 'Playing with the Play: Theatrical Self-consciousness in Aristophanes', *Antichthon* 11: 52–67.
—— (1982a) ' "I Know You – By Your Rags": Costume and Disguise in Fifth-century Drama', *Antichthon* 16: 17–34.
—— (1982b) 'A Portrait of the Artist as a Young Woman', *CQ* 32: 41–55.
—— (1986) 'Plautus and the Theater of Disguise', *CA* 17: 216–29.
Mulkay, M. (1988) *On Humor*, Oxford: Blackwell.
Mulvey, L. (1988) 'Visual Pleasure and Narrative Cinema', in C. Penley (ed.) *Feminism and Film Theory*, New York: Routledge, 57–68.
Munk, E. (1987) 'The Rites of Women', *Performing Arts Journal* 29: 35–42.
Nauck, A. and Snell, B. (eds) (1964) *Tragicorum Graecorum Fragmenta: Supplementum*, Hildesheim: Olms.
Neuberg, M. (trans.) (1992) *Aristophanes: Lysistrata*, Arlington Heights, Ill.: Harlan Davidson.
Newiger, H. J. (1957) *Metaphor und Allegorie*, Munich: Beck.
—— (1980) 'War and Peace in the Comedies of Aristophanes', *YCS* 26: 219–37.
Norwood, G. (1952) *The Nature of Roman Comedy: A Study in Popular Entertainment*, Princeton, NJ: Princeton University Press.
Nussbaum, M. (1985) 'Plato and Affirmative Action', letter, *New York Review of Books*, vol. 32, 30 Jan. 1985.
Ober, J. (1989) *Mass and Elite in Democratic Athens*, Princeton, NJ: Princeton University Press.
Oeri, H. (1948) *Der Typ der komischen Alten in der griechischen Komödie: seinen Nachwirkungen und seine Herkunft*, Basel: Schwabe.
Olson, S. D. (1987) 'The Identity of the δεσπότης at *Ecclesiazusae* 1128 f.', *GRBS* 28: 161–6.
—— (1988) 'The "Love-Duet" in Aristophanes' *Ecclesiazusae*', *CQ* 38: 328–30.
Ortner, S. B. (1974) 'Is Female to Male as Nature is to Culture?', in M. Rosaldo and L. Lamphere (eds) *Woman, Culture and Society*, Stanford: Stanford University Press, 67–87.
Parke, H. W. (1977) *Festivals of the Athenians*, Ithaca, NY: Cornell University Press.
Parker, D. (trans.) (1961) *Acharnians*, Ann Arbor, Mich.: University of Michigan Press.
Pembroke, S. G. (1967) 'Women in Charge: The Function of Alternatives in Early Greek Tradition and the Ancient Idea of Matriarchy', *Journal of the Warburg and Courtauld Institutes* 30: 1–35.
Peppler, C. W. (1918) 'Comic Terminations in Aristophanes: Part IV', *AJP* 39: 173–83.

BIBLIOGRAPHY

Phelan, P. (1988) 'Feminist Theory, Poststructuralism, and Performance', *Drama Review* 117: 107–27.

Pickard-Cambridge, A. (1946) *The Theatre of Dionysus in Athens*, Oxford: Clarendon Press.

—— (1962) *Dithyramb, Tragedy and Comedy*, 2nd edn (ed. T. B. L. Webster) Oxford: Clarendon Press.

—— (1968) *The Dramatic Festivals of Athens*, 2nd edn (ed. J. Gould and D. M. Lewis), Oxford: Clarendon Press.

Pierson, R. R. (ed.) (1987) *Women and Peace: Theoretical, Historical and Practical Perspectives*, London: Croom Helm.

Platnauer, M. (ed.) (1964) *Aristophanes: Peace*, Oxford: Clarendon Press.

Pomeroy, S. (1978) *Goddesses, Whores, Wives, and Slaves*, New York: Schocken.

Powell, A. (1988) *Athens and Sparta: Constructing Greek Political and Social History from 478 BC*, London: Routledge.

Pozzi, D. C. (1986) 'The Pastoral Ideal in the *Birds* of Aristophanes', *Classical Journal* 81: 119–29.

Price, S. D. (1990) 'Anacreontic Vases Reconsidered', *GRBS* 31: 133–75.

Pucci, P. (1977) *Hesiod and the Language of Poetry*, Baltimore and London: Johns Hopkins University Press.

Quincey, J. H. (1949) 'The Metaphorical Sense of Λ' ΗΚΥΘΟΣ and *Ampulla*', *CQ* 43: 32–44.

Rackin, P. (1987) 'Androgyny, Mimesis, and the Marriage of the Boy Heroine on the English Renaissance Stage', *Publications of the Modern Language Association* 102: 29–41.

Radermacher, L. (1940) 'Χοῖρος Mädchen?', *Rheinisches Museum* 89: 236–8.

Radt, S. (ed.) (1977) *Tragicorum Graecorum Fragmenta*, vols 3–4, Göttingen: Vandenhoeck & Ruprecht.

Rau, P. (1967) *Paratragoedia: Untersuchung einer komischen Form des Aristophanes* (Zetemata 45), Munich: Beck.

—— (1975) 'Das Tragödienspiel in den *Thesmophoriazusen*', in H. J. Newiger (ed.) *Aristophanes und die alte Komödie*, Darmstadt: Wissenschaftliche Buchgesellschaft, 339–56.

Reckford, K. J. (1987) *Aristophanes' Old-and-New Comedy*, Chapel Hill, NC: University of North Carolina Press.

Rhodes, P. J. (1972) *The Athenian Boule*, Oxford: Clarendon Press.

Richmond, H. M. (1971) *Shakespeare's Sexual Comedy*, New York: Bobbs-Merrill.

Richter, G. (1934) *De mutis personis quae in tragoedia et comoedia Attica producuntur*, Halle: Gebauer-Schwetschke.

Rösler, W. (1986) 'Michail Bachtin und die Karnevalskultur im antiken Griechenland', *Quaderni urbinati di cultura classica* 23: 25–44.

Rogers, B. B. (ed.) (1913a) *The Comedies of Aristophanes*, vol. 3, London: Bell.

—— (1913b) *The Comedies of Aristophanes: Ecclesiazusae*, London: Bell.

—— (1919) *The Frogs of Aristophanes*, London: Bell.

—— (1920) *The Thesmophoriazusae of Aristophanes*, London: Bell.

Romer, F. E. (1983) 'When Is a Bird Not a Bird?', *TAPA* 113: 135–42.

Rosellini, M. (1979) '*Lysistrata*: Une mise en scène de la fémininité', *Les Cahiers de Fontenay* 17: 11–32.

Rothwell, K. S., jun. (1990) *Politics and Persuasion in Aristophanes' Ecclesiazusae*, Leiden: Brill.

BIBLIOGRAPHY

Ruck, C. (1975) 'Euripides' Mother: Vegetables and the Phallus in Aristophanes', *Arion* 2: 13–57.

Saïd, S. (1979) '*L'Assemblée des Femmes*: les femmes, l'économie et la politique', *Les Cahiers de Fontenay* 17: 33–70.

—— (1987) 'Travestis et travestissements dans les comédies d'Aristophane', *Cahiers du groupe interdisciplinaire du théâtre antique* 3: 217–46.

Schaps, D. (1977) 'The Woman Least Mentioned: Etiquette and Women's Names', *CQ* 27: 323–30.

Schechner, R. (1988) *Performance Theory*, New York and London: Routledge.

Schmid, W. and Stählin, O. (1946) *Geschichte der griechischen Literatur*, Munich: Biederstein.

Scott, J. (1986) 'Gender: A Useful Category of Historical Analysis', *American Historical Review* 91: 1053–75.

Seager, R. (1983) 'Aristophanes *Thes.* 493–496 and the Comic Possibilities of Garlic', *Philologus* 77: 138–42.

Segal, C. (1975) 'Aristophanes' Cloud-Chorus', in H. J. Newiger (ed.) *Aristophanes und die Alte Komödie*, Darmstadt: Wissenschaftliche Buchgesellschaft, 274–97.

Seidensticker, B. (1978) 'Comic Elements in Euripides' *Bacchae*', *AJP* 99: 303–20.

—— (ed.) (1989) *Satyrspiel* (Wege der Forschung 579), Darmstadt: Wissenschaftliche Buchgesellschaft.

Shaw, M. (1975) 'The Female Intruder: Women in Fifth-Century Drama', *CP* 70: 255–66.

Sheppard, J. T. (1909) 'Tis estin he basileia?', in *Fasciculus Ioanni Willis Clark dictatus*, Cambridge: Cambridge University Press, 529–40.

Sifakis, G. M. (1971) *Parabasis and Animal Choruses: A Contribution to the History of Attic Comedy*, London: Athlone.

Simon, E. (1982) *The Ancient Theatre* (trans. C. E. Vafopoulou-Richardson), London and New York: Methuen.

—— (1983) *Festivals of Attica*, Madison: University of Wisconsin Press.

Sissa, G. (1990) *Greek Virginity* (trans. A. Goldhammer), Cambridge, Mass., and London: Harvard University Press.

Slater, N. (1985) *Plautus in Performance: The Theatre of the Mind*, Princeton: Princeton University Press.

—— (1986) 'The Lenaean Theatre', *Zeitschrift für Papyrologie und Epigraphik* 66: 255–64.

—— (1989) 'Lekythoi in Aristophanes' *Ecclesiazusae*', *Lexis* 3: 43–51.

—— (1990a) 'Performing the city in the *Birds*', paper given in panel entitled 'Aristophanes' *Birds. Nephelokokkygia*: Charting the Comic *Polis*', 122nd Annual Meeting of the American Philological Association, San Francisco, Calif., 29 Dec. 1990.

—— (1990b) 'Aristophanes' Apprenticeship Again', *GRBS* 31: 68–70.

—— (1990c) 'The Idea of the Actor', in J. J. Winkler and F. I. Zeitlin (eds) *Nothing to Do with Dionysus?*, Princeton, NJ: Princeton University Press, 385–96.

Slater, P. E. (1968) *The Glory of Hera: Greek Mythology and the Greek Family*, Boston: Beacon.

Snyder, J. M. (1974) 'Aristophanes' Agathon as Anacreon', *Hermes* 102: 244–6.

—— (1989) *The Woman and the Lyre: Women Writers in Classical Greece and Rome*, Carbondale, Ill.: Southern Illinois University Press.

Sommerstein, A. (1977) 'Aristophanes and the Events of 411', *JHS* 97: 112–26.

—— (1980) 'The Naming of Women in Greek and Roman Comedy', *Quaderni di storia* 11: 393–409.

—— (ed.) (1981) *Knights: The Comedies of Aristophanes*, vol. 2, Chicago: Bolchazy-Carducci.

—— (ed.) (1983) *Wasps: The Comedies of Aristophanes*, vol. 4, Warminster, Wilts.: Aris & Phillips.

—— (1984a) 'Aristophanes and the Demon Poverty', *CQ* 34: 314–33.

—— (ed.) (1984b) *Acharnians: The Comedies of Aristophanes*, vol. 1, Chicago: Bolchazy-Carducci.

—— (ed.) (1984c) *Peace: The Comedies of Aristophanes*, vol. 5, Chicago: Bolchazy-Carducci.

—— (ed.) (1987) *Birds: The Comedies of Aristophanes*, vol. 6, Warminster, Wilts.: Aris & Phillips.

—— (ed.) (1990) *Lysistrata: The Comedies of Aristophanes*, vol. 7, Warminster, Wilts.: Aris & Phillips.

Stanford, W. B. (ed.) (1963) *Aristophanes: The Frogs*, London: Macmillan.

Starkie, W. J. M. (1909) *The Acharnians of Aristophanes*, London: Macmillan; reprinted 1968, Amsterdam: Hakkert.

Stephens, J. L. (1990) 'Gender Ideology and Dramatic Convention in Progressive Era Plays, 1890–1920', in S.-E. Case (ed.) *Performing Feminisms: Feminist Critical Theory and Theatre*, Baltimore, Md.: Johns Hopkins University Press, 283–93.

Stevens, P. T. (ed.) (1971) *Euripides: Andromache*, Oxford: Oxford University Press.

Stone, L. (1980) *Costume in Aristophanic Comedy*, Salem, NH: Ayer.

Storey, I. (1989) 'Domestic Disharmony in Euripides' *Andromache*', *G&R* 36: 16–27.

Strauss, B. (1987) *Athens After the Peloponnesian War*, Ithaca, NY, and London: Cornell University Press.

Strauss, L. (1966) *Socrates and Aristophanes*, New York: Basic Books.

Styan, J. L. (1975) *Drama, Stage and Audience*, Cambridge: Cambridge University Press.

Sutton, D. F. (1974) 'A Handlist of Satyr Plays', *Harvard Studies in Classical Philology* 78: 107–43.

—— (1980) *The Greek Satyr Play*, Meisenheim: Hain.

—— (1984) *The Lost Sophocles*, Lanham, Md.: University Press of America.

—— (1987) 'The Theatrical Families of Athens', *AJP* 108: 9–26.

—— (1990) 'Aristophanes and the Transition to Middle Comedy', *LCM* 15: 81–95.

Taaffe, L. K. (1987) 'Gender, Deception, and Metatheatre in Aristophanes' *Ecclesiazusae*', Ph.D. diss., Cornell University.

—— (1991a) '*Lysistrata* and the Convention of Male Actors in Female Roles', paper given at Annual Meeting of the Classical Association of the Middle West and South, Hamilton, Ont., 4 Apr. 1991.

—— (1991b) 'The Illusion of Gender Disguise in Aristophanes' *Ecclesiazusae*', *Helios* 18: 91–112.

Taillardat, J. (1961) 'Ποσθαλίον et ποσθαλίσκος (Ar. *Thesm.* 292)', *Revue de philologie* 35: 249–50.
—— (1962) *Les Images d'Aristophane*, Paris: Société d'Éditions les Belles Lettres.
Taplin, O. (1986) 'Fifth-Century Tragedy and Comedy: A *Synkrisis*', *JHS* 106: 163–74.
Trendall, A. W. and Webster, T. B. L. (1971) *Illustrations of Greek Drama*, London: Phaidon.
Tyrrell, W. B. (1984) *Amazons: A Study in Athenian Mythmaking*, Baltimore: Johns Hopkins University Press.
Ussher, R. (ed.) (1973) *Aristophanes: Ecclesiazusae*, Oxford: Oxford University Press.
van Leeuwen, J. (ed.) (1904) *Aristophanis Thesmophoriazusae*, Batava: Sijthoff.
Versnel, H. S. (1987) 'Wife and Helpmate: Women of Ancient Athens in Anthropological Perspective', in J. Blok and P. Mason (eds) *Sexual Asymmetry: Studies in Ancient Society*, Amsterdam: Gieben, 59–86.
Vickers, M. (1989) 'Alcibiades on Stage: *Thesmophoriazusae* and *Helen*', *Historia* 38: 41–65.
Vidal-Naquet, P. (1981) 'Slavery and the Rule of Women in Tradition, Myth and Utopia', in R. L. Gordon (ed. and trans.) *Myth, Religion and Society*, Cambridge: Cambridge University Press, 187–200.
Walcot, P. (1971) 'Aristophanic and Other Audiences', *G&R* 18: 35–50.
—— (1976) *Greek Drama in its Theatrical and Social Context*, Cardiff: University of Wales Press.
Walton, J. M. (1980) *Greek Theatre Practice*, Westport, Conn., and London: Greenwood Press.
—— (1987) *Living Greek Theatre: A Handbook of Classical Performance and Modern Production*, New York: Greenwood Press.
Warner, M. (1985) *Monuments and Maidens: The Allegory of the Female Form*, New York: Atheneum.
Webster, T. B. L. (1953) *Studies in Later Greek Comedy*, 2nd edn 1970, Manchester: Manchester University Press.
—— (1956) 'Scenic Notes', *Wiener Studien* 69: 107–15.
—— (1967) *The Tragedies of Euripides*, London: Methuen.
—— (1970) *Greek Theatre Production*, 2nd edn, London and New York: Methuen.
—— (1972) *Potter and Patron in Classical Athens*, London: Methuen.
West, M. L. (ed.) (1966) *Theogony*, Oxford: Oxford University Press.
—— (ed.) (1978) *Works and Days*, Oxford: Oxford University Press.
—— (ed.) (1987) *Euripides: Orestes*, Warminster, Wilts: Aris & Phillips.
Whitman, C. (1964) *Aristophanes and the Comic Hero*, Cambridge, Mass.: Harvard University Press.
Wiles, D. (1991) *The Masks of Menander: Sign and Meaning in Greek and Roman Performance*, Cambridge: Cambridge University Press.
Willems, A. (1919) 'Le nu dans la comédie ancienne des Grecs', in *Aristophane*, vol. 3, Paris: Hachette, 381–95.
Winkler, J. J. (1990) *The Constraints of Desire*, New York and London: Routledge.
Zeitlin, F. I. (1978) 'The Dynamics of Misogyny: Myth and Mythmaking in the *Oresteia*', *Arethusa* 11: 149–84.

BIBLIOGRAPHY

—— (1981) 'Travesties of Gender and Genre in Aristophanes' *Thesmophoriazusae*', in H. P. Foley (ed.) *Reflections of Women in Antiquity*, New York: Gordon & Breach, 169–217.

—— (1982) 'Cultic Models of the Female: Rites of Dionysus and Demeter', *Arethusa* 15: 129–57.

—— (1985) 'Playing the Other: Theater, Theatricality, and the Feminine in Greek Drama', *Representations* 11: 63–84.

INDEX

Acharnians see Aristophanes
Achilles 94
actors: in comedy 12, 100, 107, 138, 164 n.7; convention of male 4, 17; in female roles 12, 23, 28, 33, 36, 47, 49–51, 55, 56–7, 64–5, 67, 71, 72–3, 74, 80, 82, 85, 87, 88, 89, 91, 94, 95, 96, 100, 101–2, 104, 112, 116, 118, 130, 139, 146 n.6, 148 n.7, 150 n.10; as women in Shakespeare's plays 4, 141–4, 194 n.22
actresses and Aristophanes 144–6
Adonia 63, 170 n.34
Aeschylus: in *Frogs* 136; *Oresteia* 2, 130, 169 n.27; vase illustrations of plays 6–7
Agathon 21, 78, 79–86, 87, 92, 94, 100, 177 n.20
Agyrrhios 110–11, 130
Alcestis 135
Amazons 53, 167–8 n.16
Andromeda 97
Antigone (Sophocles) 11
Aphrodite 13, 28, 29, 32, 55, 65, 67, 68, 71, 86, 106, 119, 125, 128
Apollo 86, 99, 117
Aristophanes: *Acharnians* 13, 20, 23, 24–30, 31, 37, 45, 50, 69, 95, 145; *Birds* 13, 20, 23, 41–6, 47, 69; *Clouds* 20, 23, 32–6, 47, 144; *Ecclesiazusae* (*Women at the Assembly*) 5, 9, 11, 12, 13, 19, 21, 33, 36, 50, 75, 84, 86, 87, 88, 103–33 *passim*, 134, 137, 138, 145, 146; *Frogs* 13, 22, 125, 134–6, 138, 140; *Knights* 20, 23, 30–1, 36, 69; *Lysistrata* 3, 4, 5, 11, 12, 13, 19, 20, 23, 36, 47, 48–73 *passim*, 74, 77, 78, 81, 84, 87, 89, 93, 95, 100, 101, 103, 108, 130, 138, 144–5; *Peace* 13, 20, 23, 37–41, 69; *Ploutos* (*Wealth*) 22, 124, 131, 134, 136–8, 139; *Thesmophoriazusae* (*Women at the Thesmophoria*) 5, 12, 13, 14, 19, 36, 50, 59, 74–102 *passim*, 103, 108, 134, 145, 146; *Wasps* 20, 23, 36–7, 45, 69
Artemis 99, 117
Athena 13, 45, 55, 62, 71, 144; Polias, priestess of 62

Basileia 42–5, 47, 161–2 n.48
Bdelycleon 36
beards 79–80, 81, 83–4, 108, 109, 111, 114, 130, 178 n.26, 178 n.27, 184–5 n.13, 190 n.51
Berlin Painter 6
Birds see Aristophanes
Blepyrus 113–14, 120–1, 124, 128

Chaucer, Geoffrey: the Wife of Bath 140
choregos 3
City Dionysia (Great Dionysia) 2, 3, 75
Cleon 30, 36

INDEX

Clouds see Aristophanes
Clytemnestra 14
comedy: origins of, parodied 28, 29; social role of 12, 152 n.20
cosmetics 124, 125, 126, 127, 137, 138
costume: of comic actors 4, 111–12; manipulation of 24, 29, 37, 103, 108, 111–12, 115, 124, 176 n.17
courtesans 23
cross-dressing 19, 50–1, 92, 104, 113, 133

Demeter 29, 36, 74, 75, 84, 85, 99, 117; *thesmophoros* 76
Demosthenes (*Knights*) 30
Diallage: in *Acharnians* 30; in *Lysistrata* 57, 69, 70, 93
Dikaiopolis 24–30, 79, 144
Dionysus 2, 3, 7, 26, 75, 76, 82, 85, 86, 99, 100; in *Frogs* 134–6, 137, 139, 140
disguise, 113, 114, 115, 124; gender 16, 83–4, 87, 100, 103; linguistic 112, 115, 117, 118, 120, 121, 129, 186–7 n.28; sexual 16
dramatic convention: calling into question categories of gender 19, 51; as unstable 15
dramatic illusion: disruption of 10, 49, 56, 87, 94, 115, 165–6 n.10

ecclesia 19, 88, 92, 97, 107, 108, 111, 113, 114, 115, 116, 117, 131, 179–80 n.39; parody of 174 n.7
Ecclesiazusae see Aristophanes
Echo 97, 98
Eirene 37–41
ekkyklema 80, 179 n.18
Epimetheus 34, 45
Eros 65
escape drama 98
Euelpides 41, 45
Eumenides 84
Euripides: *Aeolus* 38; *Andromache* 60, 169 n.27; *Andromeda* 97–9; *Bellerophon* 38–9; *Helen* 95–6; *Melanippe Desmotis* 91; *Melanippe Sophos* (*Melanippe the Wise*) 70;

Relative of 74–102 *passim*, 109; *Telephus* 24, 94–5; in *Thesmophoriazusae* 12, 21, 59, 74–102 *passim*, 109

falsetto 105
female figures: in Chaucer 140; in ancient Greek comedies 163–4 n.5; equated with food 26, 28, 29–30, 38, 46, 89, 120, 135, 137; exchange of 29, 30, 43, 71; functions in Aristophanes' plays 23, 46–7, 96, 100–2, 138, 139, 156 n.15; in Menander's plays 139–40; in metatheatrical context 27, 39, 46, 59, 126, 136, 139; mute 23, 30, 37, 45, 49, 51, 59, 69, 99, 158 n.25; in New and Roman comedy 140; in Plautus' plays 140; in Shakespeare's plays 140–4; in Terence's plays 140; in theatrical setting 23, 27, 29, 37, 38, 41, 46–7, 51, 54, 61, 65, 66, 68, 103, 122, 139, 143; as tricky 24, 30, 32, 34–5, 46–7, 54, 63, 67, 73, 87, 89, 90, 98, 103, 106–7, 115, 120, 122, 127, 137, 139, 164 n.6
femininity: devaluation of 113, 138, 174–5 n.9; as an element of the *polis* 13, 119; essential for comedy 85, 98, 100, 138, 139; representation of 24, 33–4, 36, 40–1, 50, 54, 72, 86, 89, 90, 93, 100–1, 138–9; symbolic of fertility 39, 46
feminization 84, 141
Frogs see Aristophanes

Ganymede 141–3
gender: ancient Greek understanding of 16; as category of analysis 19; distinguished from sex 16; as dramatic illusion 21, 50; identity (linguistic) 14, 64–5, 71, 73, 76–7, 85, 86, 88, 89, 91, 100, 115–23; as signifier of power 15, 19, 73, 78, 82, 111, 113, 129–33; *see also* disguise

INDEX

girls 23; *see also* female figures

Hades 135
Heidelberg Painter 6
Hekate 96
Helen 60, 95, 96
Hera 45, 99, 128
Heracles 135
Hermes 38, 40, 99, 138
Hesiod: *Theogony* 34, 40, 42, 43, 44, 137; *Works and Days* 34, 40, 42, 43, 44
Homer 63–4, 157–8 n.22

Iris 42, 49, 161 n.45

Kallistratos 3
Kalonike 54–8, 61
Karion 136
Khremylos 136, 137, 138
Kinesias 51, 52, 67–8, 123
Kleisthenes: in *Clouds* 33; in *Frogs* 135; in *Thesmophoriazusae* 21, 76, 78, 91–4, 96, 100
Kleonymus: wife of 93
Knights see Aristophanes
Kratinos 49
Krytilla 95–7

Lampito 56–7, 58, 60
language: manipulation of 24, 26–7, 28–9, 37, 138
Lemnian Women 53
Lenaea 2, 134
linguistic feminism 129, 190–1 n.55
Lysimache 62, 170 n.33
Lysistrata 20–1, 132, 144–5, 170 n.33
Lysistrata see Aristophanes

'male gaze' 16, 18, 67, 71, 83, 89–90, 99, 100
masculinity: in *As You Like It* 141, 143; in *Ecclesiazusae* 110, 113, 116, 118, 119, 122–3, 130, 131; in *Lysistrata* 48, 49, 51, 52, 56, 57, 59, 62, 63, 65, 66, 67, 68, 69, 70, 72, 73; in *Ploutos* 137–8, 139; in *Thesmophoriazusae* 81, 83, 84, 86, 89, 90, 93, 102
mask: comic 26, 104, 109, 116, 130; theatrical 4, 7, 10
Medea (Euripides) 11, 14, 89
Megarian merchant 28–9
Menander: *Dyskolos* 140; *see also* female figures
Menelaus 60, 95, 96
metatheatricality 27, 46, 50, 98–9, 140–1, 143, 166 n.11
Myrrhine 51, 52, 67–8, 123
Myrtia 36–7

Nicias: in *Knights* 30; peace of 40, 46
Nikon Painter 7
Nymphs 99

Old Comedy: psychoanalysis and 13–14
Opora 38–40, 49
Orestes 94

Pan 99
Pandora 34, 40, 44–5, 55
Peace see Aristophanes
Peisetairos 41–6
Penelope 128; Painter 6
Penia (Poverty): personification of 137
Pentheus 64
Pericles 32
Persephone 36, 74, 75, 117, 135
Perseus 97
Phaedra (Euripides) 11
phalloi: in *Ecclesiazusae* 105, 113; in *Lysistrata* 52, 58, 68, 69, 72; as part of comic costume 4; in *Thesmophoriazusae* 21, 81, 93
Pheidippides 32
Philocleon 36–7
Plautus 140
play-within-the-play 25, 29, 38, 52, 67, 80, 86, 95, 111
Ploutos (Wealth): personification of 137
Ploutos (Wealth) see Aristophanes
Poseidon 58
Praxagora 12, 103–33 *passim*, 145
Procne: in *Birds* 41–2; Sophocles' 89, 160 n.41

211

INDEX

Prometheus 34, 42–6, 161 n.46, 161 n.47
Python (vase painter) 10

ritual: parody of 26, 29, 61–2
role-playing 51–2, 100, 115, 132, 137
role-reversal 64, 78, 88, 94, 96, 103
Rosalind 141–3
Rural Dionysia 25, 27

satyr play 2
Scythaina 59
seduction scene: parody of 67–9, 123–9, 171 n.40
Shakespeare, William: *As You Like It* 141–3, 145; *The Merchant of Venice* 140; *Much Ado about Nothing* 140–1; *The Taming of the Shrew* 145; *Twelfth Night* 141; *Two Gentlemen of Verona* 141
Sicilian expedition 46, 72
Skira 75, 109, 184 n.12
Socrates: in *Clouds* 32–5
spectator: relationship to performance 17; 'decentered' 18
Spondai 31
Strepsiades 32–6
Susarion 174–5 n.9

Telephus 94
Telephus see Euripides
Terence 140; *see also* female figures
Theater of Dionysus in Athens 2, 17, 125
theatricality 9, 17, 19, 25–6, 27, 33, 37, 41, 51–2, 80–1, 110, 127, 139, 143
Theoria 38–40, 49, 159–60 n.36
Thesmophoria 75–6, 80, 88, 99

Thespis 2
Thucydides 30, 40, 172 n.48
tragedy: parody of 105–6, 108; *see also* Euripides
Trygaeus 37–8, 79

vase-painting: color-coded gender in 5, 150 n.11; of comic actors 5, 149 n.9; male actors dressed as women in 6–7, 9, 10

wife: of Bath *see* Chaucer; of Dikaiopolis 25, 26, 27, 49; of Strepsiades 25, 32, 36; of Tereus *see* Procne; of Trygaeus 25, 49
wives: of central male characters 23, 49; in *Lysistrata* 53, 56, 66–7
'woman' as theatrical construct 85, 86, 89, 93, 94
women: in ancient Greek tragedy 11; in attendance at dramatic festivals 17; in classical antiquity 10; in comedy distinguished from women in tragedy 11, 55; not named in public 25, 27, 148 n.6; in Old Comedy related to other literary traditions 19; representation of *see* female figures; Spartan 56, 59, 168 n.22
Women at the Ecclesia see Aristophanes: *Ecclesiazusae*
Women at the Thesmophoria see Aristophanes: *Thesmophoriazusae*
women writers (ancient) 11

Xanthias 134–6, 140

Zeus 1, 34, 37, 40, 41, 42, 43, 44, 45, 46, 136

INDEX OF PASSAGES DISCUSSED

Aristophanes: *Acharnians* 39–70: 94; 130–2: 155 n.8; 144–5: 155 n.9; 178–200: 31; 201–2: 25; 245–6: 26; 247–52: 26; 253–8: 26; 254: 155 n.11; 262: 25; 271–5: 155–6 n.13; 729–835: 28; 786–7: 157 n.19; 878–909: 30; 989–99: 69; 1198–1221: 69; *Birds* 341: 87; 659: 41; 668–74: 41; 1203: 42; 1205–6: 42; 1214–15: 42; 1233–5: 42; 1253–6: 42; 1494: 43; 1496: 43; 1497: 43; 1506: 43; 1508: 42; 1509: 43; 1516–19: 43; 1534–6: 43; 1537: 43; 1537–41: 43; 1543: 45; 1545: 44; 1546: 44; 1713–14: 45; 1706–65: 69; 1753: 45; *Clouds* 41b–55: 32; 275–313: 32–3; 340–1: 33; 348–55: 33; 316–18: 34; 331–4: 34; 355: 118; 509: 87; 1458–64: 35; 1214–1302: 36; *Ecclesiazusae* 1–16: 105–6; 6: 120; 8–9: 120; 9: 107; 10: 107; 15: 107; 20–3: 107; 24–7: 108; 31: 116; 58–60: 75; 60–4: 109; 67: 109; 69: 109; 70: 117; 73–5: 104; 74–5: 110; 90: 117; 93–7: 110; 101: 110; 102–4: 111, 130; 120: 116; 121: 111; 121–3: 116; 124–5: 116; 125: 111; 131–2: 88; 155–60: 86, 116–17; 156: 117; 190: 117; 165–8: 118; 173–88: 118; 189–92: 118–19; 204: 119; 209–13: 119; 215–18: 119–20, 122; 224–8: 120; 245–7: 120, 187 n.32; 258–60: 120; 268–79: 111–12; 285–7: 112; 295a: 108, 112; 297: 112; 299: 112–3; 318–19: 113; 332: 113; 372: 114; 383: 114; 385–7: 114; 427: 84; 442–4: 107; 481–2: 114; 486–8: 114; 496–7: 115; 501–3: 114; 506–10: 115; 519: 115; 536–8: 121; 539–46: 113, 121; 558: 121; 583–5: 122; 589: 122; 631: 123; 728–86: 123; 730–3: 125; 877–1111: 123–7; 995–7: 189–90 n.48; 1105–1111: 127; 1125–6: 128; 1141–3: 128; 1144–6: 129; *Frogs* 1–5: 134; 8: 134; 48: 135; 202: 87; 267–8: 134; 308: 134; 465–78: 135; 479–91: 134; 503–18: 135; 512: 87; 524: 87; 549–78: 135; 1479–80: 136; *Knights* 1300–15: 30–1; 1388–95: 69; 1389–91: 31; *Lysistrata* 1–3: 61, 63; 11–12: 54; 16–19: 54, 61; 20: 61; 23–4: 92; 26–7: 61; 42–5: 54; 42–8: 52; 42–9: 61; 46–8: 54–5; 51–3: 53; 79–81: 56; 83–4: 56; 87–9: 57; 91–4: 57; 99–101: 61; 107: 72; 107–10: 61; 124–8: 58; 129–35: 58; 138–9: 58, 169 n.24; 142–4: 58; 145: 59; 149–54: 52, 60; 155–6: 60, 64, 169 n.27; 184–6: 59; 191a: 61; 194–7: 61–2; 212–37: 52; 388–90: 62; 404–6: 62–3; 426–7: 59; 507–9: 63; 512: 63; 514–15a: 63; 520: 63; 530–1: 64; 532–8: 64; 549–50: 65; 554–4: 65;

INDEX OF PASSAGES DISCUSSED

567–86: 77; 600–4: 66; 678: 53; 708–9: 66, 71; 715: 66, 170–1 n.37; 717–27: 66; 770–6: 67; 829–953: 123; 831–4: 68; 839–41: 67; 841: 68; 885–8: 68; 916: 68; 921: 68; 926: 68; 929–33: 68; 931: 69; 938–45: 68; 945: 87; 950–8: 68, 69; 954–79: 69; 1105: 69; 1108–9: 70; 1115: 69; 1122–3: 69; 1124–7: 70; 1189: 71; 1713: 84; *Peace* 114–53: 38; 119–20: 38; 525: 69; 530–8: 39; 530–4: 159–60 n.36; 874–909: 39; 822–908: 69; 1329–57: 69; *Ploutos* 423–4: 138; 602: 138; 641–770: 136; 778–801: 136; 797–801: 137; 1047–65: 137; *Thesmophoriazusae* 1–2: 79; 6–12: 79; 26–7: 79; 31–5: 79; 36: 79; 50–7: 82; 85–7: 80; 93–4: 80; 96: 80; 97–8: 80, 83; 124–5: 80; 136–45: 80–1; 148–51: 81–2; 154–8: 82; 190–2: 83, 84; 200: 82–3; 204–5: 83; 218–20: 84; 222: 84; 224–6: 84; 236–48: 84; 248–31: 90; 253: 84; 254: 86; 256: 86; 260: 86; 267–9: 86; 283–8: 87; 292–3: 87; 306–9: 88; 380–2: 88; 384: 89; 392–7: 89; 396: 92; 398: 90; 407–21: 90; 467–573: 90; 531–2: 90; 533: 91; 536–9: 91; 571: 92; 574–6: 92; 580: 92; 588: 92; 591: 93; 599: 93; 601–2: 93; 605: 93; 621: 92; 636–48: 93; 644–8: 81; 647–8: 93; 654: 93; 656: 93; 658: 94; 785–803: 76; 819–29: 77; 850: 95; 853: 87; 855–8: 96; 875: 96; 861–2: 96; 879–80: 96; 897: 96; 899: 96; 916: 96; 920: 96; 929–30: 96; 934–5: 96; 939: 96; 943–4: 96; 945: 96; 946–1000: 97; 1083–97: 97; 1015–55: 97; 1022–3: 97; 1043–5: 97; 1056–132: 97–9; 1092: 92; 1136–48: 99; 1150: 99; 1151: 87; 1165–9: 99; 1178: 99; 1181–3: 99; 1189–90: 99; 1200: 99; *Wasps* 1341 ff.: 37; 1341–81: 69; 1371: 37; 1388: 36

Euripides: *Medea* 230–51: 89; *Melanippe Sophos* fr. 483: 70

Hesiod: *Theogony* 456: 40; 506–616: 42; 535–57: 44; 570–612: 34; 585: 44; 613: 43; 969: 137; *Works and Days* 42–106: 33–4; 47–106: 42; 65–6: 40; 73: 40; 75: 40; 90–104: 40; 105: 43

Hymn to Aphrodite 45–6: 67; 53–8: 67; 64–5: 67; 144: 68

Plautus: *Menaechmi* 127 ff.: 140

Shakespeare, William: *As You Like It* I, iii, 116–24: 141; III, ii, 263–4: 142; III, v, 109–23: 142; Epilogue 17–22: 143

Sophocles: *Tereus* fr. 583: 89